# Baptism and the Unity of the Church

*Edited by*

Michael Root *and* Risto Saarinen

*Institute for Ecumenical Research*
*Strasbourg, France*

William B. Eerdmans Publishing Company
Grand Rapids, Michigan / Cambridge, U.K.

WCC Publications
Geneva

Published jointly 1998 by
Wm. B. Eerdmans Publishing Co.
255 Jefferson Ave. S.E., Grand Rapids, Michigan 49503 /
P.O. Box 163, Cambridge CB3 9PU U.K.
and by
WCC Publications
World Council of Churches
150 route de Ferney, 1211 Geneva 2, Switzerland
All rights reserved

Printed in the United States of America

03 02 01 00 99 98      7 6 5 4 3 2 1

**Library of Congress Cataloging-in-Publication Data**

Baptism and the Unity of the Church /
edited by Michael Root and Risto Saarinen.
p.      cm.
Includes bibliographical references.
ISBN  0-8028-4462-6 (pbk.: alk. paper)
1. Baptism.   2. Church — Unity.   3. Baptism and Christian union.
4. Baptism and church membership.   I. Root, Michael, 1940-   .
II. Saarinen, Risto.
BV811.2.B385  1998
234'.161 — dc21                                    97-44687
                                                          CIP

WCC Publications ISBN 2-8254-1250-3

# Contents

v

# Introduction

## Michael Root and Risto Saarinen

### 1. Baptism and Unity: A Way Forward?

One, yet not one. Here lies the paradox and dilemma that drives the ecumenical movement. Does baptism offer a way out of this dilemma, or do we here encounter the same paradox of unity and division? The claim is often made that the great majority of Christian churches share a common understanding of baptism: Baptism is a sacrament of salvation and also a sacrament of initiation into the Christian community. Most churches teach these two basic meanings of baptism, even if they differ in their concrete baptismal practices.

But if we are thus united in our common understanding of baptism, why doesn't baptism have a greater ecumenical significance than it does? Why do the churches avoid drawing definite conclusions from this basic consensus, which encompasses not only baptism but also issues relating to salvation and church membership? Can an ecumenical potential be found here which has been ignored by the churches? Many theologians think so, including some of the contributors to this volume.

Or is something the matter with this line of reasoning? Is the agreement on baptism only apparent, hiding deeper differences? Even if we are one in baptism, does that unity have direct relevance for unity in the Eucharist or in the wider Christian life? Do our differing baptismal practices in fact reflect deeper divergences in New Testament interpretation, church history, and church life?

1

In recent years these questions have been especially pressing. If fellowship in the Eucharist or in ministry is not to be realized in the immediate future across the divide that separates Rome from the other churches of the West or across the divide that separates the Western churches from the Orthodox, is communion focused on baptism the ecumenical way forward? Is such a baptismal communion in fact all we really need?

This study seeks to explore these questions, which, surprisingly enough, have so far received less careful attention than they deserve. The project has had three stages, each discernible in this volume. Basic for the project is a study paper produced by the Institute for Ecumenical Research, Strasbourg, at the request of the Department for Theology and Studies of the Lutheran World Federation (LWF) through its Study Secretary for Worship and Congregational Life, S. Anita Stauffer. This study paper seeks both to lay out a particular understanding of baptism and the church as communion and to outline and analyze the various ecumenical issues raised by the interconnection of the concepts "baptism" and "communion."

After discussion within the LWF, this study paper served as a point of reference for the second stage of the project, a consultation sponsored by the Strasbourg Institute in Hvittorp, Finland, in October 1996. This consultation was designed to be ecumenical, analyzing the topic from various angles. The various contributors were asked to comment on various themes, ranging from abstract questions of ecclesiology to particular questions of practice in situations where baptism and communion have become especially live topics.

The third stage is the book you now have before you, the publication of the study paper and of the contributions to the Hvittorp consultation, revised by the authors following the discussions. We offer these reflections as a contribution to an ecumenical discussion which is only now truly beginning.

## 2. The Study Paper, Consultation, and Essays

The Strasbourg Institute's study paper has three main sections. The first, "Baptism and the Unity of the Church as a Communion," explores the biblical and theological foundations of these concepts and their interconnection. While the analysis seeks to be relevant to the wider Christian tradition, it contains a Lutheran stress on baptism as God's unconditional gift.

The second section, "Baptism and the Failures and Divisions of the Church as Communion," analyzes the various ecumenical issues that arise around the theme of baptism and the unity of the church: mutual recognition of baptism, baptism and church membership, baptism and other bonds of communion. The concern here is less to provide final answers to the questions identified than to give a clear picture of the nature of these questions.

The final section addresses the relevance of unity in baptism to the wider unity we seek ecumenically. No ecumenical panacea is to be found in baptism, but a clear recognition of our common baptism should force us to rethink the nature of our unity and division.

While the study paper served as a background for the Hvittorp consultation, it was not the focus for the various contributions. Rather, each participant was asked to discuss a specific issue related to the overall theme. Two speakers, one Lutheran and one Roman Catholic, were requested to comment on the very general theme "Baptism and the Foundations of Communion." They were asked to consider the place of baptism and unity in baptism in light of the unity of the church as a communion in Christ.

*Susan K. Wood,* an American Roman Catholic teaching at Saint John's University, USA, places baptism in the context of a rich ecclesiology of communion. She argues that although baptism brings about incorporation into the body of Christ, the communion achieved in baptism cannot be seen as complete if the particular churches lack ecumenical unity. Again, the paradox arises of baptism as entry both into the one church of Christ and into specific and divided particular churches. She then investigates as one aspect of a solution the possibilities of an "integrated rite of initiation" which would reconnect baptism with the Eucharist and restore the asymmetry between a universal baptism and a confession-bound Eucharist.

*Peder Nørgaard-Højen,* a Danish Lutheran at the University of Copenhagen, strongly supports the idea of baptism as the bond of unity par excellence. He argues that baptism should be sufficient for church unity, since what is needed to make a person a member of the church is the same as what is required for church unity. If we admit that through baptism persons enter into communion with their own church, then the mutual recognition of baptisms should in itself imply a communion between the churches.

Since this is not the case, something must be missing in the mutual recognition of baptism among the churches and perhaps also in their varying baptismal practices. He claims that the churches in reality think differently about the content of baptism and that these differences are reflected in the existing divisions between the churches. Since baptism implies a living communion, Nørgaard-Højen is also critical of practices in which the link between baptism and committed church membership has weakened. He mentions the Lutheran churches in northern Europe as a cautionary example. Even more than Wood, he thus defends a straightforward view of baptism as the foundation of communion.

The three following essays examine baptism and church unity from biblical, ecumenical, and liturgical perspectives. In his exegetical paper *James D. G. Dunn*, a Protestant New Testament scholar from the University of Durham, takes his book *Baptism in the Holy Spirit* as a point of departure. There he is critical of the way many theologians use references to baptism in the New Testament. Baptism becomes a "concertina" word: Sometimes it is used to refer only to the water rite in the narrowest sense, but on other occasions its reference expands to cover the entirety of Christian initiation. In his Hvittorp paper Dunn develops this thesis and especially pays attention to the fact that the New Testament speaks not only of baptizing in water but also in the Holy Spirit. At some points in the New Testament the outpouring of the Spirit is an event clearly distinct and separate from water baptism.

For all these reasons, Dunn warns against an overly narrow focus on baptism. In biblical times baptism was a ritual undergoing development. Moreover, the water rite alone did not yet carry the whole weight of Christian initiation; other aspects of initiation were also present. From a New Testament perspective, imposing a rich sacramental theology upon the water rite alone is thus not unproblematic.

Baptism has not gone undiscussed in the many ecumenical dialogues of recent decades, and *André Birmelé*, a Lutheran teaching at the University of Strasbourg and a consultant to the Strasbourg Institute, provides a comprehensive survey of these discussions. He affirms

Edmund Schlink's claim that the most profound difference in Christianity runs between adherents and critics of infant baptism. In his survey of dialogues with the Baptist churches, Birmelé acknowledges that both sides agree that (1) baptism is unrepeatable and that (2) faith is a necessary element in baptism. But these convergences do not yet solve the outstanding problems, for they leave open the question of what baptism actually is.

The liturgical dimension of baptism and its ecumenical implications are dealt with in *Eugene L. Brand*'s paper. Brand, former Assistant General Secretary for Ecumenical Affairs of the LWF and a liturgical scholar, points out the way our celebration of baptism often affirms distinct denominational identities rather than unity. Our practices of confirmation as a second initiation often compound these problems.

The papers of Wood, Nørgaard-Højen, Dunn, Birmelé, and Brand can be seen as the foundational or theoretical part of the consultation's reflections around baptism. Baptism is more than a theological concept, however. It is a concrete rite, celebrated by specific churches in specific ways in specific contexts. The second part of the consultation and book deals with concrete problems of mutual recognition and baptismal practice.

That we can recognize a unity in baptism that extends beyond other forms of unity presupposes that we can in fact recognize each other's baptisms as true baptisms. While this recognition is widespread, it is not universal. Three presentations address cases where mutual recognition is difficult.

The Orthodox churches have been reluctant to recognize as a matter of principle (in distinction from individual cases of economy) the validity of baptisms conducted outside the Orthodox churches. *Merja Merras*, a Finnish Orthodox teaching at the University of Joensuu, Finland, addresses these issues.

After laying out the foundations of Orthodox understanding, Merras critically discusses the Lutheran position outlined in the background paper. She is critical of the emphasis on word and faith rather than on the sacrament as such. She points out that faith needs concrete faithfulness in order to be operative as love. The problem addressed in the study paper of massive nonparticipation of the baptized in the life of the church in some countries is also related to the lack of such faithfulness.

*S. Mark Heim,* an American Baptist teaching at Andover Newton Theological School, USA, addresses the ecumenical difficulties experienced by Baptists. He outlines the Baptist viewpoint, stressing that Baptists understand themselves as presenting an "alternative ecclesiology" centered on a living church of confessing Christians. The problems of mutual recognition arise from this ecclesiology. Concrete ecumenical steps toward mutual recognition should in his view include serious reflection on the catechumenate and on the distinctions made by non-Baptist churches between baptism and confirmation. Recognition that there are gradations of membership in most churches, in spite of the fact that through baptism one enters into a "full" membership, could open new possibilities for understanding the Baptist position. Heim thinks a postbaptismal catechumenate which culminates in a confirmation of one's own (infant) baptism might meet Baptists' ecclesiological concerns.

*John Pobee,* an Anglican from Ghana working with the World Council of Churches, presents examples from the baptismal practices of African Instituted Churches. Although they have on occasion invented new practices of initiation, they are not necessarily antiecumenical in spirit. On the contrary, their ecclesiology is often marked by explicit approval of other Christian communities. They stress baptism as an entry to the immediate home community; the specifically African changes and additions in the rites are not aimed at separating these communities from others. Rather, their symbolism allows believers to identify themselves with the immediate context in which they live as Christians.

Besides problems of mutual recognition, the consultation also addressed the relationship between baptism and church membership in two countries. Much of what is said about baptism and church unity presupposes that baptism is the one means of entrance into full membership within the church. The baptized are one because baptism is or symbolizes entrance into the one church. In some situations, however, this relation has been called into question. Two papers address such situations and their implications for baptism and church unity.

In Sweden the vast majority of the population belongs to the (Lutheran) Church of Sweden. Because all children born to members of the Swedish church were automatically enrolled as members of the church themselves, a situation developed in which a significant number of church members had never been baptized. *Ragnar Persenius,* Director for Theology and Ecumenical Affairs of the Church of Sweden, describes the theological debate over "nonbaptized church members" and the final resolution of what came to be seen as an unacceptable practice. Visible here is the difficult task of mediating developing theological insights and the realities of church life.

In India, as in some other countries where the church is a small minority, some persons wish to be deeply involved in the church but for various reasons do not wish to be baptized. Baptism may bring with it significant social and political penalties. How do we understand the phenomenon of such "unbaptized Christians"? *J. Jayakiran Sebastian,* a presbyter of the Church of South India teaching at the United Theological College, Bangalore, addresses the questions raised by the Indian situation. He points out the way both secular (e.g., caste and financial issues) and religious (e.g., charismatic criticisms of the significance of baptism) realities interact in this situation. Secularism, communalism, and fundamentalism come together in the conviction that one can believe in Christ but reject baptism.

In addition to these speakers, the Hvittorp consultation was attended by the editors of this book and by Dr. Thomas Best from the Faith and Order Secretariat of the World Council of Churches. Dr. Best reported on Faith and Order activities around the issue of baptism. Especially the consultation "Becoming a Christian: Ecumenical Implications of Our Common Baptism," held by Faith and Order in January 1997, is important in this respect.

The presentations were discussed extensively at Hvittorp. Since no significant changes to the study paper itself were requested, discussions concentrated on the problems outlined in the essays. In relation to Wood's and Nørgaard-Højen's papers, many felt that the Roman Catholic recognition of other Christian baptisms, ecumenically valuable in itself, still implied unresolved problems concerning the relationship between baptism and the Eucharist. Nørgaard-Højen's straightforward assertion that the mutual recognition of baptism is the sufficient condition for church fellowship was critically debated. Although his point was considered to be well taken, the corollary claim that a baptismal recognition without eucharistic fellowship is in fact harmful for ecumenical progress was not generally shared.

James Dunn's exegetical contribution was regarded as very helpful for understanding the later doctrinal differences concerning Christian initiation as a whole. His textual evidence for "baptism in the Spirit" in the New Testament as something distinct from the water rite was convincing for many. On the other hand, the relatively great liturgical uniformity of the water rite in the early church was considered by others as important counterevidence to this thesis of Dunn.

Mark Heim's presentation prompted a discussion on the gradation of membership in Lutheran and other Protestant churches. The opinion prevailed that since baptism is in itself a "full" initiation, concrete rites of later affirmation and confirmation of this initiation can be theologically problematic. The pastoral significance of a post-baptismal catechumenate and confirmation was nevertheless considered to be of great practical importance.

The discussion of baptism and church membership revealed that in many churches the notion of membership is somewhat vague. There is often a penumbra of persons who seem to be neither simply within or without the church. A great number of situations thus exist to which no clear rules can be applied. The increasing number of catechumens and interested people who are not baptized and thus not members in the formal sense of the word further creates pastoral problems. Whether such unbaptized sympathizers can and should in practice be treated as members is a genuine pastoral problem.

### 3. Work Still to Be Done

The focus of the discussions at Hvittorp was on the foundational nature of baptism in relation to the church as communion. The discussions were sobering but also encouraging for further work. Our unity in baptism, despite all difficulties of mutual recognition, was affirmed as one of the firmest bases of and strongest witnesses to the unity that transcends our divisions. Nevertheless, baptismal unity is no magic formula that will make other problems disappear. Other issues must be addressed on their own terms on the way to a more visible unity. What baptismal unity makes clear, however, is that unity is more fundamental than division. That there is only one baptism means that we are all members of the one church. This reality cannot remain without implications for the lives of the separated churches.

As noted above, we view the publication of the study paper and essays from Hvittorp as a contribution and encouragement to further work. Our hope is that they might contribute to the ecumenical reflection and effort needed along the path from unity at the font to the wider unity we are convinced is Christ's will for his church.

# Acknowledgments

We wish to thank the Central Board of the Church of Sweden for a financial grant in support of the consultation that produced this volume. The Helsinki diocese of the Evangelical Lutheran Church of Finland provided us warm hospitality during the consultation, for which we especially thank Bishop Eero Huovinen. Thanks should be extended especially to the Reverend S. Anita Stauffer of the Lutheran World Federation, who provided the initial impetus for this project. That illness prevented her from participating in the Hvittorp consultation was a loss for us all.

# Baptism and the Unity of the Church: A Study Paper

*Institute for Ecumenical Research*

"One Lord, one faith, one baptism" (Eph. 4:5).[1] From the beginning, Christians have understood themselves as united in a single faith by the one baptism that joins them with the one Lord, Jesus Christ. Nevertheless, when one looks over the extensive recent literature on the unity of the church, especially that produced within the context of the modern ecumenical movement, baptism plays a more marginal role than one would expect. Baptism as a bond of unity is mentioned and then left to the side. When the phrase "sacrament of unity" is used, the reference is more often to the Eucharist than to baptism.

This study paper seeks to provide an initial presentation of the issues involved in the interrelation between baptism and the unity of the church. As a study paper, it aims at sparking discussion. The other essays in this volume take up other views, sometimes merely different, sometimes at odds with what we have said here. Precisely because this issue has not received the attention it deserves, different voices need to be heard.

Our presentation has two parts. The first part lays out a brief yet,

---

1. All biblical quotations in this study paper are from the New Revised Standard Version.

10

we hope, comprehensive account of the interrelation of baptism and the unity of the church. As in much recent ecumenical literature, we use the concept "communion" to understand the nature of the church's unity. The *interrelation* of baptism and communion is our focus here. No attempt will be made to provide a full account of the meaning of baptism[2] nor of the church as a communion.[3] The second section addresses specific issues and problems that relate to baptism and the unity of the church.

This paper has been written from a perspective that is Lutheran but which seeks to be ecumenically open. The first, more constructive part of the paper more obviously reflects convictions held firmly by Lutherans and shared by many but not all fellow Christians; e.g., a strongly sacramental view of baptism. We have called this paper a study paper and included it in a volume which presents other perspectives precisely because we see it as a contribution to an ongoing discussion, not as a final word.

Before we begin, a definitional question must be answered. What does the word "baptism" refer to? As James Dunn has noted, baptism is often a "concertina" word, its reference sometimes expanding to include the entirety of initiation and sometimes contracting to cover only the water rite in the narrowest sense.[4] Unless otherwise specified, "baptism" in this paper refers to the entirety of the single initiation rite centering on the immersion in water of, or pouring of water on,

---

2. For a comprehensive discussion of the meaning of baptism, written from a clearly Lutheran but ecumenically open perspective, see Edmund Schlink, *Die Lehre von der Taufe* (Kassel: Johannes Stauda Verlag, 1969); ET, *The Doctrine of Baptism*, trans. Herbert J. A. Bouman (St. Louis: Concordia, 1972). Indispensable for any discussion of baptism today is *Baptism, Eucharist and Ministry*, Faith and Order Paper 111 (Geneva: World Council of Churches, 1982), hereafter cited as *BEM*.

3. On the church as communion, see for a brief account "*Communio/Koinonia:* A New Testament–Early Christian Concept and Its Contemporary Appropriation and Significance," a study by the Institute for Ecumenical Research, Strasbourg (Strasbourg, 1990). A comprehensive account can be found in J.-M. Tillard, *Église d'Eglises. L'ecclésiologie de communion* (Paris: Cerf, 1987); ET, *Church of Churches: The Ecclesiology of Communion* (Collegeville, Minn.: Liturgical Press, 1992).

4. Dunn, *Baptism in the Holy Spirit*, Studies in Biblical Theology, 2nd ser., vol. 15 (London: SCM, 1970), p. 5.

the new Christian in the name of the triune God. If anointing and the laying on of hands occur in the context of this rite, then they are part of what we here refer to as baptism. If such rites occur at a later date as a separate rite, then we assume they are not a part of the reference of the term. This usage is only intended as an initial linguistic assumption, not as a theological assertion or definition of validity. We do not intend to prejudge, for example, whether the laying on of hands and anointing are a second sacrament in distinction from baptism, even if performed in direct connection with it.[5] As will be clear in the second part of this paper, many of the more difficult ecumenical questions surrounding baptism relate to these definitional issues.

## I. Baptism and the Unity of the Church as a Communion

### A. *Baptism into Christ and into His Church*

Baptism is both a *foundation* of the church as a communion and a *mirror* of its nature.

Baptism is, above all, the sacrament of our participation in, even unity with, Christ. We are baptized "into Christ Jesus" (Rom. 6:3). To be baptized is to be "clothed . . . with Christ" (Gal. 3:27). Lutherans have emphasized baptism as the sacrament of forgiveness,[6] but baptism mediates forgiveness precisely because it mediates unity with Christ, especially with his death and resurrection. In the baptismal waters the sinner dies with Christ (Col. 2:12), so that the new person may rise with Christ washed, regenerated (Titus 3:5). The Holy Spirit, who comes to us in baptism, brings us into unity with Christ (II Cor.

---

5. For an Orthodox argument that these events constitute a second, distinct sacrament, see Alexander Schmemann, *Of Water and the Spirit: A Liturgical Study of Baptism* (Crestwood, N.Y.: St. Vladimir's Seminary Press, 1974), p. 76.

6. "What gifts or benefits does Baptism bestow? It effects forgiveness of sins, delivers from death and the devil, and grants eternal salvation to all who believe, as the Word and promise of God declare" (Martin Luther, *Small Catechism*, IV:5f.). All quotations from the Lutheran Confessions are taken from *The Book of Concord*, translated and edited by Theodore G. Tappert (Philadelphia: Fortress Press, 1959). No attempt has been made to alter the translation in the direction of more inclusive language.

1:21f.). In participation in or unity with Christ, the many meanings of baptism find their focus.

To be baptized into Christ, however, is always to be baptized into his body, the church (I Cor. 12:13). One cannot love God and hate the neighbor; one cannot be one with Jesus without also being one body with all those who are also one with him in baptism. From Pentecost on, baptism has been the central initiation rite for virtually all branches of the church. For the New Testament, this rule would appear to be without exception.[7] The equation of baptism with entrance into the community is clear in the sentence that summarizes the response to Peter's Pentecost sermon: "So those who welcomed his message were baptized, and that day about three thousand persons were added" (Acts 2:41). To be baptized is to be added to the community.

Crucial for the significance of baptism is the intertwining of its two clusters of meanings: It is the sacrament of salvation[8] (I Pet. 3:21; cf. " 'What should we do?' . . . 'Repent and be baptized' " [Acts 2:37f.]), and it is the sacrament of initiation into the Christian community, the church. Here baptism reflects the basic structure of the church as a communion. Above all, the Christian has communion with Christ. Participation in Christ is the foundation of the church's existence. Because we each participate in Christ, we are also one with one another. The fundamental bonds of communion with Christ — faith,

---

7. That the reference to children who are holy in I Corinthians 7:14 might refer to unbaptized persons who were considered in a full sense members of the community seems speculative. The more difficult question is the status of Apollos, whom Acts 18:25 states had received only the baptism of John. He then has the Way "explained . . . to him more accurately" (v. 26) by Priscilla and Aquila, but no mention is made of his receiving another baptism. This omission is made more striking by the immediately following episode in which a group of Ephesians who had also received only the baptism of John do receive an additional baptism. If the statement that Apollos was "fervent in spirit" (RSV; "burning enthusiasm" in NRSV) implies that Apollos had, like those at Pentecost, received the Holy Spirit in some visible way (so Dunn, p. 88), then the question of the baptismal status of Apollos is a form of the question of the baptismal status of the 120 who were "brothers" prior to Pentecost and who (if they are included in the "all" of Acts 2:1) had visibly received the Spirit at Pentecost. Again, no explicit mention is made of their baptism.

8. "To put it most simply, the power, effect, benefit, fruit, and purpose of Baptism is to save" (Martin Luther, *Large Catechism*, IV:24).

baptism, the Eucharist — are also the fundamental bonds of communion with each other.

These intertwining strands of baptism and communion, both with Christ and with other Christians, come together in the close relation between baptism and the gift of the Holy Spirit. John points forward from his own baptism to the one who will " 'baptize you with the Holy Spirit' " (Mark 1:8; see John 1:33). While the connection between baptism and the gift of the Spirit is not without its complexities,[9] both the New Testament (e.g., Acts 2:38; 19:5f.; I Cor. 12:13; Titus 3:5) and tradition have stressed the granting of the Spirit in the context of the comprehensive event of baptism. The gift of the Spirit and of participation in Christ must not be played off against each other. The mission of the Spirit is precisely to lead us into Christ (John 14:26; 16:14). Within an adequately trinitarian theology, if baptism unites us with Christ, then it *must* also imply the gift of the Spirit. And this same Spirit makes us one with each other. Thus, one can say that the communion which is the church can be comprehensively described as a communion in the Holy Spirit, the Holy Spirit given within baptism.

Baptism has a foundational sense both for the individual and for the community as a whole. For the individual, baptism is the initiatory event, in which is realized and focused all that forms the foundation of the Christian life: unity with Christ, especially with his death and resurrection; the gift of the Spirit; regeneration; membership in the community. In a slightly different sense, baptism is foundational for the communion of the church. In Ephesians, Christ is said to make the community as a whole "holy by cleansing her with the washing of water by the word" (5:26). There is no single baptism in which the church comes to be, although Pentecost, the event that most accurately might be called the originating event of the church, has a bap-

9. See *BEM*, #B14, and Schlink, chap. 2, sec. 2. The relation between baptism and the Spirit is most complicated in Acts, where the reception of the Spirit and baptism in the narrow sense of the water rite seem to be closely interrelated yet distinct. (For two quite different understandings of baptism and the Holy Spirit in the New Testament, see Dunn, cited above, and Oscar Cullmann, *Baptism in the New Testament*, Studies in Biblical Theology, vol. 1 [London: SCM Press, 1950].) Especially in relation to the reception of the Spirit, the debates over the significance of anointing and the laying on of hands come to the fore.

tismal character.[10] The pouring out of the Holy Spirit that occurs then is thereafter closely associated with baptism. Among the various bonds of communion that hold the church together, the relations among Christians and between Christians and Christ that are realized in baptism are theologically basic. In this sense, one can say that baptism is the foundational sacrament of the communion which is the church.

## B. Baptism and the Structure and Life of the Church as Communion

As an event that founds and reflects the Christian's communion with Christ and the church, baptism also reflects the structure of the church as communion in various ways.

### 1. Baptism into the Local and Universal Church

It is generally agreed ecumenically that baptism is always both into a particular local church and into the church universal.[11] In normal situations, baptism is carried out by some local church and constitutes an entry into the concrete life and care of that community. One cannot belong to "the church in general" without belonging to some concrete, historically particular body (as, analogously, one cannot love "humanity in general" without loving some concrete neighbors). But as initiation into the one body of Christ, baptism is also initiation into the church universal, "the one holy catholic and apostolic church." The person baptized is united with all Christians in the one church. He or she is baptized *by* a particular church *into* the one church.[12]

The communion which is the church reflects this same interrelation of local and universal. Communion is always realized in a local

10. In I Corinthians 10:1ff., Paul does speak of all Israel being "baptized into Moses in the cloud and in the sea," presenting the early events of the exodus typologically as a sort of mass baptism of Israel.

11. See, e.g., *BEM*, #B6.

12. Particularly helpful on the issues raised in this paragraph is Eugene L. Brand, "The Lima Text as a Standard for Current Understandings and Practice of Baptism," *Studia Liturgica* 16 (1986): 40-63.

church (whether understood as parish, congregation, or diocese) as a realization of the one church catholic. The local church is indispensable. This local church, as ecumenical ecclesiology has come increasingly to recognize, is itself fully "church"; it is not just a part of the church catholic but itself a "catholic church," a church in which is found the fullness of the gifts the Spirit pours out on the church.[13] But the local church is truly catholic only in communion with other such churches. A church that chooses isolation is a church in self-contradiction. The interrelation of the church as local and as universal is a controversial theme in present discussions within and between the churches.[14] The issue is made more complicated by the divisions among the churches. In fact, one can say that baptism into the one universal church by local churches which are separated constitutes the ecumenical problem. If Lutherans, Baptists, Catholics, and Orthodox all truly baptize (a not insignificant "if"), then they all baptize into, and thus in some sense belong to, the one church of Jesus Christ. If we then cannot live out that unity in a common life of worship and mission, something is deeply wrong. How can we be one yet not one? Therein lies the fundamental contradiction that drives ecumenical efforts.

## 2. Baptism as Sacrament and the Gracious Priority of God

Lutherans, along with the majority of (but not all) other Christians, understand baptism as a sacrament. It is not a "human work," either in the sense that it is a merely human invention or in the sense that the primary agent in baptism is either the baptizing community or the baptized individual. Baptism is a work of God, both in the sense that it is divinely instituted and in the sense that the decisive agent in baptism is God, acting through the Holy Spirit within the church which

13. For an ecumenical statement and exploration of this theme, see the study document produced for the Joint Working Group between the Roman Catholic Church and the World Council of Churches, "The Church: Local and Universal," published in Joint Working Group, *Sixth Report* (Geneva: WCC Publications, 1990).

14. See here especially the discussion surrounding the letter from the (Roman Catholic) Congregation for the Doctrine of the Faith, "Some Aspects of the Church Understood as Communion" (28 May 1992), the central theme of which is the interrelation of the church as local and as universal.

baptizes. Lutherans have particularly stressed that in the sacraments, God is at work through the word of *promise,* the promise of our justification by grace through faith for the sake of Jesus Christ. What the Spirit grants in baptism is that participation in Christ which justifies "apart from works of the Law."

This understanding of baptism as sacrament undergirds its role in the life of the church. Baptism is not a rite we can use or abandon as we choose. The missionary command of the risen Christ is: " 'Go therefore and make disciples of all nations, baptizing them in the name of the Father and of the Son and of the Holy Spirit, and teaching them to obey everything that I have commanded you' " (Matt. 28:19f.). Baptism is, if nothing else, an act of obedience.[15] In this obedience, we have the assurance of the divine promise that God is at work. "To be baptized in God's name is to be baptized not by men but by God himself. Although it is performed by men's hands, it is nevertheless truly God's own act."[16]

For the Lutheran Reformation, the character of baptism as a sacrament in this sense is decisive for its evangelical significance. My assurance of the grace of Christ is not a function of some personal experience whose interpretation is open to question or of some action which may or may not be an instrument of the Holy Spirit. We can build our confidence on our baptism because here we have the divine promise: " 'The one who believes and is baptized will be saved' " (Mark 16:16). The sacrament provides the external sign so that faith has "something to which it may cling and upon which it may stand."[17]

Again, baptism reflects a fundamental aspect of the church as communion. The church is not self-constituting. Its fundamental character is given to it by God. The church is thus a dependent reality, dependent upon the institution of its essential actions by Christ and upon the activity of the Spirit within these actions. We receive the

---

15. "Observe, first, that these words [Matt. 28:19; Mark 16:16] contain God's commandment and ordinance. You should not doubt, then, that Baptism is of divine origin, not something devised or invented by men. As truly as I can say that the Ten Commandments, the Creed, and the Lord's Prayer are not spun out of any man's imagination but revealed and given by God himself, so I can also boast that Baptism is no human plaything but is instituted by God himself" (Luther, *Large Catechism,* IV:6).

16. Luther, *Large Catechism,* IV:10.

17. Luther, *Large Catechism,* IV:29.

communion which the church is. This dependent, receptive character can be seen in the days of waiting that separate Ascension and Pentecost. The apostles are not entrusted with a mission and then told to carry it out as they please and by their own strength. They are told to *wait* until they " 'have been clothed with power from on high' " (Luke 24:49). The initiative remains with God; and only when the Spirit takes up that initiative at Pentecost does the mission history of Acts begin. Likewise, the decision to baptize Gentiles was less an initiative of the community than it was the community following where the Spirit had already blazed the path (Acts 11:17). The *given* character of baptism as a sacrament points to the church as a communion in Christ and thus precisely a communion under Christ's lordship.

### 3. Baptism as Gift and the Communion Defined by Gift

Baptism as sacrament points to its fundamental character as gift and as the medium by which gifts are given. In baptism, we are receivers. In relation to baptism, faith is precisely the trustful reception of the gifts given.[18] The fundamentally receptive character of baptism is evident in its liturgical form. One cannot baptize oneself. Baptism must be received from another person.[19] (One also *hears* the Word and *eats* and *drinks* the Lord's Supper, all receptive acts.) The need for another person in baptism again indicates its communal orientation.

The gift character of baptism is also evident in the simplicity, even ease, of baptism. At the crucial moment, all one need do is be quiet and be still (and as thousands of screaming, squirming babies have shown, even these are not absolutely necessary). Baptism requires no prior physical, intellectual, moral, or religious attainments. The membership of the church is not made up of an elite who have successfully undergone some kind of initiatory ordeal. If we can boast of baptism, we can only boast of the Lord, not of anything we brought to it or achieved within it.

18. "Baptism . . . is a treasure which God gives us and faith grasps" (Luther, *Large Catechism*, IV:37).
19. On the impossibility of self-baptism, see the letter of Pope Innocent III to Bishop Bertolt of Metz, 28 August 1206, in Denzinger-Hünermann, *Enchiridion Symbolorum* (Freiburg: Herder, 1991), #788.

Precisely by looking away from human qualifications and achievements, baptism leads us into a community in which prior human divisions or distinctions are no longer of decisive significance. What is decisive is the new identity we all have been given in Christ. Twice Paul states that in Christ there is neither Jew nor Greek, slave nor free, (male nor female) (Gal. 3:28; I Cor. 12:13).[20] In both cases the statement is made in connection with baptism. Because "as many of you as were baptized into Christ have clothed yourselves with Christ," thus "there is no longer Jew or Greek, . . . for all of you are one in Christ Jesus," and thus all "heirs according to the promise" (Gal. 3:27ff.). Because in baptism all, no matter what differences they bring, receive the same fundamental, identity-defining gift, all are one. Whatever distinctions may still function in the community (because of the various, more specific gifts each receives), they must serve this more basic unity.[21]

## 4. Baptism and Communion as Gift and Call

Discussion cannot end, however, with the general statement that baptism and the communion it founds are gifts. The World Council of Churches Assembly in Canberra in 1991 spoke of the communion of the church as gift and call. The language of "gift and call" has become common in ecumenical discussions and points to an undeniable reality. The question remains, however, how gift and call interrelate in the church as communion. In baptism, gift and call interrelate in a particular way that illumines the nature of the church as communion.

As has been said, what is given in baptism is, most fundamentally, participation in Christ and his body through the Holy Spirit. Two

20. The reference to "male and female" is only in the Galatians passage. In Ephesians 2 (not by Paul?), a similar point is made without any explicit reference to baptism.

21. The argument in I Corinthians 12 leading up to the baptismal "Jew nor Greek" passage seeks a recognition both of diverse gifts within the community and of the subordination of this diversity to a more basic unity. Thus the argument opens: "There are varieties of gifts, but the same Spirit; and there are varieties of services, but the same Lord; and there are varieties of activities, but it is the same God who activates all of them in everyone" (I Cor. 12:4ff.).

aspects of this gift need here to be noted. First, if in baptism we receive Christ and his righteousness, then what we receive is not some preliminary gift, to be completed later, but the ultimate, the eschatological gift. Baptism is not simply the beginning of a process which is left behind as we progress in faith or righteousness. Rather, if in baptism we are given Christ in his fullness, then baptism is both a beginning and the presence of the end. Progress must be understood as living out of and into the gift given in baptism.[22]

But second, this gift is not a thing but a person, or, more concretely, a relation of participation in another person, Christ present through the Spirit in and as his church. A personal relation is something that must be *lived* if it is to exist. Thus, precisely as the kind of gift it is, baptism is a call, a call to life in Christ. Most fundamentally, it is a call to receive the gift given; i.e., it is a call to faith. Lutherans have sought to emphasize not only the objectivity of baptism and the grace there offered but also the necessity of faith to receive what is objectively present. The efficacy of baptism depends on faith in the recipient. We are justified by grace, *through faith*. But the nature of faith needs to be further spelled out if the relation of gift to call is to be rightly understood. Faith is never a self-subsistent achievement, an act that has meaning by itself in abstraction from that which it is faith in. Faith is the turn of the self away from the self and toward Christ, a relation of ever more perfect dependence on Christ. As a call to faith, baptism calls to dependence on the gift given. In this sense, gift has an irreversible priority to call. Not only is the nature of the call determined by the nature of the gift, but also the call is to a life that lives out the priority of the gift, the priority of grace.

An analogous relation between gift and call exists in the communion baptism founds. Our communion with Christ and with one another is a gift. What is given is not a partial communion we must

22. "Therefore, when we rise from our sins or repent, we are merely returning to the power and the faith of baptism from which we fell, and finding our way back to the promise then made to us, which we deserted when we sinned. For the truth of the promise once made remains steadfast, always ready to receive us back with open arms when we return. And this, if I mistake not, is what they mean when they say, though obscurely, that baptism is the first sacrament and the foundation of all the others, without which none of the others can be received" (Martin Luther, *The Babylonian Captivity of the Church* [American Edition, 36:59; WA, 6:528]).

then complete through our efforts. We *are* one body in Christ. We are called to live out of and into that reality. Again, since the gift is a relation of participation, it can only be received by being lived. The gift itself implies a call. But, as with baptism, the nature of the call itself points to the priority of the gift. We have communion in the Lord who remains the community's true head. The nature of the community's life in communion must constantly indicate that its communion is in the Lord and depends on the Lord for its life. Thus, word and sacrament have a theological priority over other forms of communal life because they are the events in which we have the promise of the presence of the communion-creating Christ. Throughout its life, the church is called to witness to the initiative of Christ.

### 5. Baptism and Communion in the Death, Resurrection, and Mission of Christ

The gift given in baptism is a relation of participation in a person. This person, Christ present through the Spirit, was not and is not inactive. To be baptized into Christ, to receive the gift of the Holy Spirit, is to be baptized into Christ's activity, both his earthly movement through death to resurrection and his present mission in the world through the Spirit. In relation to each, gift again implies call, a call to live out the gift given.

On the one hand, we are baptized into the event of Christ's death and resurrection. Jesus himself can refer to our following him in suffering as our being baptized with the same baptism in which he is baptized (Mark 10:38). Our participation in his death and resurrection is not a once-and-for-all event at the beginning of the Christian life. In the catechisms, Luther emphasizes baptism as a lifelong process of the death of the old person and the coming to life of the new. Baptism "is simply the slaying of the Old Adam and the resurrection of the new man, both of which actions must continue in us our whole life long. Thus a Christian life is nothing else than a daily Baptism, once begun and ever continued."[23]

On the other hand, we are not just granted a participation in the past event of Christ's death and resurrection, but also a participation

23. Luther, *Large Catechism*, IV:65.

in the ongoing activity of Christ in the world through the Spirit. The baptized is called to participation in the mission of witness and service which is the continuing work of the Spirit of Christ. As Luther put it, baptism is ordination into the priesthood of Christ, the ministry of witness and service shared by all Christians.[24] This mission and ministry is not something that stands apart from our participation in Christ, but is a concrete form of that participation. Christ is with us in such mission, "to the end of the age."

What is said about baptism must also, with some differences, be said about the communion it grounds. Whatever sense one gives to the church as the body of Christ, existing "without a spot or wrinkle" (Eph. 5:27), the church as a corporate body of forgiven sinners is called to constant conversion, a dying to the sin that is still within it and a rising to life in Christ.[25] More prominently, the church is called to participate in Christ's mission. Pentecost is both the originating event of the church and the beginning of its mission. The primary manifestation of the Spirit's presence at Pentecost is that the disciples preach and are heard (Acts 2:11). The apostles are the foundation stones of the church (Eph. 2:20), and apostles are paradigmatically and etymologically messengers, persons sent with a mission. The communion which is the church, as it is constituted by participation in Christ, is also thus constituted by participation in his mission.

## II. Baptism and the Failures and Divisions of the Church as Communion

In a world and church unaffected by sin, our comments would not require a second part. (In a world without sin, however, perhaps there would be no study papers.) Or a second part would be only an extension of the first, discussing how baptismal unity is lived out in unity

24. An excellent discussion of this theme in Luther is Hans-Martin Barth, "Allgemeines Priestertum der Gläubigen nach Martin Luther," *Una Sancta* 43 (1988): 331-42.

25. For a recent discussion of the churches' need for constant conversion, see the report from the Groupe des Dombes, *For the Conversion of the Churches* (Geneva: WCC Publications, 1993).

in the Eucharist, in common mission and service. But sin, failure, division plague both church and world. What has been said about baptism and unity is not canceled by sin and division, but we must recognize the ways in which we do not and at times cannot now live out the unity discussed above.

## A. Problems Related to Mutual Recognition of Baptism[26]

All that has been said about our unity being grounded in one baptism presumes a mutual recognition of baptism; i.e., it presumes that we all believe that we are in fact truly baptizing. If one cannot recognize the baptism carried out in a certain church as a true baptism, then one cannot see oneself as one with that church in baptism. While a mutual recognition of baptism has been extensively realized, at least implicitly, significant problems still hinder certain large groups of churches and Christians from fully recognizing many baptisms carried out in other churches.

### 1. What Are the Essential Elements of Baptism?

Mutual recognition of baptism assumes some agreement on what constitutes the identity of baptism; i.e., it assumes some agreement on what must happen for an event to be called a baptism. As noted above, the most common answer has been that a baptism must be (1) in the triune name, (2) using water, (3) with the intention to do what the church does.[27] This understanding of baptism, however, is not universal, and some churches are not able to recognize baptisms carried out in some other churches because they believe that certain elements constitutive of baptism are lacking.

Agreement on these three elements, however, does not eliminate all difficulties. For example, how must water be used? Is immersion

---

26. A useful, if by now somewhat dated, analysis and survey of ecumenical discussions on this topic can be found in Nils Ehrenström, *Mutual Recognition of Baptism in Interchurch Agreements*, Faith and Order Paper 90 (Geneva: World Council of Churches, 1978).

27. See, e.g., *BEM*, #B17; Martin Chemnitz, *Loci Communes*, locus 19, sec. 4.

the only acceptable form of true baptism, as some Baptist churches believe? If some form of pouring or sprinkling is permitted, is the mere moistening of the baptized person's forehead adequate?[28] Differences on these questions are still significant in certain contexts.

## 2. Can Baptisms Truly Occur beyond the Church?

Who can baptize? While the churches extensively agree that any member of the church can, if necessary, baptize, a more ecclesiastical question remains. Can a group of Christians whom one cannot recognize as church in the full sense or who have separated themselves from the communion of the true church of Christ (or been separated because of heresy) in fact baptize into the one church of Christ? In the church of the second and early third centuries, the answer was generally no. A community which through heresy or schism had left the community of the church could not grant entrance into the church. Heretics could not grant the gifts they had themselves abandoned; they could not truly baptize.[29]

This opinion was revised in the West during the course of the Donatist controversy, which involved the general question of the relation between the validity of the sacraments and the identity of the minister who administered them. After extensive debate, beginning with arguments put forward by Pope Stephen I in the mid–third century and culminating in the theology of Augustine a century and a half later, the validity of baptism by what one judged to be heretics and schismatics came to be generally recognized in the West.[30] In the West, any baptism carried out in the triune name, with water, and with the

---

28. Canon 854 of the Roman Catholic *Code of Canon Law* states that baptism may be "by immersion or by pouring *[infusionem]*." The 1993 *Directory for the Application of Principles and Norms of Ecumenism* warns in a footnote (n. 105) that there is "the danger of invalidity when baptism is administered by sprinkling, especially of several people at once." On this question, see the Faith and Order *Mutual Recognition* paper (above, n. 26), p. 12.

29. On these issues in the early church, the article "Ketzertaufe, und Streit darüber," in the *Protestantische Realenzyklopädie* is still worth consulting.

30. Precisely what such a baptism outside the communion of the true church communicated remained controversial. For Augustine, such a baptism did not communicate salvation (see his *De Baptismo*, bk. 1).

intention to do what the church does when it baptizes came to be generally recognized as a true baptism, regardless of the community in relation to which the baptism was performed. The Reformation churches continued this recognition, and it remains the practice of the Roman Catholic and Reformation churches.[31]

This practice does create an anomalous situation. If one believes (as was generally believed by the patristic and medieval church and is still claimed by at least the Roman Catholic Church) that one's own communion realizes the true church of Jesus Christ in a unique way, then this practice of recognizing other baptisms implies that a community in some sense outside the church can grant a kind of entrance into the one church. Even if one makes no such claim, recognition of the baptism of a community with which one is not in communion leads to the contradiction of unity in the foundational event of baptism but division in the living out of that unity.

The Orthodox churches, however, have been reluctant to accept the principle of a separation between the recognition of a community's baptisms and the full recognition of the community's reality as a church. They contend that an unqualified recognition of a community's baptisms should be part of a more general, full recognition and reconciliation of the two churches.[32] While Orthodox churches have often not insisted on a new baptism for those who come to them from other churches (or at least from those churches which they judge to have extensively preserved the essentials of the orthodox and catholic tradition), such implicit recognition of non-Orthodox baptism can be interpreted as a matter of economy, a "temporary provision for an

31. Among Lutherans, this issue has not been controversial. Of great ecumenical significance was the recognition by the Second Vatican Council of our communion in baptism: "All who have been justified by faith in baptism are members of Christ's body, and have a right to be called Christians, and so are deservedly recognized as sisters and brothers in the Lord by the children of the catholic church" (*Decree on Ecumenism*, #3). In the *Decree on Ecumenism*, see also ##4, 22-23; *Decree on the Church*, #15.

32. For a recent Orthodox discussion of this issue, see Metropolitan Damaskinos (Papandreou), "Zur Anerkennung der Taufe seitens der orthodoxen Kirche unter Berücksichtigung des heiligen und großen Konzils," *Una Sancta* 48 (1993): 48-53. For an insightful discussion of these issues, especially in relation to recent Catholic-Orthodox dialogue, see J.-M. Tillard, "Baptism: New Problems and New Questions," *Ecumenical Trends* 17 (1988): 17-20.

exceptional situation."[33] Thus, one cannot speak of an Orthodox recognition of non-Orthodox baptisms in principle in the same way as
one can speak of such a recognition by the Catholic and Reformation
churches. The idea of a unity in baptism that extends wider than the
limits of a realized full communion of the churches is not an idea
accepted without qualification by the Orthodox.

### 3. Baptism and the Confession of Faith

Who can be baptized? Most notably, must persons being baptized be
able themselves to make a confession of faith? The understanding of
baptism outlined in Part I of this paper points to the theological
grounds Lutherans and others have given to justify the practice of
baptizing the small children of Christians, children who cannot
confess the faith for themselves. For various reasons some churches
(most prominently but not only those called "Baptist") believe that
the capacity to confess one's own faith is an essential condition for
baptism. Only so-called believer's baptism is in fact baptism. The baptism of someone incapable of such confession, e.g., an infant, is simply
no baptism.[34] Those who went through a baptismal ritual as a child
must then be viewed as unbaptized. If persons baptized as infants
were to seek membership in such a church, they would need to be
baptized now as adults.

It should be emphasized that the ecumenical issue here is not
the advisability of infant baptism, but its possibility. Ecumenically, a
significant difference exists between churches which deny the validity
of infant baptism and churches such as the Disciples of Christ who,
while themselves not baptizing infants, are willing to recognize infant

33. Damaskinos, p. 50. On economy in general, see also the article "Economy
(Oikonomia)," in *Dictionary of the Ecumenical Movement,* ed. Nicholas Lossky et
al. (Geneva: WCC Publications, 1991).

34. "Baptists in general cannot regard the baptism of infants and the baptism
of adults as two different forms of one baptism. . . . In general, Baptists are unable
to acknowledge infant baptism as baptism" (Baptist-Lutheran Joint Commission,
*Baptists and Lutherans in Conversation: A Message to Our Churches* [Geneva, 1990],
#34). See also *BEM,* ##11-13. A comprehensive ecumenical discussion of these
issues can be found in *Louisville Baptism Consultation,* Faith and Order Paper 97,
in *Review and Expositor* 77, no. 1 (winter 1980).

baptism and thus accept into their membership without a new baptism persons baptized in infancy.

Most obviously, this difference over the identity of baptism means that many "believers' baptist" churches cannot recognize many, even most, of the baptisms carried out in many other churches. Talk of baptism as a bond uniting Christians becomes difficult in such a case.[35] Less obviously, obstacles can also exist for these other churches to recognize baptisms carried out in such believers' baptist churches. *If* the insistence on a capacity to confess one's own faith is a function of an understanding and practice of baptism strictly as a public profession of the faith of the baptized and their reception by the congregation, as a human response and in no sense as a sacrament understood as an act of God, then in what sense can one say that here "the same thing" is being done as in a church which clearly celebrates baptism as a sacrament in which God is the primary agent? If an essential element of baptism is an intention to do what the church does, can such an intention be reciprocally recognized in the context of such a radical disagreement over what the church is in fact doing?

## 4. New Questions about the Identity of Baptism

The problems noted in the previous three sections have been debated at least since the Reformation. New churches and new movements within the churches have more recently raised various new questions. Some Pentecostal groups insist that baptism should be in the name of Jesus alone and not in the triune name; some feminist theologians are critical of the use of "Father, Son, and Holy Spirit" as the baptismal name and prefer some less male-oriented alternative (e.g., "Creator, Redeemer, Sanctifier"); some new churches have altered other aspects of baptism (e.g., the Church of Jesus Christ on Earth through the Prophet Simon Kimbangu, a large African Instituted Church in Zaire, baptizes by the laying on of hands and prayer, without any use of water). Is the traditional list of essential elements of baptism given above still an adequate guideline for the recognition

35. See, e.g., C. B. Hastings, "The Lima Document: A Southern Baptist View," *Ecumenical Trends* 12 (1983): 24-27.

of baptism? What sorts of contextual flexibility are possible in the recognition of baptism? Both the general theological question and concrete questions of pastoral practice in particular situations need to be addressed. As a bond of communion, baptism must be such that it can be recognized as baptism by the widest possible range of Christians and churches.

## B. Baptism and the Community Which Participates in the Life of the Church

Baptism plays such a foundational role in establishing the communion which is the church, one is tempted to define the church as the assembly or community of the baptized. But other definitions are possible; other bonds of communion are important for the life of the church. One could define the church as the community which gathers around the preaching of the Word and the administration of the sacraments, i.e., as the group which participates in the defining activities of the church's life. The Augsburg Confession gives a third option: "Properly speaking, the church is the assembly of saints and true believers."[36] Ideally, the three possible definitions would be perfectly congruent. All the baptized would be believers and would gather around Word and sacrament; all who believe and gather around Word and sacrament would be baptized. In fact, such congruence is not realized. The communion realized in the daily life of the church often is constituted by a different set of people than the communion constituted by the bond of baptism. When this difference is simply a function of the fact that some will always fall away, fundamental questions are not raised. When, however, the difference between the communion defined by baptism and the communion defined by the regular life of the church comes to be a difference in principle or a difference of large proportions, the status of baptism as fundamental bond of communion is placed in question. Such a difference can arise in various ways.

36. Augsburg Confession, VIII:1.

## 1. Baptism and Full Initiation into the Life of the Church[37]

Does baptism make someone a member of the church? Is baptism the full rite of initiation into the church? One might hold that full initiation involves something beyond baptism, especially if baptism is defined strictly as the rite with water in the triune name. Orthodox churches understand full initiation to involve not only baptism so defined but also anointing (chrismation) and the first reception of the Eucharist.[38] Since all three events in the Orthodox Church typically follow each other within the same comprehensive worship service, the communion of the baptized and the community of the fully initiated remain in principle identical. A similar pattern was standard in both East and West during the first thousand years of church history.

In the West, this early rite of initiation fell apart into different rites, conducted at different times in a person's life, especially if the person was baptized as an infant. In the Roman Catholic Church, "full Christian initiation" is said to require baptism, confirmation, and the reception of the Eucharist, events often separated by years.[39] While Lutherans have not understood confirmation as a sacramental addition to baptism, they have often withheld the reception of the Lord's Supper from baptized children until some particular age or some rite of confirmation, however understood. As Eugene Brand has pointed out, neither the New Testament nor early tradition knows of a class of persons who were baptized but were not full members of the church. The creation of such a class inevitably calls into question statements about baptism as the fundamental bond of communion with Christ and his church and statements about baptism granting the eschatological gift in its fullness.[40]

A similar issue can arise in relation to claims of a "second blessing" or "baptism of the Holy Spirit" sometimes put forward by Pentecostal and Holiness churches or by charismatic movements. Charismatic movements need not call the significance of baptism into

---

37. On the questions raised in this section, see the article by Aidan Kavanagh on "Initiation, Christian," in *The Westminster Dictionary of Christian Theology* (Philadelphia: Westminster Press, 1983).

38. For a brief account of the Orthodox view, see Schmemann, pp. 115-21.

39. *Code of Canon Law*, #842.2.

40. See Brand, pp. 50f.

question and can be blessings to churches. Nevertheless, when some particular religious experience or gift is made a necessary part of full Christian identity, when the "merely baptized" are made second-class church members, then the role of baptism and the gifts given within it are denigrated.[41]

## 2. Baptism and Massive Nonparticipation

As stated above, some baptized do fall away. The circle of those who gather around the Word and the sacraments will always include fewer than the full number of the baptized. The situation changes, however, when those who participate in the life of the church with any frequency become a small minority of the baptized. What does baptism as entry into the life of the church mean if the majority of the baptized are not involved in any activity of the church: worship and sacraments, fellowship, mission, service? The link between gift and call is at best practically compromised and at worst simply denied. The bond of communion established by baptism becomes divorced from life and experience.

Such a situation arises most obviously in the folk and national churches of Europe, but is not limited to them alone. While the difficulties of the folk church are often emphasized, the often overlooked advantages and possibilities of the folk church are not to be denied. Nevertheless, a situation in which the circle of the baptized is ten to fifteen times greater than the circle of the regularly involved must be seen as theologically problematic. Pastoral sensitivity is needed, both toward individuals and toward the place of the church in the surrounding culture. The link between the gift of baptism and the call to life in Christ and in his body, the church, however, must be witnessed to by the church. Baptism must be the bond of a living and lived communion.[42]

41. For a recent Lutheran assessment of some of the theological issues raised by charismatic movements, see the study carried out in the Strasbourg Institute by Carter Lindberg, *Charismatic Renewal and the Lutheran Tradition*, LWF Report 21 (1985). This study also appeared in German in *LWB Bericht* 21.

42. A comprehensive discussion of these issues from the perspective of the German evangelical churches can be found in *Taufe und Kirchenzugehörigkeit: Studien zur Bedeutung der Taufe für Verkündigung, Gestalt und Ordnung der Kirche*.

### 3. The Participation of the Nonbaptized

From very early times, the life of the church included some persons who were not baptized, namely, catechumens. In some situations, the entrance into the catechumenate was already the social and experiential turning point on one's way into the church. A catechumen was already a Christian. Nevertheless, the catechumens' participation in the church was not full. Most importantly, they did not receive the Lord's Supper. They were still persons on their way into the community. Baptism as the sacramentally decisive entrance into the community was not called into question.[43]

A different circumstance is created when significant numbers of persons come to participate fully in the life of the church without being baptized. Usually, such a situation is a function of a particular historical context and must be interpreted in relation to the context: e.g., the history of the folk church in Sweden or the oppressive political and cultural penalties that accompany conversion and baptism in many Islamic lands. In such semisecularized societies as Europe and North America, where many may wish some connection to the church but may not be baptized, baptism as the presupposition for receiving the Lord's Supper may be difficult to realize. Pastoral sensitivity by those who must deal with such issues within a particular context and cultural sensitivity by those outside the context are of great importance. Nevertheless, certain fundamental convictions of Christian faith must somehow find expression: We do not join ourselves to Christ and the church, nor can the community join us to Christ by some action which is primarily its own. We are joined to Christ and the church through an act of God, the sacramental action of the Spirit in baptism. The church is not free to replace baptism with some other means of entrance into the community. However churches come to deal with the issue of participation by the nonbaptized, these basic convictions must not be fundamentally compromised.

---

Forschungen und Berichten der Evangelischen Studiengemeinschaft, vol. 39, edited by Christine Lienemann-Perrin (Munich: Chr. Kaiser, 1983).

43. On the status of catechumens in the patristic church, see Klaus Koschorke, "Taufe und Kirchenzugehörigkeit im 4. und frühen 5. Jahrhundert," in *Taufe und Kirchenzugehörigkeit*, pp. 129-46.

## C. Baptism and Other Bonds of Communion

While baptism can be described as a fundamental bond of communion in the church, it is not the only bond of communion. Christians are joined together in the church by a common faith, common participation in the Eucharist, a mutually recognized ministry, common participation in mission and service. As noted, these bonds of communion ideally would be fully congruent with each other. In practice they are not, creating anomalies and perplexities in the relations among the churches.

### 1. Communities Which Do Not Baptize

Baptism obviously does not form a bond of communion with Christian communities that do not baptize, e.g., the Friends (Quakers) or the Salvation Army. Nevertheless, many will feel a strong bond of communion with such communities, on the basis of shared faith, shared mission (e.g., the urban missions of the Salvation Army), or shared ethical engagement (e.g., the peace witness of the Friends). Even if the rejection of what we judge to be divinely instituted sacraments means that communion with such communities is (from our perspective) always limited in important senses (we cannot have full eucharistic fellowship with a community which does not celebrate the Eucharist), the reality and importance of the bonds of communion that exist should not be denied. In particular contexts, these bonds may be of great lived importance. Baptism is a fundamental bond of communion, but its absence does not rule out other significant forms of Christian communion.

## III. The Significance of Baptismal Unity for a Divided Church

What significance should our baptismal unity have for life in an internally divided church? This question can be addressed in many ways. Here, only two are taken up.

## A. United in Baptism, Divided at the Supper?

If churches can mutually recognize their baptisms, what follows for their relationship in the Eucharist? Any discussion of this question must recognize that eucharistic fellowship has a variety of forms and degrees. Reciprocal admission of each other's members to the Eucharist is something rather different from the common celebration of the Supper or the interchangeability of eucharistic ministers.

On the one hand, many Lutheran, Reformed, Methodist, and Anglican churches now extend eucharistic hospitality to all baptized Christians (or all baptized Christians eligible to receive the Eucharist in their own churches). In such cases, a mutual recognition of baptism is seen as having consequences for at least one sort of eucharistic fellowship. This practice, however, only admits individuals to the Supper and does not realize eucharistic fellowship between the churches as such. In addition, this practice is not shared by all Protestant churches, nor by the Roman Catholic or Orthodox churches. For such churches, the present level of unity in baptism does not justify even eucharistic hospitality on a regular basis.

On the other hand, most churches (including the Lutheran churches) have not usually understood the mutual recognition of baptism in itself to justify full altar and pulpit fellowship or full communion. If "the unity we seek" is not just "communion in holy baptism" but also "in the eucharistic meal, a communion in which the ministries exercised are recognized by all as expressions of the ministry instituted by Christ in his church," then in the pursuit of unity we must address at least our understanding and practice of the Eucharist and ministry.[44] If we are seeking "a committed fellowship, able to make common decisions and to act in common," then forms of common action and decision making need to be addressed. It is possible that differences in these areas will hinder the realization of the unity to which we are called by our common baptism. Unity in

---

44. The quotations in this and the following sentence come from the statement by the Lutheran World Federation on "The Unity We Seek" adopted at its 1984 Assembly in Budapest. See *Budapest 1984: "In Christ — Hope for the World,"* Official Proceedings of the Seventh Assembly of the Lutheran World Federation, Budapest, Hungary, 22 July–5 August, 1984, edited by Carl H. Mau Jr., *LWF Report* 19/20 (1985): 175.

baptism but not in the Eucharist, ordained ministry, or forms of common decision-making is contradictory, but the only way out of the contradiction is to seek a unity in our understanding and practice that will permit our full fellowship in these areas of Christian life. Unity in baptism is an important ground of our commitment to the ecumenical pursuit, but it does not by itself dissolve the ecumenical problem.[45]

## B. One Baptism, One Church

That unity in baptism does not immediately imply eucharistic unity should not blind us to the deep significance baptismal unity should have. As was noted above, that we are baptized into the one church by churches which cannot live out that unity is a contradiction which should drive our ecumenical efforts. As long as such a contradiction exists, we cannot comfortably accept division.

More fundamentally, baptismal unity should relativize the existing divisions by placing them in the context of the unity which is given prior to our ecumenical successes and failures. If separated churches nevertheless baptize into the one church, then the churches cannot be simply external to each other. If each church is a church only as a realization of the one church, then unity is not a matter of external relations between self-subsistent individual churches, but is an aspect of their internal reality as churches.[46] Respect for the integ-

45. Such a conclusion was already reached by the first comprehensive ecumenical study of baptism: "The discussion [at the 1957 meeting of the Faith and Order Commission in New Haven, Conn., USA] soon made it clear, however, that the widespread mutual recognition of the validity of baptism wherever administered was no solid basis for affirming the unity of the Church in practice. . . . The effort to use the rite of baptism as a simple approach to the unity of the Church turned out to be one of those apparent shortcuts which lead into a blind alley." *One Lord, One Baptism,* World Council of Churches Commission on Faith and Order Report on the Divine Trinity and the Unity of the Church and Report on the Meaning of Baptism by the Theological Commission on Christ and the Church, Faith and Order Paper 19 (London: SCM Press, 1960).

46. This argument was made in a slightly different form by the 1992 letter on "Some Aspects of the Church Understood as Communion" of the Roman Catholic Congregation for the Doctrine of the Faith (cited above, n. 14). One can accept

rity of others and for the principle of subsidiarity may well imply an attitude of noninterference in the affairs of another church, but finally all churches are realizations of the one church within which each must be concerned for the other. A recognition of our baptismal unity should undercut the false ecumenical solution of a comfortable denominationalism in which the churches each tend their own gardens, careful not to bother or insult others, but in no way living out or even seeking a truly common life.

Baptismal unity should lead also to the questioning of overly narrow understandings of church membership. As noted above, membership in the one church is lived out through participation in some particular church. If membership in any church, however, finally rests on the one baptism we share, then no Christian can look upon the life and history of another church simply as an outsider. Even in separation, a positive, internal relation exists with the life of other churches.[47] A Presbyterian should not look upon the Orthodox or Methodist traditions as something other, but as parts of the single larger tradition in which all churches share and upon which all can draw. As members of the one church, Christians are at least members-at-a-distance of all churches, even if alienated or separated members.

## IV. Conclusion

A renewed emphasis on our unity in baptism could have quite divergent ecumenical effects. If unity in baptism is equated with the unity we seek, then such a renewed emphasis could act as an ecumenical sedative, tranquilizing us to the division that yet exists. This study paper has sought to avoid such a tranquilizing effect. A recognition of our unity in baptism should be a spur that reminds us of the inherent

---

this general principle without developing it as the Congregation does in relation to the special role of the bishop of Rome.

47. What is conceptually needed here is an ecumenical extension of the assertion by the Second Vatican Council (*Unitatis Redintegratio*, #3) that "those who believe in Christ and have been truly baptized are in some kind of communion with the catholic church, even though this communion is imperfect." Those who believe and have been baptized are in some kind of communion, however imperfect, with *every* community which is church.

anomaly of divided churches. As call, our baptismal unity should move us to ecumenical engagement. As gift, however, our baptismal unity should give our ecumenical engagement confidence. "One Lord, one faith, one baptism" is not something we must achieve, but the gift in which we are called to live and rejoice.[48]

48. This study paper was prepared by Michael Root, in collaboration with André Birmelé and Risto Saarinen.

# Baptism and the Foundations of Communion

## BAPTISM AND THE FOUNDATIONS
## OF COMMUNION

*Susan K. Wood*

To explore the relationship between baptism and ecclesial unity is to ask, in effect, what baptism does and what kind of communion it creates. Even though quick catechetical responses to this question are readily available — baptism incorporates us into the church, enables us to participate in the death and resurrection of Jesus Christ, forgives sin, makes us new creatures as sons and daughters of God, signifies faith, etc. — this fundamental question, what does baptism do? appears simple and self-evident only deceptively. Such a question inquires into issues such as how grace is present in the world, how one is initiated into the life of the Christian community, and how the Christian is related to Christ. Above all, however, baptism obliges us to ask questions about the church. My charge for this conference is to address the topic of baptism and the foundations of unity from the perspective of communion ecclesiology and within an ecumenical context. I will proceed by first identifying the criteria for full communion in ecumenical statements and then examining how baptism does or does not fulfill those criteria. I will then raise two questions which relate to the relationship between baptism and the unity of the church.

First, into what are we baptized? Christ or the church or both? How are they related? Are we baptized into the universal church of Christ or a local church, a church of Christ which transcends separated ecclesial communities, or are we baptized into confessional denominations? This is the most extensive object of investigation since it requires that we wrestle with how any of these is related to the others.

Second, is it possible to consider baptism as the foundation of Christian unity in isolation from a unified rite of Christian initiation which includes baptism, confirmation, and Eucharist? What are the implications of considering baptism within an integrated rite of initiation? Liturgists are working to restore a unified practice and a unified theology of initiation. Ecumenical discussions which consider these sacraments apart from their liturgical context or in isolation from each other work at cross-purposes with this effort.

## Communion Ecclesiology

In recent years it has become common to characterize the church as a communion, although this has not been without its critics.[1] In the Roman Catholic tradition the 1985 Synod of Bishops identified *koinonia* as the dominant ecclesiological theme of the Second Vatican Council.[2] In 1993 the theme of the Fifth World Conference on Faith and Order of the World Council of Churches was "Towards *Koinonia*/Communion in Faith, Life and Witness." *Koinonia* has become

---

1. See, e.g., "*Communio/Koinonia:* A New Testament–Early Christian Concept and Its Contemporary Appropriation and Significance," a study by the Institute for Ecumenical Research, Strasbourg, 1990, in *A Commentary on "Ecumenism: The Vision of the ELCA,"* ed. William G. Rusch (Minneapolis: Augsburg Press, 1990), pp. 119-41; George Vandervelde, "Koinonia Ecclesiology — Ecumenical Breakthrough?" *One in Christ* 29, no. 2 (1993): 126-42.

2. Documents of the Extraordinary Synod, the Final Report, Rome, 1985, in *The Tablet,* 14 December 1985, II.C.1.

a recurring theme in a number of ecumenical dialogues. The 1994 Lutheran–Roman Catholic document *Church and Justification,* which notes the theological deepening of the term "church fellowship/communion" since the 1950s, figures notably among these.[3]

Within ecumenical discussions, the category of "communion" is important because it defines the church in terms of those elements of faith and grace that create community rather than in terms of ecclesiastical structures. Furthermore, the category of communion allows for various degrees of unity among the various ecclesial traditions. Restored unity can be described as "full ecclesiastical communion" and partial unity as "imperfect communion."[4]

Generally speaking, when one considers the church as a communion, this involves both visible and invisible elements of communion. The visible elements refer to the visible gathering and ordering of God's people, and the invisible to the divine, life-giving source of communion. The greatest agreement within ecumenical documents lies in the mutual acceptance of the invisible elements of *koinonia* as described in the Scriptures. For example, various ecumenical documents make the following assertions to provide the theological foundation of this *koinonia:*[5]

1. The Trinity is the interior principle of ecclesial communion. Communion means participation in Christ's own communion with the Father. This is communion with the Father, through the Son, in the Holy Spirit.[6]

---

3. Lutheran–Roman Catholic Joint Commission, *Church and Justification: Understanding the Church in the Light of the Doctrine of Justification* (Geneva: Lutheran World Federation, 1994), #74.

4. *Decree on Ecumenism,* 3; *The Church: Local and Universal,* in *Information Service* 74 (1989-90): 33.

5. A fuller analysis than is appropriate here appears in Susan Wood, "Ecclesial *Koinonia* in Ecumenical Dialogues," *One in Christ* 30, no. 2 (1994): 124-45.

6. *The Church: Local and Universal,* 1, 6; Pentecostal-Catholic Dialogue, *Perspectives on Koinonia,* in *SPCU Information Service* 75, no. 4 (1990): 29, 70-71; Anglican–Roman Catholic International Commission (ARCIC-II), *The Church as Communion,* in *SPCU Information Service* 77, no. 2 (1991): 8; Report of the Joint Commission between the Roman Catholic Church and World Methodist Council (1982-1986 Fourth Series), *Towards a Statement on the Church,* in *SPCU Information Service* 62, no. 4 (1986): 23.

2. The Holy Spirit is the source of *koinonia* or communion.[7]
3. Because it is the result of our union *(koinonia)* with God, the Christian community can also be called *koinonia.*[8]
4. *Koinonia* refers to the nature of the church as body of Christ, people of God, and temple of the Holy Spirit.[9]
5. This communion is entered through baptism and nourished and expressed in the celebration of the Eucharist (Rom. 6:4-11; I Cor. 10:17; 12:13).

The fundamental meaning of *koinonia* at the level of these invisible elements of communion is participation in the life of God in grace. This participation is mediated through the sacraments. For example, through baptism we participate in Christ's death and resurrection. In the Eucharist we participate in the body of Christ. We participate in the life of the Trinity through our union with Christ.

*Church and Justification,* the product of the most recent work of the Lutheran–Roman Catholic Joint Commission, reiterates many of these themes. Its discussion of ecclesial communion begins with the soteriological meaning of *koinonia* as communion in Christ and, through Christ, as communion in the triune God:

> However one looks at the church, whether as "people of God" or "body of Christ" or "temple of the Holy Spirit," it is rooted in the inseparable communion or *koinonia* of the three divine persons and is thereby itself constituted as *koinonia.* It is not primarily the communion of believers with each other which makes the church *koinonia;* it is primarily and fundamentally the communion of

---

7. Pentecostal-Catholic Dialogue, *Perspectives on Koinonia,* in *SPCU Information Service* 74, no. 4 (1990): 30; Baptist–Roman Catholic International Conversations, 1984-1988, *Summons to Witness,* in *SPCU Information Service* 72, no. 1 (1990): 19-23; Roman Catholic–Methodist International Commission, *The Apostolic Tradition,* in *SPCU Information Service* 78, no. 3-4 (1991): 27-29.

8. *The Church: Local and Universal,* 7; *Towards a Statement on the Church,* 1, 12; *The Apostolic Tradition,* 41; Lutheran–Roman Catholic Joint Commission, *Facing Unity: Models, Forms, and Phases of Catholic-Lutheran Church Fellowship,* in *SPCU Information Service* 59, no. 3-4 (1985): 5-6.

9. *The Church: Local and Universal,* 5; *The Church as Communion,* 7, 8; *Towards a Statement on the Church,* 11; *Church and Justification,* #64.

believers with God, the triune God whose innermost being is *koinonia.* And yet the communion of believers with the triune God is inseparable from their communion with each other.[10]

Because Christians have *koinonia* with Christ in baptism, they have communion with each other in the church. The document clearly states that the christological relationship precedes the ecclesial one. The church under the image "people of God" is "the communion of those who have been baptized in Christ's name and have received the Holy Spirit."[11] The function of the proclamation of the gospel, baptism, and the Lord's Supper is to link the individual and all believers with God in the divine trinitarian *koinonia.*[12]

The document specifies the role of baptism, which, "in the name of the Father, Son and Holy Spirit (Mt. 28:19), leads us into communion with the triune God . . . and thus also knits believers together into a communion."[13] Thus called and elected by God, we are made into the community of "God's own people" (I Pet. 2:9). We are baptized into Christ's body. The document underscores the interpretation of baptism as participation in the death and resurrection of Christ. By virtue of our participation in the body of Christ, we then constitute one body with each other (Rom. 12:4f.). This human community in the one body of Christ is then characterized as a communion "in which creaturely and social divisions no longer count for anything (cf. Gal. 3:26-28)." The bond of this communion is identified as the Holy Spirit (1 Cor. 12:12f.; Eph. 4:31). At another point the document affirms that "because the church, as communion of the faithful, is based in communion with Christ, the one Lord, there is only one single church."[14] However, the text identifies this church as the *una sancta ecclesia,* "a holy Christian people," as "persons scattered throughout the world who agree on the Gospel and have the same Christ, the same Holy Spirit, and the same sacraments." Furthermore, it states that "the church is mainly an association of faith and of the Holy Spirit in men's

---

10. *Church and Justification,* #65.
11. *Church and Justification,* #64.
12. *Church and Justification,* ##66, 67.
13. *Church and Justification,* #68.
14. *Church and Justification,* #81.

hearts." In short, it is the *invisible* elements of *koinonia*, the Holy Spirit in people's hearts, the association of faith, and agreement on the gospel that constitute this communion of the faithful.

The Lutheran–Roman Catholic Joint Commission, in *Facing Unity*, identifies more visible elements of full communion that have concrete implications for the life of the churches:

1. Community of faith, including joint witness to the apostolic faith, unity of faith in diversity of form, and the removal of doctrinal condemnations.
2. Community in sacraments, including growth in sacramental life and agreement in the understanding and celebration of sacraments.
3. Community of service, including structured fellowship, common ordained ministry, joint reflection on the early church, jointly exercised ministry, joint exercise of episcope, act of recognition, single collegial episcopé, and joint episcopé and ordination.

These elements occur in another Roman Catholic–Lutheran document, *The Ministry in the Church*, which lists as the preconditions for acceptance of full church communion "agreement in the confession of faith — which must also include a common understanding of the church's ministry — a common understanding of the sacraments, and fraternal fellowship in Christian and church life."[15]

Visible elements mentioned in these documents include a diversity of form within a unity of faith, the removal of doctrinal condemnations, jointly ordained ministry, formal acts of recognition, and, one presupposes, formal acts of agreement regarding both the understanding and celebration of sacraments. One item — common understanding of the church's ministry and sacraments — only becomes visible through formal, articulated acts of agreement and raises concerns that will be addressed later in this paper. These visible elements are not primarily soteriological, but concretely relate to church polity, structure, and practice.

For a discussion of baptism, however, the most significant text

---

15. Roman Catholic–Lutheran Joint Commission, *The Ministry in the Church*, in *SPCU Information Service* 48, no. 1 (1982): 82.

regarding visible elements of communion is found in *Church and Justification:*

> Catholics and Lutherans together understand that the communion
> with God mediated through word and sacrament leads to the com-
> munion of the faithful among themselves. This takes concrete shape
> in the communion of the churches: the one holy catholic and apos-
> tolic church, the *una sancta* of the creed, is realized in the *communio*
> *ecclesiarum* as local, regional and universal communion, and so as
> church fellowship.[16]

The problem of our unity in baptism, articulated by profession of
the *una sancta,* and our disunity as confessional communions can be
fruitfully explored, I believe, by an examination of the relationship
between the *una sancta* and the communion of churches. Communion
ecclesiology traditionally emphasizes the local church and the visible
structures that effect and signify the unity among local churches. The
paradox is that from an ecumenical point of view we enter into both
unity and disunity through baptism: unity because of our entrance into
the *una sancta,* disunity because this is inseparable from entrance into
a local church that does not fully realize the *communio ecclesiarum.*

## Baptism in the Second Vatican Council's
### *Decree on Ecumenism*

The *Decree on Ecumenism* from the Second Vatican Council is another
resource which gives some indications regarding the ecclesial communion achieved in baptism from the perspective of Roman Catholicism. The statements in the study document concerning the inade-
quate attention given to baptism in discussions of church unity are
certainly also true of Roman Catholicism. Chapter I, which gives the
Catholic principles of ecumenism, begins with the Eucharist, not baptism, as the sacrament by which "the unity of the Church is both
signified and brought about (2)." Baptism is mentioned only twice in
the chapter and not until the third article, which states that "all who

16. *Church and Justification,* #79.

have been justified by faith in baptism are members of Christ's body, and have a right to be called Christians, and so are deservedly recognized as sisters and brothers in the Lord by the children of the catholic church (3)."[17] This same paragraph states that "those who believe in Christ and have been truly baptized are in some kind of communion with the catholic church, even though this communion is imperfect."

The primary baptismal text in the *Decree on Ecumenism* is found in #22, which takes up the baptismal theology of Romans 6:4 and Colossians 2:12 and speaks of baptism as incorporation into the crucified and glorified Christ and as constituting the sacramental bond of unity existing among all who through it are reborn. The text notes, however, that it is only a beginning, an inauguration: "Baptism, therefore, is oriented towards the complete profession of faith, complete incorporation into the institution of salvation such as Christ willed it to be, and finally the completeness of unity which eucharistic communion gives."

Aside from noting the remarkable paucity of references to baptism in the chapter on the Catholic principles of ecumenism, several observations are in order. First, the text speaks of ecumenical unity as a communion. However, this document is very self-referencing with regard to the Roman Catholic Church in that it speaks of how other ecclesial communities are in (imperfect) communion with Roman Catholicism rather than how they and Roman Catholicism are in communion with each other within the church of Christ. *Lumen Gentium* offers the possibility for a more nuanced perspective when it distinguishes between the church of Christ and the Roman Catholic Church by saying that the church of Christ subsists in the Catholic Church (8). Second, the emphasis is soteriological; the text states that we are incorporated into Christ, not the church. Within sacramental theology theologians differ on whether the Christic dimension of a sacrament occurs within and through the ecclesial dimension, or whether the ecclesial dimension occurs in and through the Christic.[18] Which the-

17. Translation in the Norman P. Tanner edition of *Decrees of the Ecumenical Councils*, vol. 2 (Washington, D.C.: Georgetown University Press, 1990).

18. For an example of the first position see Karl Rahner, *The Church and the Sacraments* (New York: Herder and Herder, 1963). For a criticism of Rahner from the other perspective, see William Van Roo, "Reflections on Karl Rahner's 'Kirche und Sakramente,'" *Gregorianum* 44 (1963): 493-98.

ology prevails is a significant question for a consideration of the foundations of unity and the mediatory role of the church, but from the perspective of this text, at least, our unity is in Christ.

Finally, one can deduce from the text that unity is not found absolutely in baptism since the unity achieved is only an "imperfect" one and baptism is only a "point of departure" for full unity.[19] In other words, baptism is only one of the criteria for church unity. This conciliar text is important because, although it clearly states that baptism constitutes the sacramental bond of unity among the baptized, it distinguishes between imperfect and perfect communion and speaks of a communion created by baptism, then characterizes the communion among Christians who participate in the one baptism as imperfect.[20] We must ask ourselves what the difference is between perfect and imperfect communion and what, if anything, is missing in baptism with regard to unity.

A problem within this document, and one suspects also within discussions of ecclesial communion in general, is that there is a tension between two forms of communion, a communion envisioned between churches as institutions and a christological communion that transcends but does not bypass the churches as institutions. This tension mirrors the distinction between visible and invisible elements of communion. The document suggests a preliminary answer to this question when it states that "baptism is thus oriented toward a complete profession of faith, a complete incorporation into the system of salvation such as Christ willed it to be, and finally toward a complete participation in Eucharistic communion (22)." The unity achieved in baptism is soteriological unity in Christ. What baptism is ordered toward but cannot contain within itself, belongs to the visible elements of unity: *profession* of faith, a *system* of salvation, and partici-

19. There is a curious and rather ambiguous statement, "Although the ecclesial communities separated from us lack the fullness of unity with us which flows from baptism . . ." (Latin text: "Communitates ecclesiales a nobis seiunctae, quamvis deficiat earum plena nobiscum unitas ex baptismate profluens . . ."). The text seems to indicate a fullness of unity derived from baptism, although this is counterindicated in the preceding paragraph.

20. Edward I. Cardinal Cassidy speaks of the "significant degree" of unity shared in baptism. "Baptism and Koinonia," *Ecumenical Trends* 25, no. 2 (1996): 3/19.

pation in eucharistic communion. Yet the Christian churches affirm that unity in baptism is deeper than their divisions, and it is the unity achieved in baptism through participation in Christ that makes the divisions among Christian churches scandalous.

## One Baptism, One Church, Yet Incomplete Communion

There is a fundamental question of ecclesiality at issue beneath these differences. In ecumenical circles we expend great effort in working for unity between churches. We are trying to achieve a unity within a plurality that now experiences itself as divided. Yet the paradox is that there is one baptism and one church (Eph. 4:4-5; Nicene Creed). The oneness does not exist because of something we do or achieve as churches, but because of the one Christ into whom we are baptized. The unity is the unity of Christ. There is but one mystery of Christ and several modalities of its expression, baptism and Eucharist among them.

This was expressed by Jean Daniélou in his essay on the symbolism of the baptismal rites:

The Christian faith has only one object, the mystery of Christ dead and risen. But this unique mystery subsists under different modes: it is prefigured in the Old Testament, it is accomplished historically in the earthly life of Christ, it is contained in mystery in the sacraments, it is lived mystically in souls, it is accomplished socially in the Church, it is consummated eschatologically in the heavenly kingdom. Thus the Christian has at his disposition several registers, a multi-dimensional symbolism, to express this unique reality. The whole of Christian culture consists in grasping the links that exist between Bible and liturgy, Gospel and eschatology, mysticism and liturgy. The application of this method to scripture is called exegesis, applied to liturgy it is called mystagogy. This consists in reading in the rites the mystery of Christ and in contemplating beneath the symbols the invisible reality.[21]

21. "Le symbolisme des rites baptismaux," *Dieu vivant* 1 (1945). Translation by Robert Taft, S.J., and cited in Robert Taft, S.J., *Beyond East and West: Problems in Liturgical Understanding* (Washington, D.C.: The Pastoral Press, 1984), p. 11.

If there is one mystery, the mystery of Christ dead and risen, that mystery is present in the sacrament of baptism, as it is in the Eucharist. In our reflections on baptism and the unity of the church, we may be tempted to ask what is partial or incomplete about baptism, as if there were something deficient or partial in this sacrament since the unity achieved in baptism is incomplete or partial. To do this is to divide the mystery among its several representations, as if each were part of a whole. Within the Christian economy, it is more accurate to envision the whole present in every part, the multidimensions of the presence of the mystery emphasizing different and complementary facets of the mystery.

By way of illustration, one can cite what has been traditionally taught about baptism and church membership. We have taught that baptism makes one completely a member of a church. We acknowledge a fullness in eucharistic communion, but this has not been associated with degrees of incorporation or church membership in our various churches. Someone who has not communicated is not less a member of the church, although we acknowledge that the Eucharist is the culmination of the rite of initiation and represents a fullness. However, something has not been brought to visible, sacramental expression in the life of such a person in the absence of the Eucharist. That "something" is the visible, sacramental sign of that person's communion in the body of Christ within a concrete community which experiences its identity as the body of Christ. If the *Decree on Ecumenism* states that the unity achieved in baptism is partial, this is not because the mystery represented by baptism is partial or because our incorporation into Christ and the church is partial, but because such an incorporation requires visible expression within a eucharistic community. The Eucharist is the repeated and ongoing sacrament of the incorporation into the body of Christ achieved in baptism. Such visible expression is required for full unity, but the reason for this is rooted in the nature of the one church as a communion of particular churches. Full unity cannot be experienced in the Eucharist until the various ecclesial communities celebrating the Eucharist are in unity with one another.

Paradoxically, in spite of our disunity and inability to celebrate the Eucharist together, we confess in the creed the reality of one church. The one church is not something to be achieved at some point in the future, but exists now. How can we speak of one church being divided and yet being one? Yet that is our experience. The answer is not to look to what is incomplete in baptism. The documents affirm that the unity achieved in baptism is partial, not that the sacrament is deficient or partial. What is partial is the communion achieved by the churches, not the communion achieved in baptism. The fundamental problem is ecclesial, not sacramental or soteriological.

## Into What Are We Baptized?

We can perhaps address this paradox by asking into what we are baptized. We are baptized both into Christ and into the church. The study paper makes this point in I.A. in two consecutive paragraphs. That is the problem: These affirmations are generally consecutive and rarely, if ever, related. One is either incorporated into an ecclesial community through incorporation into Christ, or incorporated into Christ through incorporation into an ecclesial community. As we have seen, the documents cited so far here opt for the first, i.e., incorporation into the church by means of participation in Christ. However, this ambiguity is also present in the other texts of Vatican II. For example, *Lumen Gentium*, 14, states that "They are fully incorporated into the society of the church who, possessing the Spirit of Christ, accept its whole structure and all the means of salvation that have been established within it, and within its visible framework are united with Christ, who governs it through the supreme pontiff and the bishops, by the bonds of profession of faith, the sacraments, ecclesiastical government and communion."

However, into what church is a person baptized: the universal church or a local church? And what is the theology of the relationship between the two? Here the theology both within and among our various communions may differ. For example, Avery Dulles asks this question and opts for an emphasis on the universal church.[22] Although he notes that baptism is celebrated in a particular community,

22. Avery Dulles, "The Church as Communion," in *New Perspectives on Historical Theology: Essays in Memory of John Meyendorff,* ed. Bradley Nassif (Grand Rapids: William B. Eerdmans Publishing Co., 1996), p. 134.

into which the candidate is received, he holds that universal church membership is more important on the grounds that "baptism can be validly administered where no community is present" and that "some baptized Christians, while lacking any stable relationship to a particular parish or diocese, are entitled to receive the sacraments wherever they go."[23]

Jean-Marie R. Tillard represents another position. He identifies the local church as "the community of those who are 'in communion' *(communio)* through that which is 'communicated' *(communicatum)*. It receives its identity from the reality of the Body of the one who is the gift of the Father 'communicated' by the Spirit to humanity, and in which, by the same Spirit, all its members are one single body, united in the same and indivisible common priesthood."[24] The local church is a communion of the baptized. From the second point of view, the universal church is conceptualized as a communion of particular churches.[25]

The relationship between the universal and particular churches within communion ecclesiology has been a lively topic of discussion within Roman Catholicism. Actually two distinct but related ecclesial relationships are involved: the relationship between the church of Christ and the Roman Catholic Church, and the relationship between the universal church and the particular churches. Both are of considerable significance for ecumenism because the first inquires into the relationship between the church of Christ and any of our confessional communions. The second, the relationship between the universal church and the particular churches, gives us a model for the relationship of confessional communions within a reconciled church. These two relationships result in a certain ambiguity in speaking about the universal church. Sometimes "universal church" is taken to mean "worldwide" in a geographic sense. This leads to a discussion of how local churches are organized into larger regional structures.[26] At other

23. Dulles, p. 134.

24. Jean-Marie R. Tillard, *L'Église locale: Ecclésiologie de communion et catholicité* (Paris: Cerf, 1995), p. 373.

25. See, e.g., Joseph Komonchak, "The Church Universal as the Communion of Local Churches," in *Where Does the Church Stand?* Concilium 146 (Edinburgh: T. & T. Clark, 1981), pp. 30-35.

26. See, e.g., *The Ministry in the Church*, pp. 72-73.

times it may refer to "the church of Christ," meaning the church whole and entire in an ecclesiological but nongeographic sense.

*Lumen Gentium* modified an earlier claim made in Pius XII's encyclical *Mystici Corporis* (1943), that the "Church of Christ is the Roman Catholic Church." Vatican II nuanced this to the statement that "This church, set up and organized in this world as a society, subsists in the catholic church, governed by the successor of Peter and the bishops in communion with him, although outside its structure many elements of sanctification and of truth are to be found which, as proper gifts of the church of Christ, impel towards catholic unity (8)." Pope John Paul II later extended the concept by saying that the universal church subsists in the particular churches.[27] *Lumen Gentium* states that the particular churches are "formed in the likeness of the universal Church" and that "in and from these particular churches there exists the one unique catholic church (23)."

In 1992 the Congregation for the Doctrine of the Faith issued a letter, "Some Aspects of the Church as Communion," which asserts the ontological and temporal priority of the universal church (8).[28] A concern of this letter was to avoid a certain horizontalism in conceptualizing the universal church as the "reciprocal recognition on the part of the particular churches" considered as complete subjects in themselves (8). The letter notes that such a view weakens the concept of the unity of the church at the visible and institutional level.

Taking note of the first anniversary of the Congregation's letter, an unsigned letter appeared in *l'Osservatore Romano*, 23 June 1993, which both nuanced and explained the text in the *Communionis notio*. This article emphasizes the mutual interiority between the universal church and the particular churches and summarizes the relationship: "Every particular Church is truly *Church*, although it is not the *whole*

---

27. "The Catholic Church herself subsists in each particular church, which can be truly complete only through effective communion in faith, sacraments and unity with the whole body of Christ. . . . It is precisely because you are pastors of particular churches in which subsists the fullness of the universal church that you are, and must always be, in full communion with the successor of Peter." Address, 12 September 1987. The text can be found in *Origins* 17, no. 16 (1 October 1987): 258.

28. English translation in *Ecumenical Trends* 21, no. 9 (October 1992): 133-34, 141-47.

Church; at the same time, the universal Church is not distinct from the communion of particular Churches, without, however, being conceived as the mere sum of them." Because of this close relationship, the article affirms that "incorporation into the universal Church is as immediate as is incorporation into a particular Church. Belonging to the universal Church and belonging to a particular Church are a single Christian reality."

This relationship of mutual interiority between the universal and the particular churches is easily understood in terms of the Eucharist: There is but one Eucharist despite its many manifestations within particular churches. Within the Eucharist the church is present in its totality, despite the multiplicity of eucharistic communities. This is manifestly true because of the unity and indivisibility of the body of Christ.

This relationship, however, is less clear when one considers membership in the universal and particular churches through baptism, particularly if one equates the universal church with the body of Christ, the church of Christ, or the *una sancta*. Even though at some level belonging to the universal church and belonging to a particular church are a single Christian reality when viewed from the perspective of one ecclesial communion, in this instance Roman Catholicism, this poses problems ecumenically. There may be a single reality, but it is a divided reality if one can say so without self-contradiction. From the perspective of these Roman Catholic documents these problems concern ministerial structures and their recognition.

The relationship between the universal and local churches raises the issue of how ministry witnesses to church unity. The letter "Some Aspects of the Church as Communion" states that "unity or communion among the particular churches in the universal Church is rooted not only in the same faith and in the common Baptism, but above all in the Eucharist and in the Episcopate (11)." Mutual recognition of ministry is essential to a communion of particular churches if there is to be visible communion that goes beyond the fact that the Word is preached in each, and each celebrates the sacraments. As important as this is, it can in itself simply imply a coexistence side by side which is not communion, or a common participation in the Trinity which remains an invisible communion in grace. In Roman Catholicism the college of bishops visibly represents the communion of particular churches which are theologically defined as altar communities around a bishop. Thus the communion of bishops and the communion of particular churches are mutually interrelated. This recognition of ministry is why the *Decree on Ecumenism* recognizes the Eastern Orthodox churches as particular churches (17). The problems of mutual recognition of ministry and ministerial structures associated with communities issuing from the Reformation render the relationship of mutual interiority between these communities and the universal church more problematic from the perspective of the *Decree on Ecumenism* and the *l'Osservatore Romano* article.

The Lutheran/Roman Catholic commission took up this theme in *Facing Unity* and described the church as "a communion subsisting in a network of local churches" (9).[29] It seems that a viable interpretation of this relationship would be that the invisible elements of communion subsist in a concrete and specific local church similar to how the universal church subsists in particular churches. Participation in Christ and the *koinonia* that results from this occurs and finds expression in place and time within concrete faith communities.

The document *The Church: Local and Universal,* the product of a Joint Working Group of the Roman Catholic Church and the World Council of Churches, reiterates that "there is only one Church in God's plan of salvation" and that "this one Church is present and manifested in the local churches throughout the world" (2).[30] Disputes over which is prior, the local or the universal church, are neither helpful nor necessary as there is a mutual reciprocity between the two. *The Church: Local and Universal* suggests that an eschatological and pneumatological ecclesiology "does not assign a priority exclusively to either the local or the universal Church, but suggests a simultaneity of both."[31] Thus we are baptized both into a universal and a local church. One only occurs in and through the other.

29. *Facing Unity,* pp. 44-78.
30. *The Church: Local and Universal.*
31. *The Church: Local and Universal,* 22.

## Baptism into a Eucharistic Community

Most concretely, we are baptized into a worshiping assembly. Both the place, ordinarily the parish church, and the minister of baptism, the bishop, presbyter, or deacon of that place, are determined by that assembly.[32] Even though anyone can baptize in an emergency according to the intention of the church and with correct matter and form, the specificity of the local church would prohibit, for example, a Roman Catholic minister from performing a baptism in the church of another denomination when the understanding is that the person being baptized is entering that other communion. This is true even though the rites of baptism do not stipulate that a person is baptized a Roman Catholic or a Lutheran. Confessional identity derives from the particular church into which a person is baptized, and not from the rite itself.

In one sense we are baptized into the Eucharist, for baptism admits us to the Eucharist within our faith communities. This is because we are baptized into a priestly community which is deputed for eucharistic worship. In the ancient church, the first reception of the Eucharist followed baptism and any other accompanying rites immediately. Although for Lutherans this worshiping assembly is the basic unit of the church, while for Roman Catholics the basic unit is the particular church defined as an altar community around its bishop, the principle of baptism into a basic unit of the church which is fundamentally eucharistic remains the same for both confessions.

If we inquire as to what is specific within these local communities, we find that that is where the faith is professed, that is the community which receives the baptized, and that is where the Eucharist celebrates and proclaims the presence of Christ sacramentally within the community. The new rites of initiation presuppose a local church where the catechumens are evangelized and formed and where neophytes are nurtured. They are, therefore, unthinkable outside of a local community.

32. *The Code of Canon Law,* canon 857, stipulates that "adults are to be baptized in their own parish church and infants in the parish church proper to their parents, unless a just cause suggests otherwise." Canon 862 states that "outside the case of necessity, it is not lawful for anyone without the required permission, to confer baptism in the territory of another, not even upon his own subjects."

Because of the close association between baptism and the Eucharist, we must hold that there is not one *koinonia* established in baptism and another in the Eucharist. Nor is there partial first-stage *koinonia* in baptism and then complete second-stage *koinonia* in Eucharist. Rather, participation in the death and resurrection of Christ signified by the water bath in the name of the Trinity according to the intention of the church finds ongoing sacramental expression in the Eucharist, for it is there that the very body of Christ in the eschatological *pleroma* of members joined in Christ within the *totus Christus* is represented and memorialized within the eucharistic sacrament. This occurs only within a local church, for it is there that we have altar communities. The problem is not only that we have focused on the *koinonia* of the Eucharist to the neglect of baptism, but that we have failed to show their interrelationship within an integral rite of initiation and an integral theology of the body of Christ. There are undoubtedly many reasons for this failure, but the loss of an integrated rite of initiation in the Western Church culminating in the Eucharist, the relative separation of sacramental theology from its liturgical foundations, and the separation of sacramental theology from ecclesiology certainly number among them. The Eucharist, encompassing both christological and ecclesial real symbolism, signifies not only the risen Christ but also the union of all the baptized in Christ.[33] Conversely, baptism initiates us into the community identified as a priestly people (I Pet. 2:4-10). *Lumen Gentium* teaches that by virtue of this royal priesthood the faithful participate in the offering of the Eucharist (10). By virtue of the baptismal character they are appointed to Christian religious worship (11). Thus Roman Catholic teaching is clear that baptism is oriented to the Eucharist. There is an interpenetration and interrelation of sacramental real symbolism in the two sacraments rather than a simple sequencing. This is more evident in a unified rite of initiation than in the separated rite we now experience in the Western Church.

The altar communities into which we are baptized are not in union with one another. Historically, communion ecclesiology was the first ecclesiology in the church. *Communio* represented the unity between the faithful and the bishop as well as the unity between the local

---

33. See, e.g., Augustine of Hippo's instruction on the sacraments of the altar to the newly baptized in Sermons 226 and 227.

churches, represented by the unity of the bishops.[34] This *communio* was realized and represented in eucharistic communion. Miguel M. Garijo-Guembe articulates the principle thus: "Whoever sets up a distinct communion, sets up a distinct Church."[35] Note that the communion here is not the soteriological communion of participation in Christ, but the visible communion of union with a bishop and the union of local churches with each other through the *communio* of the bishops. Bishops excommunicated each other, and the church of the excommunicated bishop was then out of communion with the other local churches.

A number of practices symbolized or regulated the *communio* of eucharistic communities. For example, the fifth-century practice of the *fermentum,* where the bishop sent fragments of the consecrated bread to parish priests who were celebrating in outlying areas, signified the unity of all the faithful in Christ and the unity of the presbyterial eucharistic celebrations with that of the bishop. Another practice was the exchange of communion letters. The participants in the synod at which Paul of Samosata was excommunicated in 268 wrote to the bishops of Rome and Alexandria, requesting that they write to the new bishop and receive communion letters *(koinonika grammata)* from him.[36]

This theology and practice of early communion ecclesiology indicate that eucharistic communion, somewhat unlike baptismal communion, is strongly associated with visible ecclesial structures and ministry. While both baptism and Eucharist signify both communion in the dead and risen Christ and communion in a church, baptism effects entrance into a concrete and specific faith community which has structures and ministry which put it into communion with other faith communities or which dissociate it from those groups.[37] The emphasis on

---

34. In the ecclesiology of Vatican II the communion of particular churches is sacramentalized in the college of bishops, the union of bishops representing in their person the union of churches. See Susan Wood, "The Sacramentality of Episcopal Consecration," *Theological Studies* 51 (1990): 479-96.

35. Miguel M. Garijo-Guembe, *Communion of the Saints: Foundation, Nature, and Structure of the Church* (Collegeville, Minn.: A Michael Glazier Book, The Liturgical Press, 1994), p. 101.

36. Eusebius, *Church History* 7.30.17. Cited in Garijo-Guembe, p. 101.

37. *The Church: Local and Universal* states this principle thus: "Communion . . . refers to a dynamic, spiritual, objective reality which is embodied in ecclesial

the local church within communion ecclesiology allows us to appreciate the diversity of various communions and to envision ecumenical unity as a communion of communions, but it also points to the difficulties of communion and how those are tied to ecclesial structures. This perspective also gives us an understanding of why the profound unity achieved in baptism does not automatically result in the mutual reception of other ecclesial communities into eucharistic communion. What is lacking is not necessarily of the soteriological order, but of the order of mutual recognition of other communities. The emphasis on the visible structures of unity was a way of assuring the unity of faith among the various communities. Otherwise there could be apparent unity through the rite of baptism, but no assurance whether there was shared faith.[38] The oddity of our disunity is that we do have a profound unity with the body of Christ by participation in his death and resurrection, but since this occurs only concretely and locally, this unity needs to be sustained by visible structures of unity.

What this indicates is that the Eucharist, contrary to some more pietistic, individualistic, and mystical interpretations, profoundly embodies ecclesial symbolism. The Eucharist represents more than the presence of Christ under the species of bread and wine; it represents the unity of the baptized in the body of Christ. It also represents the communion of churches. Inadmissibility to Eucharist is not only a statement about the presence or absence of grace or incorporation into the dead

---

structures. The gift of communion from God is not an amorphous reality but an organic unity that requires a canonical form of expression. The purpose of such canonical structuring is to ensure that the local churches (and their members), in their communion with each other, can live in harmony and fidelity to 'the faith which has been once and for all entrusted to the saints' (Jude 3)."

38. The study document by the Institute for Ecumenical Research in Strasbourg (1990), *"Communio/Koinonia,"* p. 134, indicates some structures which assure a common faith. To the question of whether "communion in the confession of the faith" requires the common acceptance of the same confessional text, it notes that the LWF and its member churches have answered this question negatively, but the study document notes that the consensus in the understanding of the gospel and its proclamation in Word and sacrament should be formulated or at least be capable of formulation. Likewise the document states that the LWF Assembly in Budapest (1984) determined that the common confession of the LWF member churches permits or even demands a common declaration of altar and pulpit fellowship.

and risen body of Christ, but about the relationship of ecclesial communities. This, however, is not what is usually experienced in the pain occasioned by the absence of eucharistic hospitality between our churches. Even though we are baptized into specific concrete faith communities, our experience is not usually one of asking to be admitted to communion with another local community. In more contemporary theology and practice, our sense of universal communion in Christ wins over our sense of locality. In pastoral practice this sentiment frequently carries over into relations with other faith traditions.

The very emphasis on local communities within communion ecclesiology with the corresponding view of the church as a communion of communions gives rise to the possibility of disunity among these communions and the necessity of visible, concrete structures to assure this unity. The completion that the Eucharist brings to baptism is twofold: first, the sacramental communion in the body of Christ, the same body in which we already participate in baptism; and, second, the visible communion both within a local church and, through the local church, with the other eucharistic communions. Not to be able to concretize or sacramentalize the unity we share in baptism around a common eucharistic table represents an incongruence and self-contradiction which would be described as schizophrenia in psychological terms, but which we call sin in theological terms. Unity is given to us in baptism and the Eucharist. The disunity we experience among our various communions is our sin. Not insignificantly, Pope John Paul II calls the churches to conversion and repentance in his encyclical *Ut Unum Sint* (15).[39]

## The Impact of an Integrated Rite of Initiation

It is necessary to examine what happens to a theology of baptism and ecclesial community when viewed from the perspective of an integrated rite of initiation. One of the most important consequences of an integrated rite of initiation is that baptism and the Eucharist will reciprocally interpret each other. In other words, we are baptized into a eucharistic community, and conversely, the eucharistic community

39. 30 May 1995.

is the community of the baptized. Through baptism we are formed into a priestly people and by the baptismal character are given a place in the worship of the Christian community.[40] Within an integrated rite of initiation the spirituality of the Eucharist will retrieve its baptismal basis, meaning that once again we will understand the Eucharist as the sacramental embodiment of the body of Christ into which we are baptized, both the risen body of Christ and the ecclesial body of Christ.

Our traditions have emphasized the real presence of Christ in the Eucharist, but we have largely lost the ecclesial meaning of the Eucharist. This happened largely because of the eucharistic controversies with Berengar of Tours in the eleventh century. Originally, the term *corpus verum*, the true body, referred to the church, and the term *corpus mysticum* referred to the Eucharist because it was received *spiritualiter*. The effort to emphasize the real presence of Christ in the Eucharist resulted in a shift in the use of these terms. After the eucharistic controversies, *corpus verum* referred to the Eucharist to emphasize the real presence of Christ in the Eucharist, while *corpus mysticum* designated the church.[41] Prior to the change the three bodies — the historical body of Christ, the sacramental body of Christ in the Eucharist, and the ecclesial body of Christ — were maintained in unity. When the ecclesial body became divorced from the other two, the Eucharist lost much of its ecclesial real symbolism. Arguably this also cut eucharistic spirituality from its baptismal foundations. An integrated rite of initiation places the two sacraments back in their original proximity, enables them to mutually interpret each other, restores the unity of the christological and ecclesiological interpretations of each, and fosters a baptismal eucharistic spirituality.

Maxwell Johnson has stated that "the recovery of a baptismal spirituality calls the churches of today to a re-evaluation of communion practices."[42] He claims that the Eucharist is for all the baptized, all who are initiated into the Christian community, which he identifies

---

40. *Lumen Gentium*, 11.

41. The history of the shift in the meaning of these terms is traced by Henri de Lubac in *Corpus Mysticum: L'Eucharistie et l'Eglise au Moyen Age*, Coll. Théologie 3 (Paris: Aubier-Montaigne, 1949).

42. Maxwell E. Johnson, "We *Can* Go Home Again: A Liturgy as Welcome *Place* for the *Dis*-Placed" (presentation for the Collegeville Pastoral Institute, Collegeville, Minn., 6 July 1996).

as a continuation of the table fellowship of Jesus himself. By this John-son primarily has in mind the communicating of infants, but such a practice and a reintegrated rite of initiation will make the problem of the absence of eucharistic sharing among our churches even more acute, for the "birthright" of Eucharist table fellowship of the baptized will be denied when a person attends a eucharistic liturgy of another confession.[43] Perhaps we will continue to argue that this "birthright" only applies to the community within which a person is baptized, but none of our rites of baptism indicate ritually that a person is baptized a "Lutheran," "Roman Catholic," or "Anglican." The asymmetry be-tween a universal baptism and a confession-bound Eucharist will be-come more uneven. To continue to recognize one sacrament and not the other breaks the essential unity of the rite of initiation and, at one level, denies the initiation that has already taken place. The very es-sence and spirituality of initiation is that these be joined.

Obviously, the consequences for ecumenism are very different if one emphasizes a unified rite of initiation or if one emphasizes the structures of communion that unite disparate eucharistic communi-ties. These are two different theologies. The first will press toward intercommunion even before all the structures of mutual recognition are in place. It very well may be that the unified rite makes it more difficult to affirm that something is achieved in baptism that is not achieved in the Eucharist.[44] The second will proceed more cautiously and demand recognition of eucharistic communities before intercom-munion occurs. Related to the issue of admitting ecclesial communi-ties to communion is the question of the mutual recognition of min-istry. More study on this question is needed by liturgists, ecumenists, and ecclesiologists. The question is whether the churches will be like the donkey who is immobilized because it cannot move toward either bale of hay, one symbolizing the unity achieved in baptism and the other the requirement for recognition of the communion of churches represented in the ecclesial meaning of the Eucharist.

---

43. The *Lutheran Book of Worship* states that "Holy communion is the birthright of the baptized." Minister's Edition, p. 31. Cited by Maxwell Johnson.

44. This, however, is not the case in the Orthodox Church, which has very stringent requirements for intercommunion at the same time that it practices a unified rite of initiation.

## Conclusion

This inquiry into the relationship between baptism and communion ecclesiology results in the following observations: (1) There are both visible and invisible elements of communion. The unity we achieve in baptism as incorporation into the body of Christ is primarily soteriological and therefore belongs primarily to the invisible elements of communion. (2) Incorporation into the body of Christ through baptism is inseparable from entrance into an ecclesial community. A baptized person enters simultaneously into the universal and particular church. The churches of the various confessions are not in communion with each other, which results in the paradox of Christians being in communion with each other in baptism and at the same time finding themselves in a state of ecumenical disunity. (3) The communion achieved in baptism is partial or complete, not because the sacrament incorporates into Christ partially, but because the particular churches are not ecumenically united one with the other. This is due to a deficiency in the visible elements of communion among these particular churches. These visible elements may include professions of faith and most certainly include mutual recognition of ministry. (4) The relationship of mutual interiority between the universal and the particular churches is easily understood in terms of the Eucharist, but is less clear when one considers baptism. From an ecumenical perspective, one enters a divided church through baptism because one enters simultaneously into the one body of Christ and into a particular communion that is not in communion with other ecclesial communities of baptized persons. (5) We are baptized into the Eucharist. The Eucharist is the ongoing sacramental realization of the incorporation in Christ accomplished in baptism. A eucharistic spirituality is also a baptismal spirituality. (6) Theologies of baptism and the Eucharist, when developed independently of each other, fail to show their interrelationship. An integrated rite of initiation restores the unity of the historical, sacramental, and ecclesial bodies of Christ through the unity of the christological and ecclesiological interpretations of each.

# BAPTISM AND THE FOUNDATIONS
# OF COMMUNION

*Peder Nørgaard-Højen*

Interestingly enough, the theological literature on baptism and its bearing on the unity of the church is relatively scarce and easy to overlook. This is a surprising fact insofar as ecumenical documents in general, more often than not, do not fail to underline the importance of baptism as the sacrament of unity. With some few exceptions, however, most ecumenical statements do not go beyond this mere ascertainment and content themselves with appealing to the need for further theological clarification. We are indeed used to the idea of baptism as the foundation of communion among Christians and take it somehow for granted, and very few seem eager to dedicate thorough reflection to this issue, thereby perhaps jeopardizing a cherished and familiar concept.

After all, most churches do agree on some few but important (however more or less external or even superficial) characteristics as preconditions for the recognition of each other's baptism. It must be administered by immersion or by pouring and in the name of the triune God. But *what* we are in fact doing when we immerse a person or pour water on his or her head is seemingly not the issue at stake when churches concentrate upon baptism as the bond of unity.

This seems to be about all that the churches are able to agree upon, and therefore the presumed unity on baptism is, in the last analysis, not that far-reaching at all. It could in fact, without being too unfair, perhaps even be called a prejudice (though hopefully a positive and creative one) belonging in the area of ecumenical ideology.

This unfriendly characterization of what is normally and extensively assumed to be an asset for further rapprochement between the

61

confessions does not, however, imply any kind of depreciation, but rather a necessary theological critique of this widely held opinion. My reflections are simply based on the observation that churches often mutually recognize their baptismal practices and yet just as often resist the implementation of any kind of practical church unity. That something could thereby possibly be wrong with the conviction that baptism is a unifying factor is not the real point. I do champion that it is possible to argue in favor of that belief, but I would at the same time strongly resist its ideological devaluation. In my view, what is needed is, therefore, the theological and practical reinforcement of the vision of baptism as the unifying bond between divided churches and confessions.

In other words, my assumption is that baptism is in fact this unifying bond, and therefore I shall in a first section deal with those theological arguments that speak in favor of that proposition. In a following section, however, I intend to show the limitations of the *theologoumenon* on baptism as the foundation for church unity in order to demonstrate that this very dogma cannot possibly serve and without a second thought be accepted as a sufficient agent of ecclesial unification. Thus I intend further to fight its ideologization and to oppose the biased usage and understanding of the concept. In a concluding section I shall finally reflect positively on the understanding of baptism as instrument of Christian unity and develop in some detail what this view could realistically imply in the search for visible unity. I do not pretend to add much to what has already been said in the ecumenical discussion on baptism and church unity. Rather, I hope to reformulate in a systematic way known positions and through a fresh view contribute to a slightly different understanding of these statements and their implications and point to more realistic expectations that could possibly be drawn from them.

## What Makes Baptism a Bond of Unity between the Churches?

Baptism is the sacrament of repentance and conversion. The divine call for *metanoia* applies to the individual, but only insofar as he is a member of the chosen people of the New Covenant. In analogy to the concern for conversion in the Old Testament prophets, the call for repentance in the Gospels is primarily directed toward the people of God rather than toward its individual members. Both in the Old and in the New Covenant man is part of the chosen people (be it the Jews or the new people of God) before he becomes an individual.[1] Through baptism man becomes a Christian and is incorporated into the body of Christ. He participates in the life, death, and resurrection of Christ and receives divine grace and the forgiveness of his sins. He is purified, renewed, reborn, and sanctified, but this participation in the salvific history of Christ only becomes effective through the incorporation of the believer into his body, the church. The individual-soteriological and the social-ecclesiological dimensions are two indispensable and inextricably interrelated aspects of the same matter.

This is equivalent to the assertion that nobody receives his personal and individual salvation through baptism without being incorporated into the church. Karl Rahner stresses this fact very clearly when he writes,

> One is made a Christian and a member of the Church through baptism. Baptism is the first sacrament of the forgiveness of sins, of the communication of the divine glory of mercy, of the divine nature, of the inner, permanent equipment of faith, hope and love toward God and man. This inner, permanent and individual pardon of man, who from being a sinner turns into a justified, takes place, however, in the baptism to the effect that through this rite of initiation he is admitted to the socially-hierarchically structured people of God, to the congregation of those who believe and confess the salvation of God. God pardons man and grants him his own individual salvation in baptism by incorporating him into the *Church*.[2]

---

1. See similar deliberations in Raphael Schulte, "Die Umkehr (Metanoia) als Anfang und Form christlichen Lebens," in *Mysterium Salutis. Grundriß heilsgeschichtlicher Dogmatik V,* ed. Johannes Feiner and Magnus Löhrer (Zürich/Einsiedeln/Köln, 1976), pp. 170ff.

2. "Christ und Glied der Kirche wird man durch die Taufe. Die Taufe ist das erste Sakrament der Sündenvergebung, der Mitteilung der göttlichen Gnadenherrlichkeit, der göttlichen Natur, der inneren, dauernden Befähigung des Glaubens, der Hoffnung und der Liebe zu Gott und den Menschen. Aber diese innere, bleibende, individuelle Begnadung des Menschen, der aus einem Sünder ein Gerecht-

Human salvation cannot at all be conceived without incorporation into the Christian congregation. There exists in other words an essential relationship between being a Christian and the community of believers (the *communio sanctorum*) as the place in which the faith becomes concrete and the implications of baptism become visible. Throughout Christian history it has always been assumed that normally and as a rule church membership and baptism belong together as two sides of the same coin, and therefore it has always been regarded as an exception (though not a total impossibility) if anybody claimed to be a Christian and at the same time refused to be a member of the church of Christ. Historically and in principle church membership has been understood as the institutional embodiment of being a Christian that prevented any kind of docetic deviations of the church and safeguarded that faith in Christ is not primarily lived in the private sphere but in the midst of and together with the people of God.

Thus baptism (salvation) implies above all communion, *koinonia*, among those to whom the conviction that Jesus Christ is the savior of the world was given in the first place. Along the same line Harald Wagner argues, "God creates his people by bringing about his salvation. The new people of God, however, is the church."[3] Just as, in the nature of things, it is impossible to belong to that *koinonia* without sharing this conviction, it is fundamentally out of the question to believe in Christ without being incorporated into the hosts of those who share that belief.[4] To maintain that it is legitimate and theologi-

---

fertigter wird, geschieht in der Taufe dadurch, daß er durch diesen Initiationsritus aufgenommen wird in das gesellschaftlich-hierarchisch verfaßte Volk Gottes, in die Gemeinde der Glaubenden und das Heil Gottes Bekennenden. Gott begnadet den Menschen zu seinem eigenen individuellen Heil in der Taufe dadurch, daß und indem er ihn der *Kirche* eingliedert." Karl Rahner, *Schriften zur Theologie VII*, 2nd ed. (Einsiedeln/Zürich/Köln, 1971), p. 333. The English translation is my own.

3. "Indem Gott sein Heil wirkt, schafft er sich sein Volk. Das neue Gottesvolk aber ist die Kirche." Hans Jörg Urban and Harald Wagner, eds., *Handbuch der Ökumenik*, III/2 (Paderborn, 1987), p. 152. The English translation is my own.

4. This dogmatic statement is documented not only positively throughout history but also negatively in the fact that it can be observed mainly within the area of highly secularized churches, e.g., in Scandinavia, in which the loosened and relativized concern for the church in the second and third generation normally develops into total alienation from any kind of relationship to Christ and the Christian community.

cally acceptable to be a Christian without any relationship to the church is equal to a fatal rejection of the social, indeed incarnational, dimension of faith, and thus to an invalidation of faith itself.

This theological position is deeply challenged by the ecclesial realities, not least in the traditional folk church regions of northern Europe, where thousands or even millions of people are baptized without ever having any living relationship to the Lord of the church. Although they may (too) easily be described and dismissed as in fact apostates, even if they preserve their formal church membership by not deciding to explicitly leave the church, their very existence raises doubts as to whether baptism can really be applied as a criterion of church membership. For many of those people, who have been baptized as infants and have had no later relationship with, nor have taken any interest in upholding other than purely formal and civil religious connections to, the church, do not in fact belong to the church of Christ in any theologically valid and responsible sense of that term.

Theological reflection has to come to terms with the whole complex of problems that emerges from this situation and be open to other possible criteria of church membership.[5] But it does not, of course, affect the fundamental theological assumption that baptism creates communion and leads into a community, without which it is in danger of losing its meaning and becomes a docetic exercise with the possible purpose or at least the hidden implication of establishing a private compartment for private worship of a private God, which, however, has nothing in common with what is traditionally known as Christianity. In God's salvific history with his people, the church is the agent and intermediary of his grace and, therefore, somehow necessary. Karl Rahner rightly emphasizes the necessity of the church exactly to avoid the docetic danger:

> [O]ne thing concretely is not possible without the Church . . . : that the grace of God is present in the world as an event in historical tangibility, in incarnational corporality. . . . To the very nature of grace also belongs . . . the appearance in space and time, the existence in history, in the immanence, the shifting from any kind of

5. See Peder Nørgaard-Højen, "Die theologische und praktische Bedeutung der Taufe in den skandinavischen Volkskirchen," *Zeitschrift für kirchliche Zeitgeschichte* 8 (Göttingen, 1995): 23ff., especially pp. 38f.

mere intimacy of conscience into *all* human dimensions, into the history of man, into his sociality, his laws, his science, his art. Because salvation appears in the flesh of Christ and because man has to be saved in all dimensions of his existence, for this reason grace must become incarnate, historical, social. And when that happens, grace is called Church.[6]

I do not see any reason to weaken or even refute these wise remarks from a Lutheran point of view. On the contrary, this position has to be maintained not only within Roman Catholic ecclesiology but also as a part of Lutheran ecclesiological thinking, although there may be differences and differentiations in the more precise understanding of what *ecclesia* is all about in the two confessions. Whereas Catholic theology would underline the church as an institution willed by God and necessary for salvation, Reformation ecclesiology tends to consider the church as a more or less contingent agent for the proclamation of the gospel and the administration of the sacraments, this proclamation and these sacraments being in turn necessary for salvation.[7]

This contingency of ecclesial reality does not contradict the assumption that the church is *creatura Verbi* and thus a necessary incarnation of divine grace. It is exactly the nature of this grace to become incarnate in the contingent secular world that cannot, however, as such and in fixed historical forms, be regarded as necessary for salvation. Such deliberations, however, are not contradictory to the

---

6. ". . . eines ist konkret ohne die Kirche nicht möglich . . . : daß die Gnade Gottes in Christus als Ereignis in geschichtlicher Greifbarkeit, in inkarnatorischer Leibhaftigkeit in der Welt anwesend ist. . . . [Es] gehört zum Wesen [der] Gnade . . . auch die raumzeitliche Erscheinung, das Dasein in der Geschichte, im Hier und Jetzt, das Heraustreten aus aller bloßen Innerlichkeit des Gewissens in *alle* Dimensionen des Menschen, in seine Geschichte, in seine Gesellschaftlichkeit, in seine Gesetze, in seine Wissenschaft, in seine Kunst. Weil das Heil im Fleische Christi kommt, und weil der Mensch heil werden soll in und durch alle Dimensionen seines Daseins hindurch, in deren gegenseitiger Interferenz und gegenseitiger Abhängigkeit, darum muß Gnade leibhaftig, geschichtlich, gesellschaftlich werden. Und wenn sie das wird, dann heißt sie Kirche." Rahner, pp. 334-35; the English translation is my own.

7. See comparable reflections in Peder Nørgaard-Højen, *Wer gehört zur Kirche? Theologische Versuche XVIII,* ed. Joachim Rogge and Gottfried Schille (Leipzig, 1993), pp. 199ff., esp. pp. 204-5.

fact that people may belong to the church without ever having received the sacrament of baptism. This is certainly the case in situations in which for various good reasons the explicit performance of the sacrament is not advisable. But this anomaly, like the "baptized pagans," also raises the question of whether baptism can indeed serve as an exclusive criterion of church membership.

The preceding reflections may have clarified that baptism and communion are correlative concepts, the more so as baptism is simply inconceivable without the communion into which it incorporates. Although baptism always occurs in, and the baptized is added to, a local congregation, the believer is at the same time made a member of the universal church, the body of Christ, the *una sancta*. The local church is not only a section of the universal church, just as the latter cannot simply be identified with the local churches all together. The universal church rather becomes visible in the local congregation because of the presence of the one Lord in any *congregatio sanctorum*. This is the reason why every baptized person is through his baptism admitted to the overarching communion of saints.[8] This may even be alleged to explain the baptism as a once-and-for-all event that does not need to be repeated even in case a person leaves the church, into which he was originally baptized, and joins another confession. Baptism is thus the preeminent bond of unity, because it incorporates the believer into Christ and his body, the church, and makes him or her participate in the fellowship of salvation. Just because the one baptism belongs together with the one Lord and the one church, this church is, regardless of its confessional observance and denominational outlook, bound to admit to any person who has received the sacrament of baptism full membership rights.

## The Limitations of the Assumption of Mutual Baptismal Recognition

The latter statement reveals that the incorporation into the body of Christ through baptism is actually anything but an easy theological

8. See for further details Edmund Schlink, *Ökumenische Dogmatik. Grundzüge* (Göttingen, 1983), pp. 479ff.

matter. The believer is, as already stated, made a member of the universal church, which always, however, appears in the shape of the local, confessional church. On the practical level every baptized person is thus being incorporated into the local community. This means that baptism, which prima facie appeared to be a truly universal, ecumenical sacrament, in practice changes into a highly confessional, or even confessionalistic, self-preserving exercise that in fact is more divisive than unifying. This state of affairs is concealed through the assumption of the so-called widespread recognition of the baptismal practices among the different churches, through which the real disunity is disguised as its own contrast. In spite of the mutual recognition of each other's baptism, the churches in reality refuse to acknowledge other confessions as true and authentic expressions of the church universal.

What the highly praised and celebrated mutual baptismal recognition amounts to, in the end, is in reality the declaration of the *validity* of baptism when administered in the name of the triune God and with use of water in the form of immersion or pouring. What is recognized is not so much a theological concept of baptism, but rather a mere technical and outward matter over which even theologians may have difficulty flying into a rage. If, on the other hand, one really takes the technical performance of baptism seriously, some rather inconvenient theological implications are likely to become visible. I do not contend that the way in which we perform baptism is unimportant, and I do believe that we should baptize according to tradition in the name of the Father, the Son, and the Holy Spirit, and do so by using water. But I do contend that, as our mutual recognition of the baptismal sacrament as already mentioned practically amounts to acknowledgment of merely technical aspects, our actual agreement in reality applies to an *ex opere operato* understanding of baptism. Once the correct ritual is applied, the baptismal rite concerned is recognized and should not in case of conversions be repeated.

I do not regard this as null and void. It is not unimportant that the problem of rebaptism, at least as far as the main confessions are concerned from that perspective, is more or less excluded from the immediate and strenuous ecumenical agenda. But the great churches escape this extremely complex area at the price of suppressing the necessary debate on the content of baptism, on which they will really have to agree if they want to reach a true recognition of the sacrament. It is known that Eastern Orthodox churches in some situations take a different position, which used to deeply scandalize church people and theologians from other confessions, and insist on rebaptism of converts. This practice may rightly cause scandal. It represents, however, a certainly possible and even honest consequence drawn from the fact that followers of Orthodoxy hold another opinion regarding the content of baptism and cherish another attitude toward other confessions that do not allow them to compromise their theological principles.[9]

Christian churches still seriously diverge from one another on a number of significant areas with regard to baptismal theology: the relationship between faith and baptism, baptism and church membership, the necessity of baptism for salvation, indiscriminate baptism and rebaptism, the *fides infantium* as *fides infusa* and the sacramentality of baptism, and last but not least the understanding of the church and the disturbing contradiction between the asserted oneness of baptism and a plurality of mutually divided churches. Looking at this list of sometimes exceedingly controversial and church-divisive problems, one realizes that the alleged interconfessional agreement on baptism does not really refer to much more than the mere fact of the baptismal rite, especially as the catalogue of critical concerns could easily be enlarged. The churches do, in fact, fiercely disagree with each other on practically any important point of baptismal theology. What really leaps to the eye is not unity but disunity in the area of baptism. Nevertheless, it is not impossible for the churches to say something in common with regard to baptism, but when it comes to actual implementation, the differences are far more visible than the professed consensus. This is what today's ecumenical reality forces us to place on record in spite of any seeming agreement and fraternization, and I would dare to claim that as to the understanding of baptism the rapprochement between the confessions is in fact weaker and

9. For further details regarding rebaptism in Orthodoxy, see Dorothea Wendebourg, "Taufe und Oikonomia. Zur Frage der Wiedertaufe in der Orthodoxen Kirche," in *Kirchengemeinschaft — Anspruch und Wirklichkeit. Festschrift für Georg Kretschmar,* ed. Wolf-Dieter Hauschild, Carsten Nicolaisen, and Dorothea Wendebourg (Stuttgart, 1986), pp. 93ff.

more modest than in several other areas of interconfessional encounter, e.g., the Eucharist.

From that perspective it really seems odd and even counterproductive when the ecumenical movement insists on giving the appearance of some kind of agreement regarding baptism as the bond of unity. Still, it cannot be denied that the churches to a large extent share a common theological understanding of essential elements of baptism, to which first and foremost the Lima Statement bears an impressive witness.[10] They are agreed upon the institution of baptism (#1) and upon its meaning, insofar as they interpret it as the participation in Christ's death and resurrection (#3) and as implying conversion and conveying pardoning and cleansing (#4). They have no difficulty in asserting together that baptism as the sign of the kingdom (#7) is the gift of the Spirit (#5) and incorporates into the body of Christ (#6). What, on the other hand, strongly divides the churches are a different view on the relation between baptism and faith and last but not least the various baptismal practices, including the unsolved problem of relating the soteriological and ecclesiological implications of baptism. To be sure, the Lima Statement is honest enough to admit that, but at the same time it neglects debating in any depth some of the really church-divisive issues (e.g., the problem of sacramentality). But it overtly and courageously uncovers (though not in the main text; it is "put aside" in a commentary) the discrepancy between the churches' confession of the one baptism and the tragic divisions among them when it states, "The inability of the churches mutually to recognize their various practices of baptism as sharing in the one baptism, and their actual dividedness in spite of mutual baptismal recognition, have given dramatic visibility to the broken witness of the Church. . . . The need to recover baptismal unity is at the heart of the ecumenical task as it is central for the realization of genuine partnership within the Christian communities."[11]

In other words: The churches have no difficulty in recognizing any one baptized person as a Christian, but they passionately dispute

---

10. *Baptism, Eucharist and Ministry,* Faith and Order Paper 111 (Geneva: World Council of Churches, 1982), section on baptism, hereafter cited as *BEM.* The references to the Lima Statement are all taken from this edition.

11. *BEM,* section on baptism, #6, commentary.

the ecumenical (or rather ecclesiological) rights (inherent in baptism provided that it *really* incorporates into the *una sancta*) of that same person the moment he/she wants to make use of them. They do not doubt his/her affiliation to the *una sancta*, but they refuse to give him/her access to their particular confessional embodiments of the church universal, thus exposing him/her to an ecclesial imperialism that prevents him/her from enjoying the benefits theoretically ascribed to baptism. In terms of interchurch rapprochement it appears to be exceedingly uncostly to admit the Christian name to somebody with whom we are not prepared to share ecclesial community, let alone eucharistic fellowship. Fellow Christians — to that effect excluded from being recognized as equal members of any one church other than their own, the communion with whom they are seeking — can do nothing with the mere honor of being described as Christians, the less so as such honor will rather be conceived as supercilious contempt.

Theologically it appears hard to prove that baptism should not in fact provide a sufficient basis for church fellowship, especially since it is generally held that the sacrament makes the baptized participate in Christ and incorporates him/her into his body. To think of a more intensive unification between the believer and his/her savior than the one which is conveyed in baptism is hardly justified — at least not if the interpretation normally given is maintained. *Either* we have to abandon our present opinion on the high potentials of baptism and really regard it as the sacrament of initiation that is fully valid and effective only when followed by some other act of adherence to Christ on the side of the believer (e.g., confirmation, Eucharist), *or* we take our own high appreciation of baptism seriously and content ourselves with baptizing as prerequisite for being a member of the church of Christ. The latter solution, however, is to a considerable extent impeded in those (folk or state) churches who practice indiscriminate infant baptism that creates enormous ecclesiological problems.

In either case a thorough debate on baptism is badly needed in order to bring about a compatibility between the soteriological and ecclesiological dimensions of the sacrament. In this respect the reflections by Susan K. Wood about an integrated rite of initiation to the effect that the believer is baptized into a eucharistic fellowship as the community of the baptized appear to be creative and forward-looking and to give a considerable contribution likely to overcome the present impasse, where "one enters a divided church through baptism because one enters simultaneously into the one body of Christ and into a particular communion that is not in communion with other ecclesial communities of baptized persons."[12] Her proposal takes seriously the full weight of baptism as the sacrament of complete membership in the church that as such conveys full access to all the gifts of ecclesial community, as is the case, e.g., in the Eastern Orthodox tradition. However, her suggestion becomes less convincing because it does not seem to solve the actual conflicts among the confessions that certainly so far impede any eucharistic implication of a mere reception of baptism. On the contrary, exactly in the Orthodox tradition the unity of baptism and Eucharist is matched, logically in a sense, by an even more vehement inclination to restrict the admittance of non-Orthodox Christians to the Orthodox Eucharist. An integrated rite of initiation is not likely to guarantee the baptized person's " 'birthright' of Eucharist table fellowship" of which she speaks, since the exercise of this right is closely related to the concept of apostolicity and the apostolic succession as *the* remaining area of interconfessional divergences that no dialogue so far has been able to bridge. Compared with this fact, the quarrel on the Eucharist seems, after all, less serious and has in fact to a large extent already been overcome. A sober reflection on apostolicity appears to me, therefore, to be a necessary prerequisite for durable progress within the area of baptism — as it is for any positive result within ecclesiology as a whole.

The diverging issues are thus manifold, and the *ex opere operato* agreement on baptism, to which I referred above, is not only not much, it is probably a false thing to be agreed upon, because it has very little to do with the content of the sacrament, which we obviously do not agree upon, or else we would have no hesitations to draw our conclusions with regard to recognizing those churches whose baptismal practices we have normally no difficulties declaring valid. Some scholars are more optimistic in their judgment and dare to see a possibility of recognizing a certain measure of ecclesiality among the traditional Christian communities in addition to the acknowledgment of

12. Susan K. Wood, "Baptism and the Foundations of Communion," p. 60 in this volume.

the validity of baptism. Emmanuel Lanne concludes from the existing "technical" recognition "a fundamental community of faith in Christ as unique Lord and Saviour, in the Trinity of the Father who sent his Son for the salvation of the world and bestowed the Holy Spirit, who enables us to call on the Father . . . [and] also . . . a certain degree of communion in the one Body of Christ, the church."[13]

Without disagreeing totally with Dom Lanne, I cannot avoid the impression that his conclusion has a kind of spellbinding character that expresses his own wishful thinking with regard to what the baptismal recognition really ought to imply. His statement raises more questions than it answers, and even blurs the issues at stake with its unprecise formulations. What does, *under the present prevailing circumstances,* "a fundamental community of faith in Christ as unique Lord and Saviour" and "in the Trinity of the Father" really imply, and what is precisely meant by "a certain degree of communion in the one Body of Christ," when baptized believers are in fact mutually excluded from that communion in the one body of Christ and only admitted to the community in which they actually received their baptism, although many of them certainly share the fundamental community of faith in our Savior? So long as we do not clarify what the existing recognition of the validity of baptism implies and does not imply, such declarations will remain mere words. As the present situation is, it is certainly no exaggeration to place it on record that this recognition is not sufficient for establishing any kind of church fellowship. Rather than laying the foundations of church unity, it signalizes disunity and sharpens somehow the existing divisions.

This fact is not necessarily surprising, for it has to do with baptism as the sacrament of faith. This is to be understood to the effect that repentance and confession of faith precede the gift of baptism. In baptism the believer commits himself to Christ and confesses the faith of the church as the initiation to his lifelong commitment to the Lord. This is clearly stated in the Ecumenical Directory of the Roman Catholic Church, where it reads: "By the sacrament of baptism a person is truly incorporated into Christ and into his Church and is reborn to a sharing of the divine life. Baptism, therefore, constitutes the

---

13. Emmanuel Lanne, "Baptism," in *Dictionary of the Ecumenical Movement*, ed. Nicholas Lossky et al. (Geneva/Grand Rapids, 1991), pp. 75ff., esp. p. 79.

sacramental bond of unity existing among all who through it are reborn. Baptism, of itself, is the beginning, for it is directed towards the acquiring of fullness of life in Christ. It is thus ordered to the profession of faith, to the full integration into the economy of salvation, and to Eucharistic communion."[14] A person is thus baptized with the intention of acquiring sometime in the future this fullness of life in Christ (to which, apparently, baptism by itself grants him no access) as a precondition for being recognized as an authentic, mature member of the baptizing community.

If, at the same time, one really takes seriously the ecumenical ideology, according to which the different confessions recognize each other's baptism, the churches perspicuously baptize on a less extensive faith than the one they require for granting full communion. But this is in fact meaningless, because one cannot make a person a member of the church on the grounds of less than is required for full unity. To refuse this would be equal to rejecting that a newly baptized person would even be in communion with the community into which he was just baptized. This is, indeed, the point at which the talk about fundamental community of faith in Christ shows its harmfulness, because what is fundamental is, by its very nature, sufficient (and necessary) for becoming a member of the church as well as for remaining in communion with all those who have also been baptized on the basis of the fundamentals of Christian faith. One cannot possibly require more for reestablishing the unity among Christians than is required when the same persons are initiated to their pilgrimage and are incorporated into Christ and his body. *Fundamentum fidei satis est.*

## Implications of the Assumption
## of Mutual Baptismal Recognition

The decisive question, however, is how this *fundamentum fidei* is to be understood. What is the content of Christian faith, on which every

14. Pontificium Consilium ad Christianorum Unitatem Fovendam, *Directory for the Application of Principles and Norms of Ecumenism* (Vatican City, 1993), para. 92 (p. 57). Cf. the *Decree on Ecumenism of the Second Vatican Council (Unitatis Redintegratio)*, #22.

member of the churches has been baptized? Until this problem is solved, the mutual recognition of the Christian communions on the basis of the common baptism will certainly not be within reach. This means that the endeavors for common interpreting, regarding possibly common reformulating of the ancient faith of the church, must continue and be intensified. There is simply no ecumenical point in just stating that baptism and faith belong together, so long as we are not able to agree upon a common formula of faith to indicate the *fides quae*. In recent years appeal has repeatedly been made to the apostolic and catholic faith of the first millennium, in which the unity of the church was still unbroken, as a possible foundation for future ecclesial communion. What was actually sufficient to maintain unity in the founding era of the church is also considered sufficient to reestablish the broken fellowship.

This seems to be the conviction of the members of the International Roman Catholic–Orthodox Commission, when they in their final report, 1987, declare: "That any Church refers to the Nicene-Constantinopolitan Creed as the necessary standard of fellowship in the sole Church, which is spread in the entire oikoumene and throughout all ages, is the first precondition for true fellowship among the churches. *To that effect true faith is preconditional for sacramental fellowship.* Because of this mutual recognition of the identity and uniqueness of the faith . . . , such as it is passed on in every local Church, they mutually recognize one another as the true Church of God, and every believer from another Church is accepted as brother or sister in faith."[15]

---

15. "Die erste Bedingung für eine wahre Gemeinschaft unter den Kirchen ist die, daß jede Kirche sich auf das Glaubensbekenntnis von Nizäa-Konstantinopel als auf den notwendigen Maßstab dieser Gemeinschaft der einzigen Kirche bezieht, die über die ganze Erde und durch alle Zeiten hin ausgebreitet ist. *In diesem Sinn ist der wahre Glaube Voraussetzung für eine Gemeinschaft in den Sakramenten.* Aufgrund dieser gegenseitigen Anerkennung der Identität und der Einzigkeit des Glaubens . . . , wie er in jeder Ortskirche weitergegeben wird, erkennen sie sich gegenseitig als wahre Kirche Gottes an und wird jede(r) Gläubige in einer anderen Kirche als Bruder oder Schwester im Glauben aufgenommen." Harding Meyer et al., eds., *Dokumente wachsender Übereinstimmung. Sämtliche Berichte und Konsenstexte interkonfessioneller Gespräche auf Weltebene II* (Paderborn and Frankfurt/Main, 1992), pp. 546-47. The italics and English translation are my own.

This is a remarkably clear and honest statement: True faith is claimed as preconditional for church unity. Nothing more, nothing less! And nobody should ever fancy that real *koinonia* could possibly be established on the grounds of a so-called recognition of the common baptism that is hereby finally, though indirectly, reduced to a mere formal prerequisite for acknowledgment of baptismal validity (cf. above). Even that may under certain circumstances be questioned — e.g., as has already been mentioned, in the Orthodox Church. Also, in the relationship between churches who baptize infants and communities which practice believer's baptism this problem is still far from settled.

What is at stake is, in the last analysis, the search for truth and the quest for its exact definition and clarification. This endeavor will take different shapes, depending on the dialogue partner in question, but in any case the churches' self-understanding will be subject to revision and corrections. It will be necessary for them to abandon cherished theological ideas and to surrender superiority complexes in favor of attempts to interpret and understand anew their common theological and historical heritage. Dialogues of recent decades have made fruitful experiences in common Bible study that could probably in the case of baptism reveal a variety of biblical approaches to baptismal theology and thus promote a healthy relativism likely to subvert petrified attitudes developed in the course of history. The most decisive hindrances for a successful rapprochement between the confessions are without any doubt the different hermeneutical codes by which the churches traditionally uncover and formulate the truth — the Reformation principles *(solus Christus* and *sola scriptura)*, the Catholic teaching authority, ecumenical councils, etc. — and make their authoritative decisions. Somehow the churches will have to come to terms with one another and consider realistic possibilities for common decision making. Otherwise they will continue to prevent themselves from making progress with regard to the highly controversial issues that still divide the confessions in the area of baptismal theology.

As I have tried to show, the upholding of the appearance of baptismal agreement among the confessions tends to promote ideological support to an ecumenical inflexibility that does not go beyond a safe and self-sufficient status quo. To that effect the dogma on the assumed recognition of the baptismal practice in the churches is detrimental to any serious change in favor of the authentic unity we are still bound to seek and realize. On the other hand, the idea of baptism as the bond of unity is not just nothing, and it by no means implies that baptismal unity is a phantom, as I have also tried to show. Theologically it is a given fact, just as it is a prerequisite for ecclesiology to base the actual search for church unity on the oneness in Christ. To that effect the assertion of baptismal unity is, in fact, theologically reasonable, although the churches fail to draw the relevant practical and ecclesial conclusions, and it certainly possesses a strong and pragmatic appeal to overcome the divisions and thus to implement what is already inherent in the very concept of baptismal recognition. "Baptism is an incentive to definitely and energetically promote the work of unification. In this whole area theological and pastoral differences are of no really profound significance, let alone a significance of such kind that it might legitimate the divisions."[16] The latter sentence is, to be sure, regrettably enough, not yet a description of the situation in which our churches find themselves. On the contrary, in the actual interconfessional relations the differences are, indeed, allowed to play an overwhelmingly church-divisive role. Against this obscure background the statement of Harald Wagner gives all the more reason to emphasize the normative weight of his appeal.

So far, however, theological and pastoral differences did legitimate the divisions and impeded any real progress in an area where most people concerned for Christian unity presumed they had reason to believe that unity already existed. What remains is the task to unravel the tangled threads of a case, in which an ideology disguised as argumentative theology threatens to freeze interconfessional progress and to release the ecumenical potentialities inherent in the idea of baptism as the bond of unity par excellence.

16. "Taufe ist Ansporn, das Werk der Einigung dezidiert und energisch voranzutreiben. Theologische und pastorale Differenzen haben in diesem ganzen Komplex keine sehr tiefgreifende, gar die Trennung legitimierende Bedeutung." Wagner, in Urban and Wagner, eds., p. 149; the English translation is my own.

# Baptism and the Unity of the Church in the New Testament

*James D. G. Dunn*

## 1. Introduction

There is general agreement that our key doctrines and practices should be either based on or in conformity with the NT Scriptures. This principle should not be understood in a narrow way, as though only formulations and practices actually attested to in the NT were thereby validated by the NT. Creeds and confessions, liturgy and praxis have all developed over the centuries — inevitably and necessarily so. Nor is it to beg any questions about the relation of Scripture and tradition. Scripture needs to be interpreted. It does not always speak clearly or with a single voice. Tradition (different church traditions!) is bound to have a crucial (some would say determinative) role in the process of interpretation.

Yet, at the same time, anyone who takes the concept of the canon seriously has to allow the possibility, not to say the requirement, that Scripture should function as a critical principle against which subsequent tradition(s) can be measured in some realistic way — "the norm (Scripture) that norms the norm (Scripture and tradition)." For a faith which centers so much on the incarnation it can hardly be otherwise, since that faith invests paramount and normative significance in the revelation of a specific life and ministry in a particular time and place in history, and our only witness/access to that life and ministry is through the NT.

I presume also that biblical (here NT) specialists have a role to play within the teaching ministry of the church at this point. Since the text (NT) was brought into existence as authoritative text within particular historical contexts, the NT specialist may be said to have the competence to illuminate the meaning of the text in context and thus to indicate and even delimit the meanings which can legitimately be read from the text. I do not wish to become sidetracked into issues of current hermeneutical theory and debate, but it is difficult to see how Scripture could function as a critical norm otherwise.

Let us take baptism as a test case. How might such an exercise speak to the issue of baptism and unity? Given the importance of the issues raised in the initial study paper, it might be of value to test the scriptural foundations of baptism to reassure ourselves that they will bear the weight which the different Christian traditions have put upon them. I confess to some misgivings here, since I have found the questions raised in this way surprisingly disturbing in their implications, and I would not want to distract this consultation from its real business. On the other hand, if the questions do arise from the texts themselves, perhaps they need to be asked.

I begin by stating the questions as they have arisen for me over the years, then I will develop the points by looking at the key NT texts. In each case my concern is to be as clear as possible on what this baptism is which is a basis of unity and what its NT foundations are, and whether there are NT nuances and emphases which speak to our present concerns.

## 2. Preliminary Questions

My starting point is the observation made at the beginning of my *Baptism* and cited also in the study paper: that the central term, "baptism," is a "concertina" word. "It may be used simply for the actual act of immersion in water, or its meaning may be expanded to take in more and more of the rites and constituent parts of conversion-initiation until it embraces the whole."[1] Several problems or issues arise from this initial observation.

1. J. D. G. Dunn, *Baptism in the Holy Spirit* (London: SCM, 1970), p. 5. In

a. "Baptize, baptism" are, of course, loanwords from the Greek *(baptizein, baptisma)*. In secular usage *baptizein* meant to "dip, plunge." In the passive it is used in the sense "be drowned, sink."[2] It gained its particular prominence for Christians from John the Baptist: His practice was so distinctive that he was nicknamed from it — "John the baptizer/the one who dips/immerses" (Mark 1:4), "John the Baptist" (Matt. 3:1; Luke 7:20; etc.). The practice was taken over into Christianity and the term into Christian vocabulary, with this distinctive meaning, so that subsequently the only way to translate it effectively was by continuing to use the Greek term. In other words, the basic meaning of the term is given by the water rite which was John the Baptist's hallmark.

This obviously contrasts somewhat with the characteristic usage in contemporary discussion, where the expanded sense "to include the entirety of initiation" is almost universal. Thus in the study paper, "baptism" (1) "refers to the entirety of the single initiation rite centering on the immersion in water of . . . the new Christian in the name of the triune God"; (2) mediates "forgiveness" and "unity with Christ"; (3) "must also imply the gift of the Spirit . . . the Holy Spirit given within baptism"; (4) "is a work of God . . . the decisive agent in baptism is God"; etc.

These two usages are manifestly different. How do we get from the one usage to the other? How are the two related? Would clarification here be of help to us?

b. A second issue immediately follows. In using the single term "baptism" to cover a range of texts, which goes from the Baptist's original usage to more developed use (as in Paul), are we in danger of homogenizing what are in fact different usages? This is partly a question about the legitimacy of drawing on texts from different NT writers within a single paragraph, on the assumption (presumably) that the texts all function on the same level.[3]

More serious is the danger of "illegitimate transfer of meaning."

---

*Baptism* I coined the term "conversion-initiation" to embrace the total event of becoming a Christian with as little question-begging as possible.

2. H. G. Liddell, R. Scott, and H. S. Jones, *Greek-English Lexicon,* 9th ed. (1940), *"baptizo."*

3. One paragraph in the study paper (p. 14) draws freely on texts from Mark, John, Acts, Paul, and deutero-Paul.

I refer here to one of the criticisms leveled against the Kittel *Wörter-buch:* that the meaning of a word may be seen (illegitimately) as the sum of its usages; that all the dimensions and nuances of the term may then be claimed as present or implicit in every individual usage. Whereas, in reality, as even a brief acquaintance with a Greek NT lexicon will illustrate, the same term can have a range of meanings, which are often discrete from each other, or if they lie on a continuous spectrum can still be used in specific contexts with nuances specific or even distinctive to that context. The key consideration, as James Barr insisted, is the use of the term in each specific context — the sentence (not the word) as the unit of meaning.[4]

The question to be asked in this case, then, is whether the expanded sense of "baptism" can and should be read legitimately into all the uses of *baptizein/baptisma*. If there is a spectrum of meaning in the usage of the Greek terms from the Baptist to Paul, say, do we not have to ask of individual references where they stand on that spectrum, and whether different usages on one part of the spectrum are in fact distinct from other usages on another part of the spectrum?

c. A further concern is that an illegitimate transfer of meaning in this case may also involve some degree of theological sleight of hand. For at one end of the spectrum we are talking simply of a rite of immersion in (or effusion with) water — a rite triggered by human request and implemented by human action. At the other we are talking about an action of God. In running the spectrum together (squeezing the concertina) into a single usage ("the sacrament of baptism"), are we in danger of confusing human action and divine?

The point is that the water ritual always stand at the center of "baptism," no matter how much we insist that the focus is on God's action. And the water rite is what *we* control. By *our* decision to baptize X or Y in water, we in effect dictate to God to act upon X or Y in accordance with the fuller theology of the sacrament of baptism which we confess. We say it is *God* who acts in baptism, we delight in a sacrament (infant baptism) which mirrors the initiative of grace, but the actual initiative is all *ours*.[5] Of course, we can make theological

4. J. Barr, *The Semantics of Biblical Language* (Oxford University, 1961).
5. The sharpness of the issue here posed is only partially resolved by appeal to the general commission of Matthew 28:18-20; see also below, §4.a.

capital from the situation by meditating humbly and gratefully on a God who thus commits himself to act in a sacrament whose happening is at our command. At the same time the disparity between numbers baptized and the much smaller numbers of those who subsequently take up active Christian discipleship must at least raise the question as to whether God has indeed acted with any great efficacy in the baptisms of the apostatizing (?) majority.[6]

d. This line of reflection in turn raises what became the most important issue for me from my earlier work on this subject. That is, whether by taking up this word "baptism" we are focusing on baptism to an extent not justified by the NT. Two things became quite clear to me from my research in this area thirty years ago.

First, that the decisive factor in conversion-initiation was the gift of the Spirit. This was the message from the beginning. The Baptist characterized the Coming One as he who will baptize in the Holy Spirit (and fire). It is clear again and again from Acts that everything hung on the gift of the Spirit — whether the Samaritans in Acts 8, Cornelius and his friends in Acts 10, or the Ephesians in Acts 19. "Can any one forbid water for baptizing these people who have received the Holy Spirit just as we have?" asked Peter (Acts 10:47). "Did you receive the Holy Spirit when you believed?" asked Paul (Acts 19:2).

As regards Paul I could go on at some length. But let me just highlight a few references. In Galatians it is striking how Paul's main argument starts from the well-remembered (on both sides) fact of their reception of the Spirit (3:1-5). In the event, everything stood or fell on this. In II Corinthians 1:21-22 Paul piles up the imagery — confirmed into Christ, anointed, sealed, and given the *arrabon* of the Spirit in their hearts. The Spirit is the "down payment," the "first installment" — in other words, the beginning of the salvation process. That the Spirit is to be seen as the defining mark of the Christian is put in blunt terms in Romans 8:9: "You are not in the flesh but in the Spirit, assum-

---

6. Since parallels are often drawn between baptism and circumcision, we should perhaps note the contrast at this point with circumcision. Circumcision was not seen as a sacrament in the Christian sense. It was not a rite of entry into the people of the covenant; that happened by birth. It was rather the first act of Torah obedience of the new member of the covenant people.

ing that[7] the Spirit of God does indeed dwell in you; if anyone does not have the Spirit of Christ, that person does not belong to him." In this verse, in fact, Paul provides the nearest thing to a definition of a Christian (someone who is "of Christ"). And the definition is in terms of the Spirit. It is "having the Spirit" which defines and determines someone as being "of Christ"; it was by receiving the Spirit that one became a Christian.

Second, the other feature which came home to me with considerable force was the fact that the coming of the Spirit into a life in those early days was itself a recognizable event. The Spirit was known by the impact on that life and the transformation thus effected. This is an observation which is more or less common to all modern studies of the Spirit in the NT. As Eduard Schweizer put it at the beginning of the NT section of his well-known Kittel article on *pneuma* — but he was simply echoing the consensus since Hermann Gunkel: "Long before the Spirit was a theme of doctrine, he was a fact in the experience of the community."[8] The most recent thorough study begins on the same note: "Whatever else, for Paul the Spirit was an *experienced reality*"; "For Paul the Spirit, as an experienced and living reality, was the absolutely crucial matter for Christian life, from beginning to end."[9]

7. The *eiper* ("assuming that") denotes a necessary condition for the validity of the preceding assertion — "since" (NRSV, REB); see further my *Romans*, Word Biblical Commentary, vol. 38 (Dallas: Word, 1988), p. 428.

8. E. Schweizer, *Theological Dictionary of the New Testament*, 6:396. H. Gunkel's *Die Wirkungen des Heiligen Geistes nach der populären Anschauung der apostolischen Zeit und der Lehre des Apostels Paulus* (Göttingen: Vandenhoeck, 1888) is generally regarded as the beginning of the modern treatment of the Spirit in the NT.

9. G. Fee, *God's Empowering Presence: The Holy Spirit in the Letters of Paul* (Peabody, Mass.: Hendrickson, 1994), pp. xxi, 1. Y. Congar likewise finds it necessary to begin with "A Note on 'Experience' " (*I Believe in the Holy Spirit*, 3 vols. [New York: Seabury; London: Chapman, 1983], 1:xvii). J. Moltmann opens with the sentence: "The simple question: when did you last feel the workings of the Holy Spirit? embarrasses us" (*The Spirit of Life: A Universal Affirmation* [Minneapolis: Fortress, 1992], p. x). And M. Welker attempts as his starting point to take seriously "the broad spectrum of experience of God's Spirit," "the rich reality and vitality of the Holy Spirit," "the appearance of God's reality and God's power in the midst of the structural patterns of human life" (*God the Spirit* [Minneapolis: Fortress, 1994], pp. ix-xi).

This is evident in the episodes in Acts which focus on the coming of the Spirit. I cannot refrain from citing here the comment on Paul's encounter with the Ephesian "disciples" made by one of the doyens of ecumenical Christianity — Lesslie Newbigin:

> The apostle asked the converts of Apollos one question: "Did ye receive the Holy Spirit when you believed?" and got a plain answer. His modern successors are more inclined to ask either "Did you believe exactly what we teach?" or "Were the hands that were laid on you our hands?," and — if the answer is satisfactory — to assure the converts that they have received the Holy Spirit even if they don't know it. There is a world of difference between these two attitudes.[10]

The same point follows from the "definition of a Christian" in Romans 8:9 and 14. Paul does not say: "If you are Christ's, you have the Spirit; since you are sons of God, you are led by the Spirit." In both cases, Paul puts it the other way round: "if you have the Spirit, you are Christ's; if you are being led by the Spirit, you are God's sons." The fact which was immediately discernible was not whether they were Christ's — attested to by baptism or confession — a fact from which their possession of the Spirit could be deduced as a corollary. That which was ascertainable was their possession of the Spirit; that was the primary factor from which their relation to Christ could be deduced. Their Christian status was recognizable from the fact that Christ's agent was in evident control of their lives.[11]

Such acceptance of religious experience, and indeed reliance on it as a sign of God's action on and in a life — need this be said to Lutherans! — has something unnerving about it. Anyone familiar with the history of "enthusiastic" sects within Christianity (as in other religions and ideologies) is bound to recognize danger signals. Paul, how-

---

10. L. Newbigin, *The Household of God* (London: SCM, 1953), p. 95. Again, as Newbigin well realized, the issue is only partly softened by noting the difference between the missionary situation of the beginning church and the situation today (which is more a missionary situation in western Europe than we Europeans care to admit).

11. See further below, §5. I need not go into "the evidences of the Spirit" at this point. In the NT they range from ecstatic phenomena (speaking in tongues) to intellectual illumination and moral transformation.

ever, was well aware of the danger and provided several "tests" by which the presence and inspiration of the Spirit might be discerned. This is not a subject we can pursue here. I mention it only to prevent a too speedy discounting and dismissing of the point being made. For the point is that the coming of the Spirit was in itself a memorable experience in the lives of the first Christians. They did not need to be reminded of it by means of a reference to their baptism. As Paul shows, when he recalled his readers to their beginnings as Christians, the recall was most often to the gift of the Spirit itself, and not to baptism.

And that poses the question for us today: In including so much in baptism, are we giving baptism the prominence due to the Spirit?[12] In seeing the gift of the Spirit as a function of baptism (baptism as bestowing or mediating the Spirit), are we subordinating the Spirit to a rite which we humans decide to administer? Are we compromising the sovereignty of the *pneuma* to "blow where it wills" (John 3:8)? Are we putting too much emphasis on the ritual moment? Perhaps by clarifying such issues some of the problems confronted in the study paper can be set in a fresh light, or some of the elements can prove to be less intractable.

## 3. Precursors of Christian Baptism

Since the Christian sacrament originates in the baptism of John the Baptizer, it is well that we become as clear as possible on what the texts say about it and about the Coming One's baptism. Still more important, John's baptism of Jesus is generally regarded as the vital precedent for Christian baptism. So we need to be clear on what the Gospels actually say about it and what sort of precedent it provides.

a. *John's baptism.* It is worth reminding ourselves that the NT consistently regards John's baptism as the beginning of the gospel (Mark 1:1; Acts 1:22; 10:37; 13:24). It is described consistently as a

---

12. I note, e.g., how the study paper speaks of "baptism as a lifelong process of the death of the old person and the coming to life of the new" (I.B.5.). Despite its pedigree, such talk confuses the once-for-all imagery of baptism. The ongoing process of "being saved" is better described with other imagery, particularly that of transformation, and again is more appropriately referred directly to the Spirit (as, e.g., in II Cor. 3:18).

"baptism of repentance" (Mark 1:4; Luke 3:3; Acts 13:24; 19:4), or more fully as a "baptism of repentance into forgiveness" (Mark 1:4; Luke 3:3). Does this mean that John's baptism conveyed forgiveness? That is, was it already a sacrament and an embryonic Christian baptism? Such is often thought to be the case. But the relevant texts point to a different conclusion.

For one thing Luke's usage makes it fairly clear that the phrase "into forgiveness" goes with "repentance" rather than with "baptism." The basic concept is of a "repentance which receives forgiveness" (Luke 24:47; cf. Acts 5:31; 11:18). So far as the verb is concerned ("repent"), Acts 2:38 is ambiguous, but again Luke's other usage implies that the primary relation is between repentance and forgiveness (Luke 17:3; Acts 3:19). We should also note that Jesus is remembered as calling for repentance although he himself did not baptize (Mark 1:15). In other words, we should probably take the phrase "baptism of repentance for the forgiveness of sins" as "baptism which expresses the repentance to which God gives forgiveness," rather than as "baptism for forgiveness."[13]

Matthew's language seems to confirm this. He omits talk of "forgiveness" from his account of the Baptist, and is the only one to include the same phrase ("for the forgiveness of sins") in his account of the Last Supper (Matt. 26:28). Does he thereby indicate his belief that forgiveness was possible only as a result of Jesus' death? Moreover, he has John describe his baptism again in distinctive terms: " 'I baptize you in water into repentance' " (Matt. 3:11). In other words, for the Matthean Baptist, baptism was a means to repentance (not forgiveness), i.e., a means of bringing to climactic or visible expression the repentance response to his preaching.

b. *"He will baptize you in the Holy Spirit' "* (Mark 1:8). Traditionally, this promise is taken as a prediction of Christian baptism. There are two flaws in this reasoning.

One is the contrasting or antithetical form of the Baptist's statement:

13. An offer of forgiveness of sin without reference to the required sacrifice and the formal absolution of the priest (Leviticus 4–5) would probably have caused some hostile comment (cf. Mark 2:7; Luke 7:49). The silence of the Baptist tradition on this point leaves the issue obscure.

I            baptize you    in water,
but he will    baptize you    in the Holy Spirit.

In the first line the medium into which "you" are to be plunged/dipped/immersed is "water"; in the second, the medium into which "you" are to be plunged/dipped/immersed is "the Holy Spirit." The evident simplicity of the contrast would be distorted if we actually read the second line as "he will baptize you in water and the Holy Spirit." Nor does the term "baptize" of itself mean "baptize in water." On the contrary, the Baptist was evidently taking the ritual act which was his hallmark and "punning" on it. He was using his distinctive rite as a metaphor of what the Coming One would do. The fact that Jesus himself is remembered as taking up the imagery of baptism and using it in a similarly metaphorical way — in speaking of his coming death as a " 'baptism with which I must be baptized' " (Mark 10:38; Luke 12:50) — simply confirms the point. In other words, what we are seeing is the key term "baptize" beginning to move along the spectrum of meaning. And in this first, rather crucial broadening out of the term, it is clear that the metaphorical usage ("in Holy Spirit") is not a broader usage which includes the narrower ("in water"). On the contrary, the broader usage is set over against the narrower, in contrast to it.

The other flaw is the failure to note the background of the Baptist's imagery. This comes out most clearly in the fuller Q version of the Baptist's prediction — " 'he will baptize you in the Holy Spirit and fire' " (Matt. 3:11/Luke 3:16). This powerful combination of imagery — river, *ruach/pneuma*, and fire — is evidently drawn from scriptural language. The most striking parallel is Isaiah 30:27-28:

> Behold, the name of the Lord comes from afar,
>     burning with his anger, and in thick rising smoke;
> his lips are full of indignation,
>     and his tongue is like a devouring fire;
> his *ruach* is like an overflowing stream that reaches up to the neck;
> to sift the nations with a sieve of destruction,
>     and to place on the jaws of the peoples a bridle that leads astray.

Almost certainly we have here the imagery on which the Baptist was drawing, and by combining it with the metaphor drawn from his own distinctive rite he was able to coin one of the most powerful images in all the Bible — the Coming One's ministry characterized as a sifting/purgative/destructive experience as though one had been plunged into a river of the Lord's fiery *ruach*.[14] That the Markan and subsequent Christian version of the saying (Acts 1:5; 11:16) omit talk of "fire" does not affect the central point that the Baptist's image of one who would "baptize in Spirit" was a powerful metaphorical use of the term "baptize."

c. *Jesus' baptism by John* (Mark 1:9 and pars.). On this point tradition is even clearer: that Jesus' baptism by John is the precedent for Christian baptism. Or, more specifically, that Jesus' baptism by John was the first fulfillment of the Baptist's prediction: Jesus was "baptized in the Spirit" in John's baptism (in water). That is, Jesus' baptism brought the two together — baptism in water and Spirit. Somewhat distinctive in emphasis but not untypical in character is the comment of Kilian McDonnell and George Montague:

> The Spirit not only anointed Jesus but in some way effected a sanctifying of the baptismal water through him. Far from the water sanctifying Jesus, Jesus sanctified the water for all subsequent baptisms in his name.[15]

It is doubtful, however, whether the resulting emphasis properly reflects the focus and weight of the biblical narratives.

In Mark 1:9-11 it is certainly quite appropriate to read the descent of the Spirit in close conjunction with his baptism by John. Jesus "was baptized [aorist] in the Jordan by John. And immediately as he was

---

14. See further my *Baptism*, pp. 10-14; also "The Birth of a Metaphor — Baptized in Spirit," *Expository Times* 89 (1977-78): 134-38, 173-75; also "John the Baptist's Use of Scripture," in *The Gospels and the Scriptures of Israel*, ed. C. A. Evans and W. R. Stegner, Journal for the Study of the New Testament, Supplement Series, vol. 104 (Sheffield: JSOT, 1994), pp. 42-54.

15. K. McDonnell and G. T. Montague, *Christian Initiation and Baptism in the Holy Spirit* (Collegeville, Minn.: Liturgical Press, 1991), p. 28. McDonnell and Montague deny that in Luke-Acts the Spirit was mediated through John's baptism (p. 28), but want to claim that in Luke's understanding, Christian initiation "is only one baptism, an integral rite that involves water and the gift of the Holy Spirit" (p. 39).

coming up from the water [present], he saw the heavens split open. . . ." We note that the baptism could be taken as already completed (aorist), and the following events as subsequent to, and not (properly speaking) "part" of, the baptism. Nor is it clear whether the "coming up" denoted Jesus' resurfacing, or actually climbing back on the bank. And Mark's "immediately" is a well-known feature of his narrative, which may often serve to give pace to his narrative rather than to indicate continuity of the action. On the other hand, the text could be read as the "coming up" which completed the baptism and thus the heavenly voice and descent of the Spirit as "part" of the baptism. Matthew 3:16-17 is close to Mark's text and raises the same possibilities and questions.

Luke 3:21-22 is noticeably different:

> It came about that, in the being baptized of all the people, and, Jesus having been baptized and while he was praying, he saw the heaven opened and the Holy Spirit descend in bodily form like a dove upon him. . . .

The immediate context and structure of the text itself makes Luke's point. He has already narrated the Baptist's imprisonment (3:18-20); the Baptist has been removed from the scene. So Luke does not actually describe John's baptism of Jesus. In the text itself it is clear that the baptism has already taken place, and Jesus is now praying when the Spirit descends upon him. In other words, the focal point of the sequence of events is the descent of the Spirit. The baptism is simply part of the buildup to the event which really counts. This is confirmed by the emphasis which Luke later puts upon the key feature — Jesus' anointing by the Spirit (Luke 4:18; Acts 10:38).

In John's Gospel the point is still clearer. John never mentions John's baptism of Jesus. He was well aware that John baptized (1:25, 26, 31). He uses the tradition of John's prediction that Jesus would baptize in the Holy Spirit in contrast to John's own baptizing in water (1:33). But all he records of John's encounter with Jesus is that John saw the Spirit descending upon him. In other words, the focus is exclusively on the descent of the Spirit. Had we only John's Gospel we could not even speak of the event as "the baptism of Jesus."

If all this evidence counts for anything, we should be cautious about (a) attributing forgiveness to baptism, (b) deducing that the metaphor of baptizing in Spirit was intended in its first coining or subsequent Christian usage as part of a complex event of baptism in water and Spirit, and (c) concluding that the Evangelists intended Jesus' baptism by John to be the archetype of the Christian sacrament of baptism (in water and Spirit). If anything, we are encouraged *not* to make too much of the ritual of baptizing in water (as conveying forgiveness or mediating the Spirit). The emphasis falls clearly on the coming of the Spirit, whether expressed metaphorically ("baptize in") or as described in the "anointing" of Jesus.

## 4. The Importance of Christian Baptism

There can be little doubt as to the importance of Christian baptism within the NT.

a. We may note, first, that so far as we can tell, the beginning of Christian baptism coincided with the beginning of Christianity. The biblical tradition attests that the Christian practice of baptism was authorized by Jesus himself. The "great commission" (Matt. 28:18-20) is certainly quite late.[16] And the commission to baptize in the threefold name sits awkwardly with a uniform tradition that the first Christians baptized "in the name of Jesus (Christ)" (Acts 2:38; 8:16; 10:48; 19:5; I Cor. 1:13). But very few doubt that baptism in the name of Jesus was practiced from the beginnings of Christianity. Overlap anomalies like the Ephesian disciples aside (Acts 19:1-7), we know of no unbaptized Christians even in the first generation of Christianity. The fact that Paul, in writing to churches with which he had no personal contact, could simply assume that all had shared a common baptism (Rom. 6:4; Col. 2:12) confirms that baptism in the name of Jesus must have been the rite of acceptance into the new movement both from the beginnings in Jerusalem and in all the subsequent missions of outreach to Jew and Gentile. There are not many features of Christianity which we can trace back to the very beginnings with such confidence. The fact that we can do so in the case of baptism makes it a powerful

---

16. Mark 16:16 is still later; the longer ending of Mark's Gospel (Mark 16:9-20) should not be regarded as part of the canonical text.

focus of continuity with those beginnings and with all traditions which claim and rejoice in that continuity. Whatever we make of Matthew 28:18-20 in its present form, therefore, the fact that it attributes the earliest practice of baptism to a command from Jesus himself has to be respected.

b. Second, we should give due weight to what must have been the social significance of baptism from the first. Conversion typically was not some private spiritual transaction. It involved baptism. But baptism usually involved a public act, probably a public confession (Rom. 10:9). The imagery of I Corinthians 1:13 — "baptized into the name of"[17] — was of a transfer of ownership and allegiance to the person named. That is to say, it constituted almost literally a "rite of passage." Those baptized were thereby renouncing old allegiances and old ways of life and committing themselves to a new Lord and to a new way of life. That is precisely why Paul referred to their common baptism in Romans 6:4 — "so we also should walk in newness of life." The social consequences of their common baptism is one of the main themes of I Corinthians, beginning with Paul's plea for an end to factionalism.[18] Not only so, but different nationalities were also thereby pledging allegiance to what was still seen as a Jewish messianic sect. And adoption of "Jewish ways" was a frequent cause of disparagement among Rome's intellectuals.[19] It would hardly be surprising then if baptism was in most cases an event of profound significance to which Paul and his converts could and did often revert when reflecting on the beginnings of their Christian discipleship and its consequent character.

c. Third, the exegetical basis for a "high" view of baptism is quite strong. However we read the precedent of Jesus' baptism by John, the precedent set by Peter on the birthday of the church can certainly be taken to indicate at least a very close conjunction between repentance, baptism, forgiveness of sins, and reception of the gift of the Holy Spirit (Acts 2:38):

17. The imagery is the same as when we today write a check "to the name of" as means of transferring funds to the person named.

18. See particularly M. M. Mitchell, *Paul and the Rhetoric of Reconciliation: An Exegetical Investigation of the Language and Composition of 1 Corinthians* (Tübingen: J. C. B. Mohr; Louisville: Westminster, 1992).

19. See, e.g., the data collected in my *Romans*, pp. xlvi and xlviii, and the brief catena of vituperation from Roman authors in my *Romans*, pp. l-li.

"Repent and be baptized each of you in the name of Jesus Christ for the forgiveness of your sins, and you shall receive the gift of the Holy Spirit."

Similarly, the words of Ananias to Saul/Paul in Acts 22:16 are quite naturally read as the action of baptism effecting the washing away of sins: "Rise, be baptized and wash away your sins, calling on his name." Here is a good basis for a doctrine of the sacrament of baptism. Elsewhere we might simply note I Peter 3:21: "Baptism saves...."

The most powerful witness is provided by Paul. He clearly links talk of "baptized into Christ" with talk of (the rite of) baptism (Rom. 6:3-4):

> Are you unaware that all we who were baptized into Christ Jesus were baptized into his death? So then we were buried with him through baptism into death, in order that as Christ was raised from the dead . . . so we also should walk in newness of life.

It is hardly forcing the sense to see the two phrases as equivalent: "baptized into his death" = "buried with him through baptism into death." In other words, the "into Christ" of participation in Christ was effected "through baptism." Colossians 2:12, so similar to Romans 6:4, invites a similar line of interpretation. And Galatians 3:27 ("as many of you as were baptized into Christ have put on Christ") is usually cited in the same breath.[20] Similarly in I Corinthians 10:2: "all were baptized into Moses in the cloud and in the sea." If the imagery of passing through the Red Sea ("under the cloud" and "through the sea")[21] is equivalent to baptismal immersion (in water), and if Moses typologi-

---

20. Cf. E. Dinkler, *Die Taufaussagen des Neuen Testaments*, in *Zu Karl Barths Lehre von der Taufe*, ed. K. Viering (Gütersloh: Gütersloher, 1971), p. 86: "The becoming sons of God happens subjectively in faith, objectively through baptism."

21. The allusion to the cloud and sea may have been prompted by Wisdom of Solomon 19:7 in particular. That Paul saw the cloud as a symbol of the Spirit is less likely (*pace* McDonnell and Montague, p. 45; I was more open to this possibility in *Baptism*, p. 127 n. 34, with further bibliography). The implication of the "under" and "through" is that Paul saw the cloud above and water on either side as a prefiguring of baptism by immersion. See also G. Fee, *1 Corinthians* (Grand Rapids: Eerdmans, 1987), pp. 445-46.

cally represents Christ ("into Moses" on the analogy of "into Christ"),[22] then Paul presumably had in view the experience of being baptized (in water) into Christ.

In the light of such material it is easy to see how a strong sacramental theology of Christian baptism can be founded upon the NT. To be baptized means to be baptized into Christ. From which it would follow quite naturally that the "one baptism" of Ephesians 4:5, which is one of the bases of Christian unity, is the full sacrament of baptism, the entirety of Christian initiation.

## 5. The Danger of a Too Narrow Focus on Baptism

At the same time, some cautionary words are also called for by the evidence.

a. First, we should not assume that baptism was an already well developed, and always or necessarily, public ceremony. The information provided by the NT itself suggests rather that for the first half-century or so at least, the initiation ceremony was still simple and spontaneous. Certainly the testimony of Acts points firmly in that direction: three thousand received the word and were baptized in the same day (2:41); both the Ethiopian eunuch and Lydia heard the gospel, responded immediately, and were baptized there and then (8:36, 38; 16:14-15); similarly the Philippian jailor believed and was baptized — his baptism evidently taking place in the middle of the night (16:31-33); the story is repeated in Corinth, including one of the cases mentioned by Paul himself (18:8; I Cor. 1:14). As Johannes Munck observed:

22. First Corinthians 10:2 ("baptized into Moses") is obviously modeled on "baptized into Christ" (Rom. 6:3-4; Gal. 3:27; I Cor. 12:13). It would be exegetically fallacious to derive the sense of the more common phrase elsewhere from a meaning permitted by the historical relationship between Moses and the Israelites (*pace* G. Delling, *Die Zueignung des Heils in der Taufe: Eine Untersuchung zum neutestamentlichen "taufen auf den Namen"* [Berlin, 1961], pp. 79-80; C. Wolff, *Der erste Brief des Paulus an die Korinther*, in *Theologische Handkommentar zum Neuen Testament*, 7/2 [Berlin: Evangelische Verlagsanstalt, 1982], p. 41 n. 231). In I Corinthians 10:1-4 Moses, like the journey through the Red Sea and the food and drink in the desert, functions as a type of the eschatological reality now experienced in and through Christ. See also my *Baptism*, pp. 112, 125-26.

In Acts, as in the rest of the New Testament, there seems to have been no hesitation about baptizing. In a way that is remarkably casual compared with the modern formal ceremony, one baptizes and goes on one's way.[23]

This ties in with the lack of any clear reference to a catechumenate before about 200 C.E. That there was instruction of new converts from the first can hardly be doubted.[24] What is hardly clear is that such instruction was regarded as a necessary *preparation* for baptism. Which again raises the question as to whether baptism was thought of as quite such a climactic and dramatic event in the crucial transition to membership of the new sect.[25]

Consistent with this is the cautionary note Paul repeatedly records in the letter which has most to say on baptism. Paul himself was evidently anxious lest the Corinthians make too much of their baptism. It would appear that some of them were too ready to interpret their own baptisms in the light of similar or equivalent practices in other cults. In I Corinthians 1:12-13 we learn that baptism by someone (or his associate) was grounds for allegiance to that person. The logic is clear: "I am of Paul" because I was baptized by Paul. "I am of Apollos" because I was baptized by Apollos. Baptism, in other words, was thought to form some kind of mystical bond between baptized and baptizer. In 10:1-12 the implication is that baptism (and the Lord's Supper) were being regarded as a kind of spiritual inoculation and guarantee against subsequent rejection by God. And in 15:29 the mysterious baptism "on behalf of the dead" presumably indicates the baptismal rite undertaken by one and regarded as effective for another already dead.[26]

23. J. Munck, *Paul and the Salvation of Mankind* (London: SCM, 1959), p. 18 n. 1.

24. Clearly implied in Galatians 6:6 and Paul's reference to traditions passed on to and received by new established churches.

25. Still greater uncertainty attaches to the role of laying on of hands, apparently an occasional feature in initiation procedures (only clearly in Acts 19:6), and the still more obscure issue of when anointing was first linked with baptism (cf. I John 2:20).

26. This deduction regarding the views of the Corinthians regarding baptism (1:12-13; 10:1-12; 15:29) follows the main consensus.

In each case Paul deliberately de-emphasizes baptism. It was Paul himself who resisted any possible analogy between Christian baptism and equivalent cultic rites in the mysteries. Baptism provided no such bond, only a bond with the name of Jesus. Baptism provided no such guarantee. Paul even expresses his gratitude that he baptized so few. He could recall baptizing only Crispus and Gaius, and he almost forgot to mention the household of Stephanas (1:14-16) — so, not a series of particularly memorable events so far as Paul was concerned. So far as he was concerned, his mission was to preach the gospel, not to baptize (1:17) — an interesting comment on the role and relative importance attributed by Paul to baptism within the complex of conversion and initiation.[27]

b. Second, alongside Romans 6:3-4 we have to set I Corinthians 12:13. In contrast to the other *baptizein* references just noted, this is the only unqualifiedly positive reference to being baptized in I Corinthians.

> For in one Spirit we were all baptized into one body, whether Jews or Greeks, whether slaves or free, and all were irrigated with the one Spirit.

On any analysis of the tradition history lying behind this talk of being "baptized in the Spirit"[28] there is one obvious trail to be followed — though surprisingly neglected by most commentators.[29] It is the

---

27. See also my *Baptism*, pp. 118-20. To be noted is the fact that it is baptism which Paul sets as a lower priority than preaching, not just baptism misunderstood — a clarification Paul could have made had he thought baptism so salvation-effective as the usual interpretations of Romans 6:3-4, etc., assume. Cf. C. K. Barrett, *Church, Ministry, and Sacraments in the New Testament* (Exeter: Paternoster, 1985), p. 66: "I cannot understand 1 Cor. 1.14-17 as implying anything less than a relative depreciation of baptism."

28. *En* with *baptizomai* ("baptized") is most naturally taken as "baptized in" rather than "baptized by." This is the consistent usage in the NT, with *hypo* ("by") indicating the baptizer. NRSV has improved RSV at this point.

29. So, e.g., R. Schnackenburg, *Baptism in the Thought of St. Paul* (Oxford: Blackwell, 1964), pp. 26-29; H. Ridderbos, *Paul: An Outline of His Theology* (Grand Rapids: William B. Eerdmans Publishing Co., 1975), p. 398 ("baptism is simply qualified as the baptism of the Spirit"); G. Haufe, "Taufe und Heiliger Geist im Urchristentum," *Theologische Literaturzeitung* 101 (1976): 561-66; McDonnell and

trail which we have already followed a little way, beginning with the Baptist's first coining of the metaphor ("he will baptize in the Holy Spirit") and continuing through the two most decisive events in the Acts account on Christian beginnings — Pentecost (1:5) and the crucial precedent of the Gentile Cornelius's conversion (11:16).[30] The most obvious interpretation of I Corinthians 12:13 is that Paul himself was aware of this tradition and deliberately alludes to it at this point.

As we saw, a feature of the imagery of "baptized in Spirit" is that it was both coined as a metaphor from the rite of baptism and set in some distinction from or even antithesis to the rite of baptism ("I in water, he in Spirit"). In the metaphorical usage, Spirit takes the place of water as that "in" which the individual is immersed. And the two Acts accounts to which the reworked metaphor is applied are both notable for their descriptions of an outpouring of the Spirit quite separate and distinct from baptism (2:1-4; 10:44-48). In the light of such a tradition-history of the motif ("baptized in Spirit"), it is at least likely that Paul in his own use of it likewise alluded simply to the Corinthians' experience of receiving the Spirit.[31] Too often neglected is the fact that the emphasis clearly lies on the "one Spirit" (twice repeated), rather than the verb: It was by being baptized in *one* Spirit that they had been constituted *one body*.[32]

We may even have to draw in Romans 6:3 here, with its talk of being baptized into Christ's death. For, as we also noted above, Jesus himself was remembered as having taken up and adapted the Baptist's metaphor and applied it to his own death — his death as a baptism

---

Montague, pp. 42-43. G. R. Beasley-Murray, *Baptism in the New Testament* (London: Macmillan, 1963), pp. 167-71, at least raises the issue.

30. That the prediction is remembered in Acts as a saying of Jesus only underlines its importance for Luke.

31. See further my *Baptism*, pp. 129-30; Fee, *God's Empowering Presence*, pp. 179-82, 860-63. Presumably it does not need to be said again that the term "baptize" itself means simply "baptize, immerse" and not "baptize in water." Josephus, e.g., can talk of people flooding *(ebaptisen)* into a city (*War* 4.137).

32. This also has bearing on the parallel Galatians 3:27-28, since the implication there too is that it is not so much baptism which is "the soteriological principle of equality" (P. Stuhlmacher, *Biblische Theologie des Neuen Testaments. Band 1: Grundlegung. Von Jesus zu Paulus* [Göttingen: Vandenhoeck, 1992], p. 353) as the commonly experienced Spirit (3:2-5, 14).

with which he himself was to be baptized (Mark 10:38-39 and pars.).[33] Here, too, then, we might well find the background to Paul's talk of being baptized into Christ's death — as an adaptation of the Baptist's metaphor attributed to Jesus himself. It was probably because Jesus was recalled as having used the metaphor of being baptized in this way that Paul felt free to adapt it afresh to his own theology. As Christ had spoken of *his death* as a *baptism,* so Paul could speak of the beginning of salvation as a *baptism* into *Christ's death.* In which case it is relevant to note, once again, that the metaphor of baptism had been quite far removed in conception from the actual performance of baptism in water.[34]

This also suggests a resolution to the dispute whether "baptized into Christ" is in effect an abbreviated form of the fuller "baptized into the name of Christ." For the latter ("to the name of"), as already mentioned, is a metaphor drawn from business and commercial life — baptism seen as a transfer, as we would say, "to the account of Christ." In this case the metaphor is contained in the attached phrase — "to the name of." The verb itself seems to be a straightforward reference to the act of baptism itself. In contrast, in the briefer phrase, "baptized into Christ," it is the term "baptized" itself which seems to carry the metaphorical force. And its outcome is the "mystical," and far from immediately public, participation in Christ. "Baptized into Christ" carries all the overtones of Adam Christology (Romans 6:3 follows directly from 5:12-21). And "baptized into his death" leads directly into the profound motif of sharing in Christ's sufferings (6:5).[35] In short, the two phrases function within different imagery, and, as with other metaphors of salvation, an attempt to blend or identify them may simply result in the confusion of the image conveyed by each.[36]

c. Third, we need to recall, not least, the evidence indicated above regarding the gift and reception of the Spirit. Even the abbreviated survey should have made two things clear: that reception of the Spirit was generally a vivid experience in the remembered beginnings of Christian commitment; and that Paul refers to it repeatedly, and could

---

33. For more detail see my "The Birth of a Metaphor."
34. See further my *Baptism,* pp. 139-41.
35. See further my *Jesus and the Spirit* (London: SCM, 1975), pp. 330-38.
36. See again my *Baptism* with bibliography on both sides.

do so, precisely because it was such a striking highlight in that crucial transition. This is in striking contrast with the relatively few "baptize/baptism" references, however they are interpreted. Later generations, for whom the central or even only remembered experience of Christian beginnings was their baptism, need to take care lest they assume that it was ever thus. Paul's testimony is quite to the contrary. It was the experienced Spirit which made the greatest impact on their lives and in their memory. Presumably, then, the reason why Paul does not refer so much to baptism is that for him, as for most of his converts, baptism was not the focal or most significant feature of his conversion and initiation. The focal and most memorable feature of most of his converts' conversion and initiation was the gift of the Spirit.[37]

This finding also indicates the resolution to the reference of some other disputed metaphors. In particular, the "seal of the Spirit" (II Cor. 1:22; Eph. 1:13; 4:30), despite later application to baptism,[38] should almost certainly be seen as a reference to the marked effect of the Spirit's impact on the individual life. To receive the gift of the Spirit was to be stamped with the seal of new ownership, a stamp whose effects made visible who it was to whom the individual now belonged.[39] "Anointing" likewise is more naturally linked with the Spirit.[40] In the sole occurrence of the imagery (II Cor. 1:22) there may indeed be a further echo of the claim that Jesus himself had been anointed by the Spirit.[41] They had been anointed into the anointed one (II Cor. 1:22 — ". . . eis Christon kai chrisas hemas theos").

37. This was the main finding of my *Baptism*, though the full scope of the experiential character of the gift of the Spirit only became clear to me in the further study which resulted in *Jesus and the Spirit*.

38. See particularly G. W. H. Lampe, *The Seal of the Spirit*, 2nd ed. (London: SPCK, 1967); Dinkler, pp. 95-96; others in Fee, *God's Empowering Presence*, p. 294 n. 38. For U. Schnelle, II Corinthians 1:21-22 makes clear that "baptism and Spirit belong inseparably together" (*Gerechtigkeit und Christusgegenwart: Vorpaulinische und paulinische Tauftheologie* [Göttingen: Vandenhoeck, 1983], p. 125).

39. See my *Baptism*, p. 133; Fee, *God's Empowering Presence*, pp. 294-96.

40. Indicative of the loss of the power of the metaphor in later generations is the inference by some that the reference must be to a rite of anointing (see those cited by McDonnell and Montague, p. 48 n. 14); but see Dinkler, p. 95.

41. The reference to Isaiah 61:1-2 is most explicit in Luke 4:18, but is also implied in Luke 6:20/Matthew 5:3 and Luke 7:22/Matthew 11:5. Luke also alludes to it in Acts 4:27 and 10:38, the latter itself an early formulation.

Similarly with the imagery of putting on Christ. There is no evidence that a change of clothes was part of the earliest baptismal ceremonies. Rather, the metaphor of "putting on Christ" gains more illumination by reference to the similar talk of an actor getting fully into his part.[42] It is also notable that while Paul can use it for the once-for-all of Christian beginnings in Galatians 3:27, he can use it also in the subsequent call to responsible living (Rom. 13:14). In other words, there is nothing inherently baptismal about the imagery. In Galatians 3:27, indeed, it is of a piece with "baptized into Christ," but perhaps primarily because the metaphor of immersion into Christ is equally close to the actor's total immersion in the character being played on stage.

The imagery of washing is more naturally seen as an allusion to baptism (I Cor. 6:11; Eph. 5:26; Titus 3:5).[43] But even here we have to recall the extent to which Paul had spiritualized issues of ritual purity and sanctification. All believers were "saints" (Rom. 1:7; 8:27; etc.), in complete independence of the Jerusalem cult. Their bodies were now the only temple of which they need take account (I Cor. 3:16-17; 6:19; II Cor. 6:16). All things were "clean" simply because they were made and given by God, irrespective of Jewish tradition.[44] So, quite probably, the washing in view was that of heart and conscience, without specific reference to or dependence on the act of being baptized in water.[45] A

42. A similar phrase is attested in the first century B.C. by Dionysius of Halicarnassus 11.5, used of acting: "to put on Tarquin" = "to play the role of Tarquin" (Liddell, Scott, and Jones, *endyo*). Note also that the metaphor can be used to indicate an inward and spiritual change (e.g., Isa. 61:10; Zech. 3:3-5), or alternatively, the Spirit's "enclothing" of human individuals (Judg. 6:34; I Chron. 12:18; II Chron. 24:20; Luke 24:49; Hermas, *Sim.* 9.24.2) (Dunn, *Baptism*, p. 110). H. Lietzmann, *An die Galater*, 4th ed., Handbuch zum Neuen Testament 10 (Tübingen: J. C. B. Mohr, 1971), p. 23, suggests that "put on Christ" is another expression for "receive the Holy Spirit."

43. Direct reference to baptism is an almost universal assumption. E.g., Schnackenburg begins with the theme "baptism as a bath," referring to these texts; Ridderbos, p. 397: "That the expressions 'to wash' and 'bath of water' refer to baptism cannot be doubted."

44. *Katharos/katharizo* — Romans 14:20; Ephesians 5:26; I Timothy 1:5; 3:9; II Timothy 1:3; 2:22; Titus 1:15; *koinos* — Romans 14:14; cf. I Corinthians 10:26.

45. See also my *Baptism*, pp. 121-22; similarly M. Quesnel, *Baptisés dans l'Esprit* (Paris: Cerf, 1985), pp. 165-66; Fee, *God's Empowering Presence*, pp. 130-31.

similar case could be made with regard to Acts 22:16, though the imagery within Acts is too isolated for us to be able to read Luke's mind with confidence at this point.

d. Finally we should note an aspect too often ignored in these discussions. In some ways the most obvious role for baptism in Paul's gospel was as the equivalent to and replacement for circumcision. So the assumption often runs: that Paul replaced the ethnically constricted (or legalistic!) requirement of circumcision with the more universally applicable baptism.[46] However, this is precisely what we do *not* find. It is *faith* which Paul contrasts so sharply with the works of the law, of which circumcision was a primary obligation. And it is *the gift of the Spirit,* not baptism, which provides the new covenant answer to the old covenant circumcision (cf. Rom. 2:29; Phil. 3:3). The eschatological newness of Christianity, their movement on to a new plane as the first Christians so experienced it, had been accomplished through faith and by the Spirit. Whereas Paul says in effect to the Galatians, "You do not need circumcision because you believed, because you have received the Spirit, have become part of Christ, have been justified" (Gal. 3:1-5, 14; 5:2-6; 6:13-15), he never says, "You do not need to be circumcised because you have been baptized." Of course it is true, speaking sociologically, that Christian baptism in effect formed as effective a group boundary as circumcision. But so far as Paul's theology was concerned the only answer to any call for circumcision which really mattered was the reality of grace through faith, of Christ through the Spirit in his converts' lives.

Paul, like Luke, repeatedly emphasized these two features of Christian beginnings — faith and the Spirit. Quite how he correlated baptism within the process is less clear. That he saw baptism as the expression of faith is quite probable. This seems to be implicit in his talk of baptism in I Corinthians 1:13: The baptizand handed himself over (in and by baptism) to belong to the one named over him. Other-

---

46. Cf., e.g., the fairly typical handling of Colossians 2:11-12. P. Pokorný, *Colossians* (Peabody, MA: Hendrickson, 1991), p. 124: "the writer explains that baptism is the true circumcision"; M. Wolter, *Kolosser* (Gütersloh: Kaiser, 1993), p. 130, speaks of *Taufbeschneidung* ("baptismal circumcision"); see further my *Epistles to the Colossians and to Philemon,* New International Greek Testament Commentary series (Grand Rapids: William B. Eerdmans Publishing Co., 1996), p. 157 n. 18.

wise Paul says nothing explicit about the correlation of faith and baptism — itself an interesting feature in one who saw the response of faith as such a crucial and sole defining element in the acceptance by God and the reception of the Spirit. But baptism as the expression of faith commitment would correlate with the understanding of the Baptist's baptism as the expression of repentance. And it would accord also with the nearest thing we have to a definition of baptism in the NT — I Peter 3:21: baptism saves "as an appeal to God for a good conscience" (NRSV) or "from a good conscience" (REB), or "as the pledge proceeding from or to maintain a good conscience" (NJB).

## 6. Conclusion

So far as testing the NT foundations of Christian theology of baptism is concerned, then, the strongest support is probably given by the two references to baptism in Romans 6:4 and Colossians 2:12. What happened in the beginning event happened "through baptism" (Rom. 6:4) and "in baptism" (Col. 2:12). Baptism was in some sense the medium through which God brought the baptizand into participation in Christ's death and burial. There are probably echoes here (for some at least) of moving memories of the experienced symbolism of sinking below the surface of the water of baptism in immersion.[47] Alternatively expressed, baptism was the moment and context in which it all came together, so that the image of "baptized into" Christ was given its deeper resonance. Equally significant is the testimony of Acts 10:44-48 that reception of the Spirit prior to baptism did not render baptism in Christ's name unnecessary.

At the same time, our brief study has indicated some dangers of overstressing the ritual moment. First, are we indeed using the term "baptism" appropriately? Are we too quickly imposing rich sacramental theology upon texts which speak only of the water rite? Are we in danger of succumbing to the age-old temptation to control the means of grace by our ecclesiastical rubrics? Second, a theology of baptism which hopes to function as a unifying factor among churches which

---

47. Hence, we may suppose, the particular association of baptism with burial more than death (Rom. 6:4; Col. 2:12).

honor the biblical canon as a norm also needs to observe the relative weight and emphasis which the NT writers placed on the different elements in conversion-initiation. The centrality and sovereignty of the Spirit is particularly prominent, as also its correlative of faith. Whatever weight we judge ought to be placed on baptism should not be allowed to obscure or diminish these centralities.

The embarrassing question thus arises: Is our discussion of baptism and unity unhelpfully, or even misleadingly, focused? We say baptism is an act of God. But our disputes are all about the *humanly devised* rubrics which control the administration of the sacrament. Should our discussion not take our *theology* more seriously and orient itself in relation to *God's* action? What matters is whether God has acted in a human life. And where God has so acted, baptism is (properly speaking) a secondary consideration — still of major importance, but secondary.

I am fully aware, of course, that in posing these questions I am in effect questioning the traditional theology of baptism. And for many that fact may rule my questions (and paper) out of order from the start. But the challenge which came home to me from my study of the NT teaching in this area is whether the canonical witness does not require us to look again at even this basic feature of sacramental theology. Consider, after all, the clear lesson of the most significant development in earliest Christianity — the breakthrough to the Gentiles. What settled all the questions was the manifest action of God in the life of Cornelius. Peter argued not *from* baptism, but from the evident work of the Spirit *to* baptism: " 'Can anyone forbid water for baptizing these people who have received the Holy Spirit just as we have?' " (Acts 10:47). Similarly in Paul's account in Galatians 2:7-9, with regard to the crucial question whether Gentile believers must be circumcised. It was the manifest grace of God through Paul and Barnabas in the conversion of Gentiles which settled that question; baptism is not even mentioned. The point is confirmed by one of Christianity's favorite phrases — "the fellowship *(koinonia)* of the Holy Spirit" (II Cor. 13:14; Phil. 2:1). As repeated studies of *koinonia* have shown, the word itself means "participation in," "the shared experience of." The basis of Christian *fellowship* is the *shared experience of* the Holy Spirit.

If this is so, then the conclusion is clear. Ought we not to orient our conclusions to this most fundamental Christian datum? Ought we not to be discussing such questions as: How may we better recognize the grace of God in a human life, and give that greater prominence as a criterion of unity than we have given it hitherto? And how may we better correlate the importance of "the shared experience of the Spirit" for unity, with the issue of baptism and unity?

# Baptism and the Unity of the Church in Ecumenical Dialogues

*André Birmelé*

The second section of the German study *The Condemnations of the Reformation Era*[1] is dedicated to the sacraments. Eucharist, confirmation, anointing of the sick, marriage, and ordained ministry are each considered. Baptism is not explicitly taken up. It is dealt with by only a few references in the chapter on confirmation.

This state of affairs is characteristic of the modern ecumenical movement. Baptism is not a central theme because it has not led to doctrinal condemnations. In contrast to the Eucharist, which has been the occasion for an endless series of dialogues, it has not been a locus of visible division. For the majority of Christian churches the continued existence of a common baptism is a decisive factor of unity beyond the divisions. A common baptism is an important, already-given impulse on the way to the reestablishment of a single church.

This valuation, which has long held sway among the Reformation churches, has also become characteristic for the Roman Catholic Church, at least since the Second Vatican Council. "Baptism establishes a sacramental bond of unity existing among all who have been

1. *The Condemnations of the Reformation Era: Do They Still Divide?* ed. Karl Lehmann and Wolfhart Pannenberg, trans. Margaret Kohl (Minneapolis: Fortress Press, 1989).

reborn by it" (*Unitatis Redintegratio,* 22; cf. *Lumen Gentium,* 15). Ultimately, it is Christ himself who baptizes (cf. Sacrosanctum Concilium 7), and so there is only one Christian baptism. "Those who believe in Christ and have been truly baptized are in some kind of communion with the catholic church, even though this communion is imperfect" (*Unitatis Redintegratio,* 3). Progress in living out baptism is a growing assimilation to Christ and thus a growing communion among the churches. This common starting point provides a basis on which one can build, for baptism is oriented toward "the complete profession of faith, complete incorporation into the institution of salvation such as Christ willed it to be, and finally the completeness of unity which eucharistic communion gives" (*Unitatis Redintegratio,* 22). This perspective of the Council was and is of the highest significance for the ecumenical movement.

There are ecumenical partners, or course, who are not prepared to speak of a common baptism. Baptists and traditions with a baptist orientation (e.g., Pentecostal churches) raise questions about the legitimate recipient of baptism.[2] In dialogues involving these churches, problems are discussed of infant or adult baptism, of the relation between grace and faith, and ultimately of the understanding of sacrament. Nevertheless, such baptist churches assign a relatively small place to baptism in the general life of the church and so do not make a common understanding of baptism a precondition for their participation in the ecumenical movement.

For the Orthodox churches, on the other hand, baptism is of the greatest importance. They have raised questions in dialogues with other churches about the unity of the sacraments of initiation (baptism, anointing, Eucharist): Must not baptism take place within the ritual structure followed by patristic tradition, an initiation rite not maintained by the West? The question is also repeatedly raised about who baptizes: Can a schismatic administer true baptism?

Against the background of these introductory remarks, the shape

---

2. Translator's note: The capitalized word "Baptist" will refer throughout to those churches which call themselves Baptist; the noncapitalized word "baptist" will refer to non-Baptist churches which share with the Baptists an affirmation of believer's baptism only. When the word falls syntactically at a point that demands capitalization, it is hoped that the context will clarify who is meant.

of the *status questionis* of the ecumenical dialogue over baptism becomes clear:

1. First, the results of multilateral and bilateral dialogues which as
   a rule proceed from a far-reaching consensus in the understanding of baptism will be discussed.
2. Second, the dialogues with baptist churches will be taken up.
3. Third, the dialogues with the Orthodox churches will be analyzed.

## I. Convergence and Consensus in the Understanding of Baptism: Multilateral and Bilateral Dialogues

At the center of this section must stand the baptism section of *Baptism, Eucharist and Ministry* (hereinafter *BEM*-B), the convergence
document of the Faith and Order Commission of the World Council
of Churches (WCC).[3] This is the most complete modern ecumenical
text on baptism. That almost all Christian traditions took part in its
development gives it added significance. The theme of baptism, however, is not a manifestly central theme within the WCC, as can be seen
in the work of the Fifth World Assembly on Faith and Order (Santiago
1993). Despite the theme "On the Way to Fuller Koinonia," baptism is
hardly mentioned in the preparatory documents. The Assembly's Final
Report deals with baptism in a few short references.[4]

### A. The Content of BEM-B

*BEM*-B first recalls the institution of baptism: "Christian baptism is
rooted in the ministry of Jesus of Nazareth, in his death and in his
resurrection" (1). It "is the sign of new life through Jesus Christ" (2).

---

3. Faith and Order Paper 111 (Geneva: World Council of Churches, 1982).
4. With the exception of four short paragraphs in the Report of Section III.
See *On the Way to Fuller Koinonia*, official report of the Fifth World Conference on
Faith and Order, ed. Thomas F. Best and Günther Gassmann, Faith and Order Paper
166 (Geneva: WCC Publications, 1994), pp. 247f.

Appealing to the Scriptures, *BEM*-B describes baptism as "participation in Christ's death and resurrection (Rom. 6:3-5; Col. 2:12); a washing away of sin (I Cor. 6:11); a new birth (John 3:5); an enlightenment by Christ (Eph. 5:14); a re-clothing in Christ (Gal. 3:27); a renewal by the Spirit (Titus 3:5); the experience of salvation from the flood (I Peter 3:20-21); an exodus from bondage (I Cor. 10:1-2) and a liberation into a new humanity in which barriers of division whether of sex or race or social status are transcended (Gal. 3:27-28; I Cor. 12:13)" (2). These biblical images are commented on and completed with a reference to incorporation into the body of Christ (6) and to baptism as a sign of the kingdom of God (7).

Within this basic theological description, the existing differences between the churches are said to be differences of "practices of baptism" (6c). Disputed questions do not concern fundamentals, and it should not be too difficult "to recover baptismal unity" (6c).

In its more systematic section, however, *BEM*-B does not appear to avoid the theological difficulties. Part III addresses the problem of gift and faith, the classic problem of the dialogues involving the baptist churches (see below). "Baptism is both God's gift and our human response to that gift" (8). *BEM*-B rightly emphasizes the necessity of faith (8) and the understanding of baptism as "life-long growth into Christ" (9). In addition, baptism calls for the realization of the will of God in all realms of life (10). Against this background, the problem of infant and believer's baptism is discussed (11, 12). *BEM*-B recommends a common recognition of both practices (12c).

The basic question of the dialogue with the Orthodox also here becomes explicit. This problem, however, is not treated as a basic question but as a practical one, as is already clear in its placement in section IV, "Baptismal Practice." Not only Baptists but also most Western churches have reservations about an initiation which does not at some point include a personal confession of faith. The Orthodox, however, do not understand why most Western churches deny communion to baptized children. *BEM*-B attempts to bring these positions closer together and formulates a basic consensus: "that Christian baptism is in water and the Holy Spirit" (14). It attempts to overcome the more difficult questions by the statement that baptism must be "constantly reaffirmed" and that the baptismal vow requires "renewal" (14c). The request for the Western churches to reflect anew on communion by children (14b) stands in a certain contradiction, however, to the earlier strong emphasis on the faith of the person baptized. In addition, the statement in the concluding paragraphs that "baptism is normally administered by an ordained minister, though in certain circumstances others are allowed to baptize" (22) might have better been explained, since this is a debated point in the dialogue with the Orthodox.

## B. Comments on BEM-B

1. As is well known, the Lima Document is often misunderstood. Although the authors have repeatedly emphasized that they have worked out convergences and in no sense a consensus, the responses of many churches show how this statement has often not been heard.[5] Here lies an important difference from the bilateral dialogues, which mostly have worked toward consensus. The result of *BEM*-B is convergences of the highest importance. They demonstrate, in fact, a far-reaching common understanding of baptism, especially in relation to the biblical witness to baptism, which each tradition, however, interprets in its own way.

2. *BEM*-B strives for a mutual recognition of baptism. One senses a certain anxiety to burst barriers. This naturally means that when "hot potatoes" are taken up, they are not touched where they are hottest. Typical examples are:

- The interplay of gift and faith in the baptismal action. That both are essential, as *BEM*-B stresses, is agreed by all. The articulation of these two realities, however, is not addressed. Whether baptism itself "effects" grace or is only the ethical answer of the baptized remains open. Is the validity of baptism dependent on the faith of the baptized?
- The concept "sacrament" appears for the first time only in 13c. It is avoided in the main text and relegated to the commentary.

5. See the six volumes edited by Max Thurian, *Churches Respond to BEM* (Geneva: WCC Publications, 1986-88).

- The same is true for "sign" (2). Does the sign effect what it signifies? The question remains open.
- Do the "open questions" really all belong to the area of practice?

3. Such an ecumenical method also runs the danger of imprecision. Two examples can be given by way of illustration:

- *BEM*-B works with the alternative infant baptism — believer's baptism. Would it not be more correct to differentiate between infant and adult baptism (as the French translation of *BEM* in fact did)? For *BEM*-B, it appears that infant baptism is never the baptism of a believer. Through this false alternative the real problem is misperceived. Theologically it is a matter of two different understandings of baptism which are prior to the problem of infant baptism: Ultimately it is a matter of the difference between what adult baptism means for each. The different traditions do not always mean the same thing when they use the word "baptism."
- Something similar is the case in the important assertion that baptism is unrepeatable (13). All agree that this is so. But here again, all do not mean the same thing. A baptist church is baptizing a convert for the first time when it baptizes someone already baptized as an infant in another tradition. Since in the understanding of the baptist church this earlier baptism was in fact no baptism, it can also reject rebaptism.

Thus, despite its significant development of many convergences, *BEM*-B in the end avoids the questions which stand in the way of communion between the Western churches and either the baptist churches or the Orthodox.

## C. Consensus in the Bilateral Dialogues

This first section, which has so far focused on the convergences in *BEM*-B, should conclude with a discussion of the dialogues which have been able to speak not simply of convergence but of consensus in the understanding of baptism. As a rule, these involve Western traditions whose differences in the understanding and practice of baptism are and have been without church-dividing effect. As a result, any section on baptism in these dialogue reports, when present, has been small. The mutual recognition of baptism is normal.

We will look at the international dialogues conducted under the official mandate of the churches and briefly cite their statements on baptism. Afterward, some national or regional dialogues of these same families will be mentioned. Not their great numbers but rather the fact that these latter dialogues have formulated no new initiatives on the theme of baptism permits a selection of a few important examples.

### 1. Anglican-Lutheran: Pullach 1972 (Paras. 64-66)[6]

Baptism, administered with water and the threefold name, is the effective means by which God brings a person into the covenant of salvation wrought by Christ and translates him from darkness and bondage into the light and freedom of the Kingdom of God. The baptized are grafted into the church, adopted as children of God, brought into a relation with him which means justification, the forgiveness of sins and exposure to the sanctifying power of the Holy Spirit in the believing, witnessing and serving community.

Faith is necessary for the right receiving of the sacrament. . . . The practice of infant baptism necessitates the provision of opportunity for personal profession of faith before the congregation. In both our traditions this has been associated with confirmation. . . .

This same consensus in the understanding of baptism is repeated in the later Niagara Report (1987).[7]

At the level of the regional dialogues, the statements of the Porvoo Common Statement (British-Irish/Scandinavian-Baltic) or of the Meissen Declaration (Church of England–Evangelical Church in Ger-

---

6. In *Growth in Agreement: Reports and Agreed Statements of Ecumenical Conversations on a World Level*, ed. Harding Meyer and Lukas Vischer (New York: Paulist; Geneva: World Council of Churches, 1984), p. 22. Misprint of "exposure and" corrected to "exposure to."

7. Anglican-Lutheran International Continuation Committee, *The Niagara Report: Report of the Anglican-Lutheran Consultation on Episcope*, Niagara Falls, September 1987 (Cincinnati: Forward Movement Publications, 1988), p. 35.

many)[8] are in their content simply repetitions of the international dialogue.

## 2. Anglican-Reformed: God's Reign and Our Unity, 1984

This dialogue perhaps offers — next to *BEM* — the most detailed unfolding of a theology of baptism. It repeats on several pages a consensus in a way similar to *BEM* or the Lutheran-Anglican dialogue. New in this report is the appearance of the problem of the relation between baptism and church membership (para. 57). This connection is controversial in many Reformed communities. The dialogue is of the opinion that this problem is simply a function of context. It notes that in many congregations baptism has become a problem since many members have become influenced by newer movements, especially charismatic ones, which communicate more baptist ideas (para. 58).[9]

On the regional level, reference should again be made to the Meissen Declaration (see above), in which the German Reformed churches participated.

## 3. Anglican–Roman Catholic: Ministry and Ordination: Elucidation, 1979 (Para. 2)

"The priesthood of the whole people of God (1 Peter 2:5) is the consequence of incorporation by baptism into Christ. This priesthood of all the faithful . . . is not a matter of disagreement between us" (para. 2).[10]

This is later expanded in the document *Church as Communion* (1990) (para. 15): "Visibly, this communion is entered through baptism and nourished and expressed in the celebration of the eucharist. All

---

8. Porvoo Common Statement in *Together in Mission and Ministry: The Porvoo Common Statement with Essays on Church and Ministry in Northern Europe* (London: Church House Publishing, 1993); Meissen Declaration in *Ecumenical Bulletin* 103 (January 1991): 4-9.

9. Anglican-Reformed International Commission, *God's Reign and Our Unity:* The Report of the Anglican-Reformed International Commission, 1981-1984 (London: SPCK; Edinburgh: St. Andrew Press, 1984), pp. 36f.

10. *Growth in Agreement,* p. 85.

who are baptized in the one Spirit into one body are united in the eucharist by this sacramental participation in this same one body."[11]

### 4. *Lutheran-Methodist: The Church: Communion of Grace, 1984 (Paras. 44-51)*

Here again a far-reaching consensus in the understanding of baptism is formulated. But differences are also described: Lutherans endorsed the emergency baptism of small children in special situations, which Methodists reject. More important, however, is the appearance again of the problem of baptism and church membership (parallel to the Anglican-Reformed): "We agree in looking upon baptism as entrance into the church. However, there is a difference among us about the way in which we more precisely define the relationship between baptism and church membership. For Lutherans, baptism establishes church membership. Most Methodists distinguish between preparatory and full membership. The former is given through baptism, the latter through explicit admission on profession of faith."[12]

The international *Reformed-Methodist* dialogue ("Together in God's Grace, 1987")[13] did not deal with baptism. The national dialogues also emphasize on the one hand the consensus in the understanding of baptism and on the other the different understandings of the interrelation of baptism and church membership. Such occurred, e.g., in the German dialogue[14] and in the pan-European declaration of church fellowship between Lutherans and Reformed on the one side and Methodists on the other.[15]

---

11. Second Anglican–Roman Catholic International Commission, *Church as Communion: An Agreed Statement* (London: Church House Publishing; Catholic Truth Society, 1991), pp. 14f.

12. Lutheran-Methodist Joint Commission, *The Church: Community of Grace* (Geneva: Lutheran World Federation; Lake Junaluska: World Methodist Council, 1984), pp. 18f.

13. *Reformed and Methodists in Dialogue:* Report of the Reformed/Methodist Conversations, 1985-1987, Studies from the World Alliance of Reformed Churches (Geneva: World Alliance of Reformed Churches, 1988).

14. *Vom Dialog zur Kanzel- und Abendmahlsgemeinschaft* (Hanover/Stuttgart: Lutherisches Verlagshaus, 1987), sections 16ff.

15. In *Wachsende Gemeinschaft in Zeugnis und Dienst. Reformatorische Kir-*

The Methodist–Roman Catholic dialogue (Nairobi Report 1985, para. 12) limited itself to the following remark: "Baptism initiates the individual into the koinonia of the Church."[16]

### 5. Lutheran–Roman Catholic: Facing Unity, 1984 (Para. 75)

Lutherans and Catholics are conscious that they participate in one and the same baptism. In keeping with the statement BEM, we jointly confess that "Christian baptism is rooted in the ministry of Jesus of Nazareth, in his death and in his resurrection. It is incorporation into Christ, who is the crucified and risen Lord; it is entry into the New Covenant between God and God's people." This common understanding of baptism is expressed in the manner in which baptism is administered and is confirmed by the fact that almost everywhere our churches have officially recognized each other's baptism. Moreover, our churches are faced by common or similar pastoral tasks concerning the understanding of baptism, and how it is expressed and concretized in baptismal practice, faith-life and the piety of congregations and the faithful.[17]

National dialogues between these two traditions have on occasion treated the theme in detail (e.g., the dialogues in the USA[18] and in Germany).[19] These simply reached the same conclusion as that of the international dialogue.

---

*chen in Europa.* Texte der 4. Vollversammlung der Leuenberger Kirchengemeinschaft, ed. W. Hüffmeier and C. R. Muller (Frankfurt: Lembeck Verlag, 1995), p. 171.

16. In *Information Service,* Secretariat for Promoting Christian Unity, 62 (1986 IV), p. 208.

17. Roman Catholic/Lutheran Joint Commission, *Facing Unity: Models, Forms, and Phases of Catholic-Lutheran Fellowship* (n.p.: Lutheran World Federation, 1985), p. 38.

18. Paul C. Empie and T. Austin Murphy, eds., *One Baptism for the Remission of Sins: Lutherans and Catholics in Dialogue II* (Minneapolis: Augsburg Press, 1966).

19. *Kirchengemeinschaft in Wort und Sakrament* (Paderborn: Bonifatius Verlag, 1984), sections 24-30.

### 6. Reformed–Roman Catholic

The first international dialogue of these two families ("The Presence of Christ in Church and World 1977") has long sections on Scripture, salvation, Eucharist, and ministry; the theme of baptism does not appear. Only in the conclusion to the second dialogue ("Toward a Common Understanding of the Church 1990") is the desire expressed for a general, mutual recognition of baptism, "provided that it has been celebrated in the name of the Father, the Son and the Holy Spirit and with the use of water."[20]

Mutual recognition is also the major concern of national dialogues, e.g., the French dialogue (in which Lutherans participated) which declared such a recognition already in 1973 after a common exposition of a theology of baptism.[21]

## II. The Dialogues of the Reformation Churches and the Conversations with the Baptist Churches

### A. A Settled Controversy of the Reformation Period?

1. In 1969, E. Schlink wrote: "The most profound difference runs its course not between the Eastern Church and Augustine, nor between Thomas and Luther, nor even between Luther and Calvin, but between all of these on one side and Zwingli and the Baptists on the other. The most profound difference is not the acknowledgment or nonacknowledgment of infant Baptism, but the understanding of Baptism either as God's deed or as the deed of human obedience."[22]

Even if formal doctrinal condemnations in relation to baptism did not exist between the major streams of the Reformation, this topic was more controversial than one usually assumes. Its consequences can be found in the Reformation churches through the present. The Marburg

---

20. In *Information Service,* Pontifical Council for Promoting Christian Unity, 74 (1990 III), p. 116.

21. See A. Birmelé and J. Terme, eds., *Accords et Dialogues Oecuméniques* (Paris: Les Bergers et les Mages, 1995), section 8, pp. 235-38.

22. Edmund Schlink, *The Doctrine of Baptism,* trans. Herbert J. A. Bouman (St. Louis: Concordia Publishing House, 1972), p. 169.

Colloquy between Luther and Zwingli (1529) centered on the Eucharist. The mediation of salvation was the issue. Since nothing less than the general understanding of sacrament was under debate, baptism also was involved.[23] Luther, the former Augustinian monk, certainly sought to avoid a false, "magical" understanding of sacrament, yet it was clear for him that God has chosen certain means of communicating himself to persons. God had thus bound himself to the word of Scripture, the elements of the Lord's Supper, and the water of baptism. The word of God occurs not only in the audible word of the sermon but also in the visible word of the sacraments, which can never be separated from the spoken word. The gift of God in the sacrament is not dependent on faith, even if this gift can only be received in faith. Zwingli, however, differentiated the external sign (water, bread, wine) from the "inner" spiritual gift, which alone is finally important. The former are not the bearers of the latter. Sacraments are not gifts of salvation but signs of a salvation already worked in Christ. The salvation effected by Christ is given and received in faith in the proclaimed word. There is thus no special gift of salvation in the sacraments, whose meaning is then limited to that of *initiatio* and *oppignoratio* (pledge).[24] The sacrament presupposes faith and is a celebration of faith. It is the confirmation of an already-present inner reality whose existence is independent of this sign.

On the basis of the *Consensus Tigurinus* (1549), it has often been assumed that Calvin shared Zwingli's approach in this area. Calvin's refusal to bind the infinite God to finite realities indicates a similarity and has strengthened the suspicion of a common outlook. Nevertheless, Calvin's emphasis on baptism as covenantal bond is much closer to Luther than is at first apparent. Statements such as "a sacrament is . . . a visible form of an invisible grace"[25] and "it is therefore certain that the Lord offers us mercy and the pledge of his grace both in his Sacred Word and in his sacraments"[26] are common in his writings. It

---

23. See my study "Le debát entre Luther et Zwingli. Une contribution au dialogue oecuménique sur la baptême," *Positions luthériennes* 39 (1991): 41-59.

24. H. Zwingli, *Sämtliche Werke* (Zürich: Theologische Verlag, 1959-60), vol. 3, pp. 757f.

25. John Calvin, *Institutes of the Christian Religion*, trans. Ford Lewis Battles, Library of Christian Classics, 20-21 (Philadelphia: Westminster Press, 1960), 4.14.1; p. 1277.

26. Calvin, *Institutes of the Christian Religion*, 4.14.7; p. 1282.

is thus no surprise that "Calvinist" Reformed confessions, such as the Confession of La Rochelle, explicitly condemn the Zwinglian "Sacramentarians."[27]

This difficult theological situation in the sixteenth century was made more complex by the presence of Anabaptist streams. The latter were influenced by Zwingli's approach, but did not simply derive from it.

That this controversy is not limited to the Reformation era but continues in the life of the church of the Reformation into the present is shown by statements of such famous theologians of the twentieth century as K. Barth, E. Brunner, and J. Moltmann.[28] Baptism is sometimes understood as the first, ethical answer of the believer to whom God has given grace through the word.

It was the task of modern ecumenical dialogues to overcome the controversies which had arisen through these questions.

2. The controversy with the Anabaptists of the sixteenth century over the understanding of baptism (and rebaptism) continued with their immediate successors in this stream, the Mennonites. All dialogues with this stream have confirmed the disagreement in the understanding of baptism. For example, in the French dialogue the Mennonites emphasized: "Being baptized is an act of confessing the faith: it means that we wish to reject the past life in order to live the new life which has been poured into us by Jesus Christ through the Holy Spirit. . . . Baptism thus brings to expression the will of those who publicly respond to the grace of God, wish to serve the life and witness of a local community through their gifts, and intend to live with their brothers and sisters in accord with the rules of fraternal behavior (Mt. 18)." On the Lutheran side such an emphasis on faith is not to be rejected, but baptism cannot be so limited. The Mennonites explicitly separate themselves from the sacramental Lutheran understanding of

27. In *Confessions et catéchismes de la foi réformée*, ed. O. Fatio (Genève: Labor et Fides, 1986), pp. 126f. See also Calvin's *Catechism* (1545), in *Confessions*, p. 96, and the *Heidelberg Catechism*, in *Confessions*, p. 156.

28. K. Barth, *Die kirchliche Lehre von der Taufe*, Theologische Studien 14 (Zürich: Evangelischer Verlag, 1953); see also *Church Dogmatics*, IV/4 (1967); E. Brunner, *Dogmatik* III (Zürich: Zwingli Verlag, 1960); J. Moltmann, *The Church in the Power of the Spirit* (San Francisco: Harper, 1977), pp. 199-206, 226-42.

baptism.[29] The dialogue in the Netherlands[30] and the dialogue recently completed in Germany confirm this still-existing divergence.

3. Particular interest is merited by the *Lutheran-Reformed* dialogue, since many of these churches appeal to Luther, Calvin, and also Zwingli. The questions were first worked through in national European dialogues (France and Germany)[31] and then in pan-European dialogues (Arnoldshain Theses 1959).[32] A notable consensus was reached. Proceeding from an exegetical basis, they understood baptism as participation in Christ's death and resurrection: "We are grafted into Christ through baptism. This is a non-repeatable event. . . . The righteousness which our Savior has won on the cross is reckoned to us and so our sins are forgiven. We are now liberated from the domination of all alien powers and free for walking in newness of life."[33] The concept *promissio* helped to bridge the divide between a causative and a cognitive understanding of baptism:

> Through the preached Word and the water-bath connected to it, God pledges to those baptized that they will be children of God and in baptism he grants such. In faith we are certain that what God promises, God does in the power of the Holy Spirit, prayed for by us and promised by God. . . . The special feature of baptism is that here, through a Word clothed in an action and in a unique, unrepeatable, and irrevocable way, new life is given to the individual and sealed. Christ is himself the agent in baptism. Therefore, it cannot be understood as an event separated from the acting Christ and guaranteed through the mere performance of a ritual or through the power of human faith. Baptism thus cannot be understood only as

29. Text in *Wachsende Kirchengemeinschaft: Gespräche und Vereinbarungen zwischen evangelischen Kirchen in Europa*, ed. C. Nussberger (Bern: Evangelisch Arbeitsstelle Oekumene, 1992), pp. 178f.

30. *Wachsende Kirchengemeinschaft*, p. 195.

31. France: "Lyons Theses," in *Accords et Dialogues Oecuméniques*, part 2, pp. 170f.; Germany (Westphalia), in *Auf dem Weg I: Lutherisch-reformierte Kirchengemeinschaft* (Zürich: EVZ Verlag, 1967), pp. 81f.

32. Original German in E. Schiefer, *Von Schauenberg nach Leuenberg: Entstehung und Bedeutung der Konkordie reformatorsicher Kirchen in Europa* (Paderborn: Bonifatius Verlag, 1983), A1-A4.

33. Schiefer, A1f. (II, 1 and 2).

a symbolic act separated from the promise of God and representing a mere illustration of the event of salvation.[34]

In the conclusion, various themes were emphasized: the necessity of faith as answer to baptism; incorporation through baptism into the church, the body of Christ; the eschatological orientation and ethical consequences of baptism.[35]

The consensus reached at Arnoldshain is of the highest significance for the Lutheran, Reformed, and United churches of Europe. The Leuenberg Agreement of 1972 could simply adopt these results without further dialogue: "In preaching, baptism, and the Lord's Supper, Jesus Christ is present through the Holy Spirit. Justification in Christ is thus imparted to men, and in this way the Lord gathers his people. . . . Baptism is administered in the name of the Father and of the Son and of the Holy Spirit with water. In baptism, Jesus Christ irrevocably receives man, fallen prey to sin and death, into his fellowship of salvation so that he may become a new creature. In the power of his Holy Spirit, he calls him into his community and to a new life of faith, to daily repentance, and to discipleship."[36] After the ratification of this agreement by the synods of the Lutheran, Reformed, and United churches in Europe, the theme of baptism was taken up in further dialogues. The results of the Arnoldshain discussions have been repeatedly affirmed.[37]

The *international Lutheran-Reformed dialogue* also was satisfied simply to repeat the statements of the Leuenberg Agreement.[38]

---

34. Schiefer, A2 (III, 1-3).

35. Schiefer, A3f. (IV, 1-3).

36. Paras. 13 and 14, in *An Invitation to Action: A Study of Ministry, Sacraments, and Recognition,* ed. James E. Andrews and Joseph A. Burgess, Lutheran-Reformed Dialogue Series III, 1981-1983 (Philadelphia: Fortress Press, 1984), p. 68.

37. For example, in the document "Lehre und Praxis der Taufe," approved by the Assembly of the signatory churches of the Leuenberg Agreement in Vienna, 1994. In *Wachsende Gemeinschaft in Zeugnis und Dienst,* pp. 63-72.

38. Lutheran-Reformed Joint Commission, *Toward Church Fellowship* (Geneva: Lutheran World Federation, 1989), para. 59, p. 22. In this context it is important to note that the Lutheran-Reformed dialogue in the USA did not address the theme of baptism *(An Invitation to Action).*

## B. The Dialogues Involving Baptist Churches

After these Lutheran-Reformed dialogues, we need to look at the dialogues involving churches of a baptist character. These churches do not go back directly to the sixteenth century but nevertheless belong to the Reformation tradition. In this category belong above all the international dialogues between Pentecostal churches and the Roman Catholic Church (P-RC I, P-RC II, P-RC III),[39] between Baptist and Reformed (B-R),[40] between Baptist and Lutheran (B-L),[41] between Baptist and Roman Catholic (B-RC),[42] and dialogue of the Disciples of Christ with the Catholics (D-RC)[43] and with the Reformed (D-R).[44]

A chronological rather than confessional ordering recommends itself for an analysis of these results. It is interesting to note that the dialogues which occurred during the run-up to the Lima statement exhibit a different fundamental outlook than those which took place after Lima. The one exception is the 1987 dialogue of the Disciples with the Reformed, which clearly wished to remain on the line of the Lima text and is to be placed with the first group.

1. The first series of dialogues, those which occurred prior to the Lima statement, are oriented toward consensus and are concerned to demonstrate convergences.

Agreement exists that baptism is an incorporation into the body of Christ, the church (P-RC I, 19; D-RC 23; B-R 15). The foundation of every Christian baptism is the baptism of Christ in the Jordan and the practice spoken of by the Scriptures (D-RC 26). Baptism is carried out in the name of the triune God (D-RC 28). It is not only water baptism

---

39. *Growth in Agreement*, pp. 421ff.; *Information Service*, Secretariat for Promoting Christian Unity, 55 (1984 II-III), 72-81; *Information Service*, Pontifical Council for Promoting Christian Unity, 75 (1990 IV), 179-91.

40. *Growth in Agreement*, pp. 131-51.

41. Joint Commission of the Baptist World Alliance and the Lutheran World Federation, *Baptists and Lutherans in Conversation: A Message to Our Churches* (Geneva: Lutheran World Federation, 1990).

42. *Information Service*, Pontifical Council for Promoting Christian Unity, 72 (1990 I), 5-13.

43. *Growth in Agreement*, pp. 153-66.

44. *Towards Closer Fellowship:* Report of the Dialogue between Reformed and Disciples of Christ, Studies from the World Alliance of Reformed Churches, 11 (Geneva: World Alliance of Reformed Churches, 1988).

but is always connected to baptism in the Holy Spirit (P-RC I, 11-15). It places the baptizand into a new relation to God and to other believers (B-R 16) and has ethical consequences (D-R 23).

Even when one turns to the traditional controversial questions, one still finds agreement. Baptism must not be understood magically (P-RC I, 22), but must be connected to faith (P-RC I, 21-25; D-RC 31; B-R 9; D-R 23). It is not clarified, however, whether baptism is simply the confirmation of faith or mediates salvation to the believer. It is also not clarified whether this faith perhaps is, as with Luther, a *fides aliena*. What exists are simply convergences that faith is necessary and that grace has the priority, since the grace of God always comes before human faith (P-RC I, 23; D-RC 38). This prevenient grace, however, is not explicitly connected to baptism. Throughout these dialogues, it can be understood as the grace out of which the faith arises which baptism presupposes. Only the Baptist-Reformed dialogue really addresses the question whether baptism is to be understood as an action of God or a human action. This alternative is rejected. Human and divine action occur here always together, so that "baptism is a powerful sign and effective means of grace" (B-R 14, 21). Such a statement is, taken in itself, real progress. It must, however, be read in the general context of the document, which limits its significance. The Baptists add that grace is given in the gospel of the cross and resurrection and that baptism is a means of grace only insofar as the faithful there express their "appropriation of God's gift through faith" (B-R 9). All these traditions finally agree that any re-baptism is to be rejected (P-RC I, 27; D-RC 30; D-R 27). This rejection of rebaptism, however, is only relative, since the churches which reject infant baptism emphasize that infant baptism is no baptism and thus the baptism of an adult already baptized as an infant is in their eyes not a rebaptism (P-RC I, 27).

In these dialogues, as similarly in *BEM*, the points of divergence are seen primarily in open questions of baptismal practice. Two are stressed: the form of the rite of baptism and the age of the baptizand. In relation to the rite, Pentecostals and Disciples require that other traditions return to baptism by immersion (P-RC I, 21; D-RC 37). On the age of the baptizand, these churches are of the opinion that all infant baptism is to be excluded since they believe that this practice is in contradiction to the biblical witness (D-RC 33; P-RC I, 27). Only the Baptist-Reformed dialogue saw in this question more than a problem of practice. For the Baptists, infant baptism is unacceptable because it contradicts the necessary temporal sequence of the preaching of the gospel which awakens faith, which then leads to confession, expressed in baptism (B-R 9). This temporal order excludes all infant baptism. The dialogue between the Pentecostal churches and the Catholic Church established the same divergence, but it appears there to be a question of form (P-RC I, 21).

The basic question whether baptism is to be understood as a means of grace or as a confirmation of faith is not really addressed. The possible recognition of a church with a different understanding of baptism and a different baptismal practice could not yet be addressed in this first phase. D-RC 39 envisaged the possibility; B-R 17 excludes it until the dialogue has made greater progress; D-R 24 emphasized the mutual recognition of baptism and the invitation to the Eucharist.

The Italian dialogue among Waldensians, Methodists, and Baptists, which led to an important agreement in 1990, also belongs to this category.[45] The locus of important differences is found only in practice and not in basic questions. It sees a temporal separation of water baptism and Spirit baptism as possible (3.4) and understands water baptism as both a sealing of and an invocation of Spirit baptism. Against this background, a twofold practice is possible, even if the Waldensians and Methodists continue to advocate infant baptism and the Baptists reject such (3.7f.). For all the participants, what is decisive is less baptism itself than the value of the fruits of baptism. When these fruits are present, then "a mutual recognition" is possible (3.10).

2. The dialogues pursued after Lima are more open to expressing differences. A clear hardening of the lines can be observed. The most recent dialogues do not avoid labeling the divergences by name.

The *Baptist-Lutheran* dialogue completed in 1990 mentions the convergences emphasized by previous dialogues (shared understanding of faith and discipleship and their necessity, B-L 22f.). In distinction from *BEM*, this dialogue differentiates between infant or adult baptism on the one hand and believer's baptism on the other (30). Recent developments in Lutheranism have led to an increasing

45. Text in *Wachsende Kirchengemeinschaft*, pp. 155-67.

number of adult baptisms, but "the traditional point of disagreement between Lutherans and Baptists still remains" (30). The dialogue "could not bridge the gap" (33). "Lutherans stress that baptism is a form of God's word — a visible word, the expression of the priority of divine grace. It is God who through baptism incorporates the person baptized into the kingdom and thus into the community of the church. In baptism, therefore, God gives the gift of salvation, a gracious gift which only faith can receive. Baptism and faith belong together, for without faith God's baptismal gift is of no use. But lack of faith cannot nullify God's action; as God's gracious action baptism remains valid even without faith" (39). "Baptists do not recognize a biblical foundation for such an interpretation of baptism as a visible word of prevenient grace. They do not attribute to baptism the place the gospel occupies, the gospel which is proclaimed and testified to. Baptists must regard the Lutheran understanding as altering the character and place of baptism in the biblical order of salvation. Baptism is not the first step. For Baptists, the Lutheran view isolates and overestimates baptism, giving it an independent theological weight and function. They fear this could lead to attributing to baptism the place reserved for Christ and his cross" (40). This difference has consequences also for understanding the person's "free decision" (41ff.) and for ecclesiology (50ff.), especially the emphasis on the universal church on the one side and on the local community — congregationalism — on the other. This was already emphasized in the earlier national dialogue in Germany.[46]

The *Baptist–Roman Catholic* dialogue (1984-88) stressed the same difference. "Baptists emphasize the importance of an initial experience of personal conversion in which the believer receives the gift of God's saving and assuring grace. Baptism and entrance into the congregation are witnesses of this gift, which expresses itself in a life of faithful discipleship. For Catholics, baptism is the sacrament through which a person is incorporated into Christ and born again in order to take part in the divine life" (B-RC 18). Both emphasize the necessity of faith. Nevertheless,

---

46. "Baptisten und Lutheraner in Gespräch: Schlussbericht eines offiziellen Gesprächs (1980-81)," in *Texte aus der VELKD* 17/1981. Summary in *Wachsende Kirchengemeinschaft*, pp. 142ff.

the heart of the problem which one must address in this connection appears to be the nature of faith and the nature of the sacraments, which most Baptists name "ordinances." Thereby a series of questions are raised which Baptists and Catholics must deal with together. Is faith simply the individual's answer to God's gift? Can the faith of the community replace the personal faith of the infant? Can one speak of a *community of faith,* i.e., of the Body of Christ, as the subject of a common faith in which the individual participates? Are the sacraments external signs of a prior inner commitment? Are they means through which Christ effects his saving and redeeming work? What is meant by the phrase that baptism is "the sacrament of faith"? (51)

These questions stand on the agenda of further dialogue.

In their third dialogue (1989), Pentecostals and Catholics repeat their earlier essential convergences (the unity of baptism and faith, P-RC III, 43f.), but at the same time emphasize a basic problem: "the meaning of the concepts *sacrament* and *rite*" (41). It therein becomes clear that for most Pentecostals baptism is "a visible symbol of rebirth" (47). They "reject the Roman Catholic teaching of baptism as a constitutive mediation of the salvation worked by the life, death, and resurrection of Christ" (51). Catholics understand "conversion as a process of the incorporation of the individual into the church through baptism. Even in infant baptism, a later, personal appropriation or acceptance of one's own baptism is an absolute necessity" (48). For them "baptism is the sacrament of entry into the church, the *koinonia* of those saved in Christ and taken into his death and resurrection." In this sacrament "faith is given to the child" (61).

Particularly important in this dialogue is the connection between the theology of baptism and ecclesiology. Catholics emphasize that the recognition of Pentecostal baptism is the basis of the ecumenical dialogue. This has as a consequence "a real even if imperfect *koinonia.*" "The unity of baptism constitutes and demands the unity of the baptized" (54). The Pentecostals, however, do not attribute to baptism such a significance for the nature of the church and its unity. More important is "unity in faith and in the experience through the Holy Spirit of Jesus Christ as Lord and Savior" (55). The end result is neither a mutual recognition nor a clear rejection of baptism within the other tradition.

## III. The Dialogues with the Orthodox

The third and concluding section of this investigation takes up the dialogues with the Orthodox tradition. It will be less detailed, not because the questions are less important, but because significantly fewer dialogue results exist.

### A. *The Problem*

A major concern of the Orthodox is to stress the unity of the sacraments of initiation: baptism, anointing (chrismation), Eucharist. The immersion of the baptizand under the water signifies insertion into Christ's death; coming out of the water signifies rising with Christ. In baptism it is a matter of an ontic unity with Christ through the Holy Spirit. In the accompanying anointing with oil, the Holy Spirit is mediated, in dependence on the Pentecostal event. Baptism and anointing follow one another in a single liturgical celebration and are the basis for membership in the church, the body of Christ. Since this membership is represented and strengthened in the Eucharist, the newly baptized can immediately participate in the Eucharist. The celebration of baptism continues into the celebration of the Eucharist, a practice of the ancient church which in Orthodoxy is still carried out even in the case of infant baptism. In ecumenical dialogues, the Orthodox state their expectation that all churches will return to this practice. "Strictly speaking, the eastern churches require (in dependence on Cyprian of Carthage) a full initiation when heretics or schismatics convert. Even when they show 'leniency' and limit themselves to the administration of a penitential-pneumatic chrismation, they avoid saying that the previous baptism had any value before the person's conversion."[47] Against this background one can understand why some Orthodox churches (e.g., the Greek) baptize all converts, even if they have already been baptized in some other Christian tradition, while others (e.g., the Russian) forgo a new baptism and only anoint, without pronouncing upon the earlier baptism and its schismatic administration.

---

47. G. Wainwright, "Taufe," in *Evangelisches Kirchenlexikon,* s.v. See also G. Wainwright, *Christian Initiation* (London: Lutterworth Press, 1969).

This Orthodox understanding has been questioned by Western theology. Even theologians sympathetic to Orthodoxy (e.g., G. Kretschmar) have questions about this unity of the initiatory sacraments and ask whether "here something is being ascribed to confirmation which in reality belongs to baptism."[48]

The question repeatedly is asked whether a deep theological difference really exists between the Eastern and Western understandings of baptism. Or is it a matter of a different question: the recognition of the Western Church as a true form of the one church of Christ?

Nondoctrinal factors also play an important role in this dialogue. For example, the open questions between Orthodox and baptists are not first those about baptism but those relating to baptist evangelization and mission in traditionally Orthodox countries.

Against this theological background, besides the Orthodox participation in *BEM* only two international dialogues involving the Orthodox have directly addressed the question of baptism: the Old Catholic–Orthodox[49] and the Roman Catholic–Orthodox[50] dialogues. The Anglican-Orthodox dialogue, which has continued already for twenty years, has only one short reference to baptism, which states that "the Church baptizes her members into the death and resurrection of her Lord, bringing them from the state of sin and death into membership of his body and participation in his eternal life."[51]

For the sake of completeness, reference must be made to the regional dialogues of the Evangelical Church in Germany with the Russian Orthodox Church and with the Romanian Orthodox Church. The former, pursued since 1969/70, has not led to a common declaration. Six series of short convergence theses have been signed only by two theologians from the two traditions.[52] The dialogue with the

---

48. G. Kretschmar, "Firmung," in *Theologische Realenzyklopädie*, s.v.

49. German original with French and English translations in *Koinonia auf altkirchlicher Basis*, ed. Urs von Arx, supplementary issue to *Internationalen Kirchlichen Zeitschrift* 79 (1989).

50. "Faith, Sacraments and the Unity of the Church," *One in Christ* 23 (1987): 330-40.

51. *Anglican-Orthodox Dialogue: The Dublin Agreed Statement 1984* (London: SPCK, 1985), para. 60, pp. 32f.

52. *Taufe, Neues Leben, Dienst: Das Leningrader Gespräch über die Verantwortung der Christen für die Welt* (Witten: Luther Verlag, 1970), pp. 26-32.

Romanian church led to a detailed report.[53] The results, however, did not go beyond the convergences formulated in *BEM*. The temporal unity of baptism, anointing, and Eucharist remains a "difficult unsettled question."[54] A strength of this dialogue is that pastoral and ecclesial questions of baptismal practice are considered in the present social context.

## B. The Old Catholic–Orthodox Dialogue

This dialogue, already with a long history, completed in 1985 a declaration on baptism. Its content is classic: emphasis on incorporation into the church (12), baptism as necessary to salvation (13), stress on the apostolic practice of a threefold immersion (14f.), the necessity of a "personal acceptance of the divine gift in faith, conversion, and works of love" (16).

What is not said in this dialogue is also important. The declaration states that "baptism has as a natural and immediate consequence the possibility and necessity of the baptized partaking in the gift of the Holy Spirit poured out at Pentecost and acceding to the sacrament of Eucharist" (2.3). This is confirmed in the immediately following statements on anointing and Eucharist. Nevertheless, the dialogue never speaks of the temporal unity of the three sacraments of initiation. The dialogue emphasizes the spiritual and theological unity of the three actions of the church, but the necessity of a unified celebration is not addressed. The question remains open. The dialogue also states that "in emergency cases" baptism can be administered by a deacon or a layperson, even if the rule is that a bishop or presbyter administers it (2.4). It is not clear whether this statement is merely descriptive or represents a theological conviction. No theological consequences are drawn from it. In particular, the question of a possible mutual recognition of baptism remains unclarified.

53. *Die Taufe als Aufnahme in den neuen Bund und als Berufung zum geistlichen Kampf in der Nachfolge Jesu Christi*, ed. K. Schwarz (Hermannsburg: Missionshandlung Hermannsburg, 1995), pp. 191ff. (second section of a volume, the first section of which is entitled *Rechtfertigung und Verherrlichung [Theosis] des Menschen durch Jesus Christus*).
54. *Die Taufe als Aufnahme*, p. 195.

## C. The Roman Catholic–Orthodox Dialogue

After conversations about church and ministry (Munich 1982), these two traditions in 1984 began a dialogue about sacraments. The theological views of this dialogue offer for the present no totally new insights.

"Faith is a presupposition of baptism and the entire sacramental life which follows it. Indeed, one participates through baptism in the death and resurrection of Jesus Christ (Rom. 6). Thus begins a process which continues all through Christian existence" (12). This faith is passed on in the sacrament itself through the church to the recipient of baptism (13). The liturgical tradition itself is a passing on of the faith (14). Through the Holy Spirit the Lord "makes his work pass into the Church's celebration. The sacraments of the Church transmit grace, expressing and strengthening faith in Jesus Christ, and are thus witnesses of faith" (17).

It should be added that this understanding of faith does not correspond to that of a baptist tradition. In this dialogue, however, precisely this understanding of faith is the first condition for a true communion among the churches: "the true faith is presupposed for a communion in the sacraments" (21). The basic orientation of this dialogue thus becomes clear: Its goal is the declaration of a communion in the sacraments on the basis of an ascertainment of true communion in the faith and so a mutual recognition as church of Jesus Christ. Yet just this important goal, built on a common understanding of baptism that this dialogue at first systematically pursues and in the end almost reaches, is suddenly interrupted . . . by a renewed reflection on baptism (37ff.). The spiritual unity of the three sacraments of initiation is emphasized by both Catholic and Orthodox (38). The model of their temporal unity in a single liturgical celebration "remains the ideal for both Churches since it corresponds as exactly as possible to the appropriation of the scriptural and apostolic tradition accomplished by the early Christian churches which lived in full communion with each other" (46). Since in the West this tradition has not been maintained, a consensus does not exist in the understanding of baptism and sacrament. This is not formulated *expressis verbis*, but it appears that on the basis of this divergence the dialogue broke off at this point (48). In the concluding paragraphs the items of consensus in the understanding of baptism are listed without further elucidation: "1. the necessity of baptism for salvation; 2. the effects of baptism, particularly new life in Christ and liberation from original sin; 3. incorporation into the Church by baptism; 4. the relation of baptism to the mystery of the Trinity; 5. the essential link between baptism and the death and resurrection of the Lord; 6. the role of the Holy Spirit in baptism; 7. the necessity of water which manifests baptism's character as the bath of new birth" (49). "On the other hand, differences concerning baptism exist between the two Churches: 1. the fact that the Catholic Church, while recognizing the primordial importance of baptism by immersion, ordinarily practices baptism by infusion; 2. the fact that in the Catholic Church a deacon can be the ordinary minister of baptism" (50).

The crisis situation that led to this breaking off of the conversation is difficult to interpret. The clear systematic construction building toward a consensus in the understanding of baptism ends in an attached listing of points of consensus and difference in the understanding of baptism, which does not really belong at this place. Why are precisely the questions which appeared solved in the dialogue with the Old Catholics now again the locus of radical conflict? Why did the later dialogue, begun again after a certain period of time, not take up these questions anew? Much suggests that this listing is a pretext for other problems which suddenly hindered the dialogue.

Here is not the place to speculate on the internal problems of this dialogue. The Benedictine Dom Emmanuel Lanne, who participated in this dialogue, refers to the unspoken questions which stood in the background. In his opinion nothing less was at stake than mutual recognition and sacramental communion. In order to avoid this, the dialogue had to be broken off and the difference in the understanding of baptism played up.[55] Whether this assumption is correct is not here to be debated, but such a background would explain the peculiar development of this dialogue. In the end, it was a matter not of the understanding of baptism, but of basic ecclesiological questions which had been settled to the point that sacramental communion became possible. The time for this, however, did not appear ripe.

---

55. E. Lanne, "Catholiques et orthodoxes, un dialogue exigeant à un tournant capital," *La nouvelle revue théologique* 107 (1985): 87-100.

This dialogue with its peculiar history is additional evidence for the significance of baptism in the ecumenical dialogues. The question of baptism is not as such absolutely central. It is so, however, in its significance for church communion and mutual recognition.

# Rites of Initiation as Signs of Unity

*Eugene L. Brand*

Baptism is an *act* of the church which is performed in obedience to a dominical command.

Together with the Eucharist, it belongs to the core of Christian worship. Baptism is not just a biblical teaching or a theological concept. Since baptism is a ritual or liturgical act, our teaching about it and our discussion of it must be rooted in what we as church do when we baptize. While that may seem self-evident, even a cursory perusal of the literature on baptism, ecumenical and otherwise, indicates the opposite. It is salutary, therefore, that the planners of this conference noted the connection.

It is also salutary that the theme for this presentation departs from the otherwise consistent use of "baptism" to speak of "rites of initiation," because dealing with the subject in a satisfactory manner takes us beyond baptism in the narrow sense of the term.[1] It is necessary not only to consider the sequence — to use the shorthand of the Western tradition — of baptism, confirmation (chrismation), first communion and how coming to faith fits into it, but it is also necessary

---

1. Perhaps especially among Lutherans, "rites of initiation" is not uncontested terminology. But some term is needed to refer to a complex of rites, and "initiation" is the term generally in current use.

to consider the preaching and instruction which form the ecclesial context for the rites of initiation.

Rites of initiation are signs of unity when they themselves and their use reinforce — in the midst of divided churches — the biblical teaching that there is but one baptism which incorporates those baptized into the one Lord and thus into the one church of God. Seen this way, Christian initiation — and especially baptism — continually calls ecclesial divisions into question. And the reverse is also true. Christian initiation administered — as it must be — by divided churches mutes the force of the question because it diminishes the impact of the ritual action.

One could deal with the theme by looking at as many liturgical texts for initiation as possible to discover what they say or imply about the unity of the church. That is not the path I have followed for at least four reasons: (1) based on research I have done, I know that it is not particularly fruitful;[2] (2) such an approach assumes a burden that the texts themselves cannot bear, both because liturgical texts are not (should not be) didactic or homiletical and because the words spoken are not necessarily the most significant part of the rite; (3) such an approach tends to divert attention from the ecclesial context of the rite; and (4) such an approach cannot deal with the varying ecumenical contexts of the local churches. Therefore, I have instead opted for a series of points or assertions about Christian initiation and church unity which are intended to stimulate discussion.

1. The liturgical texts *are* important. They must neither state nor imply that the candidate is being initiated or baptized into anything other than the "one holy catholic and apostolic church." If they do, baptism as the fundamental expression of unity is contradicted. One is not "baptized Lutheran" or "baptized Catholic"; one can only be "baptized Christian" because that is the only confessionally neutral term which remains.

1.1. The use of the Apostles' Creed both in the rite of baptism and in the catechisms makes the point regarding unity most clearly (in the Orthodox churches, the Nicene Creed is used). Not just any confession of faith will do. It must be an *ecumenical* creed. It must be

---

2. See my "The Lima Text as a Standard for Current Understandings and Practice of Baptism," *Studia Liturgica* 16, no. 1-2 (1986): 40ff.

a creed confessed by the "one holy catholic and apostolic church." If a confession with "confessional" associations or some more "relevant" contemporary confession is substituted, the rite is robbed of a fundamental ingredient.

1.2. Without itself becoming didactic or homiletical, the liturgical text can also provide a point of contact for preaching or teaching about baptism and unity. Among the many examples which could be cited[3] is the rite of the Church of Christ in Thailand. The text begins, "In baptism we become part of the people of God, members of the Body of Christ, the Church . . . ," and the introduction to the final prayer states, "This child of God is a member of the Holy Catholic Church. . . ."

1.3. In the performance of the liturgy, the Apostles' Creed and other texts which reinforce the point of church unity cannot, however, by themselves bear the whole burden of expressing unity. While ritual texts are important, Christian initiation requires the context of a ministry of preaching which is both baptismally and ecclesially oriented, drawing out and enhancing baptism's sign character and its implications for the individual and for the church. A few pious words in connection with baptisms and confirmations are insufficient to create the needed context. Baptisms cannot be isolated moments which occur when one must "have a child done" or when an adult "joins the church." Baptism requires an ecclesial context which itself is baptismal. Emphasizing the context should be a reminder that the whole church or congregation celebrates the rites of initiation. The assembled community are not simply passive observers of an action which concerns only the candidates themselves.

2. The minister and the assembled congregation are today a potential problem because they both carry confessional or denominational labels. I say "today" because prior to the sixteenth century at least, the presence of an ordained minister would have been a sign that baptism is an act of the *whole church* administered locally. The point registered even more clearly when the bishop was the minister of chrismation. But today one is, for example, baptized in a *Lutheran* church by a *Lutheran* pastor. Given that situation, how can it be made

---

3. See Max Thurian and Geoffrey Wainwright, *Baptism and Eucharist: Ecumenical Convergence in Celebration,* Faith and Order Paper 117 (Geneva: WCC Publications, 1983).

clear that the confessional labels must not contradict the intention of the baptismal act? Even though the normal minister of baptism is a person ordained in the one church of Christ and even though he or she acts on behalf of the whole church, since that minister is under the discipline of a confessional communion and functions within a local church/congregation which itself is part of the structure of a confessional communion, the impact of the confessional context easily drowns out the intention stated in the text. The problem also arises when adults "join the church" and are baptized, especially in multidenominational situations where they decide to associate themselves with one denomination and not another. Again a vital context of proper preaching and teaching may be the answer (see 5. below).

3. Since individual persons are baptized, the rite is all too easily seen and understood individualistically. The problem is exacerbated where infant baptism is the norm. The primary emphasis on baptism as incorporation into Christ and *therefore* as initiation into the one church is contradicted by two caricatures. One regards baptism as personal salvation insurance, the antidote for the poison of original sin, the ticket to heaven. The other reduces baptism to a name-giving rite and/or gaining membership in the ecclesial expression of a national culture. While this is not the place to deal theologically with the first caricature, it is the place to assert that neither of them contributes anything to the theme: the relationship between baptism and Christian unity. Both promote an individualistic baptismal concept, and the toxin of individualism requires powerful antidotes. The liturgical texts, bereft of their proper context, cannot themselves do what is needed. Their use must be explained and reinforced in teaching and preaching.

3.1. What has been said about the assembled church as baptismal context reinforced by preaching and teaching applies here also. Though the liturgical texts do not speak individualistically, by themselves they are not enough. It is questionable whether any person should be baptized where the ecclesial context is ignored or even spurned. At the very least that means prebaptismal instruction for the parents and sponsors of infant candidates.

3.2. The practice of "private baptisms" should be discouraged, especially if they are not administered in church. They tend conceptually to connect baptism to the birth of infants and to be experienced as family celebrations. Folk or state churches where this practice is most deeply rooted are generally now making serious attempts to overcome it.

3.3. The optimal baptismal context is most pointedly experienced at certain times in the church year. The most potent of these is the vigil of Easter. Whether or not the connection of baptism with Easter is primitive,[4] it is an ancient connection which carries strong theological conviction. Pentecost affords another opportunity, as do All Saints' Day and the Baptism of Our Lord. The proclamatory and didactic impact of these days literally forces a different conceptualization of what is going on in baptism. Relating baptisms to the kerygmatic unfolding of the gospel in the church year provides a clearer link with church unity than relating them to birth and family. The former emphasizes the corporate while the later reinforces the tendency toward individualism. Baptism should not be classified with the "occasional services" of marriage and burial.

4. Lutherans inherited the separation in time of the rites of initiation — baptism, confirmation (chrismation), first communion — which had become characteristic of the Latin Church.[5] The roots of this state of affairs were often accidental or due to practical rather than theological difficulties. After the fact, of course, the separation was often justified theologically. Again, this is not the place to go into the history of this separation or the theological reasons which have been offered for it, but it is the place to assert that where the temporal sequence of the rites of initiation is interrupted, their ecclesial impact is diminished, and the claims we make about them regarding church unity are thereby weakened. In what follows I can speak only to the Lutheran situation, which in some ways is typical of the Latin Church but in other ways is not.

4.1. Judged by our theme, the most serious separation is that between baptism and first communion because it creates a two-tiered membership in the church for which there is no justification in the

---

4. Paul Bradshaw, " 'Diem baptismo sollemniorem': Initiation and Easter in Christian Antiquity," in *Living Water, Sealing Spirit,* ed. Maxwell Johnson (Collegeville, Minn.: Liturgical Press, 1995), pp. 137ff.

5. I have sometimes used "baptism" in a broad sense as synonymous with "initiation." Here I shall use it in the narrow sense, differentiating it from chrismation.

New Testament. If the church baptizes infants, it should also admit them to the Lord's Table.[6] One should not regard baptized persons as outside the membership of the church or as some sort of second-class members. "Baptized members" can only mean full members. And, except for reasons of discipline, one cannot exclude a member of Christ's body from participation in the sacramental body of Christ. If all the baptized *within* the discrete confessional communions are not eligible for eucharistic communion, how can one put forward convincingly the baptismal argument for unity; i.e., that baptism constitutes the communion in Christ which we call the church, and therefore that recognition of baptism across confessional lines is a powerful argument for sacramental communion in the Eucharist? Those Lutherans are headed in the right direction who have lowered the age of first communion and separated it from confirmation as precondition. Until now, the Evangelical Lutheran Church in Canada is the only Lutheran church to sanction the communion of infants, though infant communion does happen elsewhere.

4.2. Lutherans have objected to any theology of initiation which connects the *gift* of the Holy Spirit to confirmation (chrismation)[7] and which waffles on its bestowal in baptism. Baptism itself is full initiation, and no baptized person lacks the gift of the Spirit. Confirmation (by the sixteenth century a separate sacrament from baptism) cannot be a sacrament because it has no scriptural warrant (Apology of the Augsburg Confession, XIII, 6) and because it adds nothing to baptism.[8] Abolishing the link between confirmation and first communion has diminished the problem character of the rite, though, as it is often administered, confirmation has sacramental impact. But confirma-

6. See my "Baptism and the Communion of Infants: A Lutheran View," in *Living Water, Sealing Spirit*, pp. 350ff.

7. Though the prayer in the rite of the Lutheran Church — Missouri Synod reads, ". . . God, the Father of our Lord Jesus Christ, give you his Holy Spirit. . . ." *Lutheran Worship* (St. Louis: Concordia, 1982), pp. 206f.

8. Where "confirmational" chrismation is reintegrated with baptism, Lutherans need to be careful to regard the rite whole so that chrismation is not understood as a separate moment, albeit immediately sequential, which adds the gift of the Spirit. See the criticism of the work of the Inter-Lutheran Commission on Worship (North America) in Maxwell Johnson, "The Shape of Christian Initiation in the Lutheran Churches: Liturgical Texts and Future Directions" (unpublished paper, 1995).

tion for Lutherans can be only a reaffirmation of baptism, and it is usually the climax of concentrated catechetical instruction. For one baptized in infancy, confirmation instruction becomes the focus of the context of baptismal preaching and teaching, as was mentioned several times above. And precisely here problems regarding baptism and church unity may arise, for confirmation instruction can be the time when we "make Lutherans." Of course Lutheran catechists will instruct adolescents and adults from the standpoint of the Lutheran Confessions. But *how* this is done or perceived can be crucial for people's understanding of unity. It makes all the difference whether the confessional viewpoint is presented in order to erect a Lutheran fortress or in order more clearly to confess the faith of the "one holy catholic and apostolic church." A question to candidates in the confirmation rite of the Lutheran Church of Australia illustrates the problem: "Do you intend to remain faithful to the teaching of the Lutheran church, as you have learnt it from Martin Luther's Small Catechism?"[9] In other words, the unity which is established by baptism may be, in practice, called in question by confirmation.

5. The place where baptism is administered may militate against its potentiality as a sign of unity. That is especially true in multiconfessional areas (as opposed to areas where there is, for all practical purposes, only one confessional communion present). Where each church building represents not only a different congregation but a different confessional communion, and where each church has a font, the "baptized Lutheran" syndrome is reinforced. Though similar things could be said about altars and eucharists, more people experience intercommunion or eucharistic hospitality than "interbaptism." To the *Lutheran* midwife and the *Lutheran* family (see 2. above) is added a *Lutheran* womb. If baptism is really commonly acknowledged across confessional boundaries, what would prevent baptisms being celebrated together, administered by ministers of several confessional families, even taking place in a baptistery the congregations have in common? An ecumenical celebration of the Easter vigil would be a grand occasion for that. Separate processions from a common baptistery to different eucharistic halls would, after a time, become unbearable. If such intercelebration is impractical for all baptisms, doing it

9. Johnson, p. 14.

occasionally could influence how baptism is perceived. Of all the chief rites of the church, I suspect baptism tends to be celebrated and experienced in the most sectarian manner. If so, how can one expect it to be perceived as the base upon which church unity can be established?[10]

In these assertions, two underlying convictions should have become clear: (1) rites of initiation are or should be signs of unity; (2) the obstacles relate more to the lack of a baptismal understanding of the church than to how the church understands baptism.

10. *The Celebration of Holy Baptism* of the Caribbean Conference of Churches (Thurian and Wainwright, pp. 89ff.) and the North American *A Celebration of Baptism* (Consultation on Common Texts, 1988) illustrate the possibilities of intercelebration.

# Problems of Mutual Recognition

## BAPTISMAL RECOGNITION AND THE ORTHODOX CHURCHES

### Merja Merras

There is every reason to greet with pleasure the effort the Lutheran World Federation has taken up by organizing this consultation, for it shows serious concern for our problem. The unit which convenes the consultation can determine the premises for it, and thus our starting point is "a perspective that is Lutheran, but which seeks to be ecumenically open." We are here trying to answer the Lutheran church as to why we have been unable to express a common view of baptism. This setting dictates something of the way one approaches this question.

First, I shall briefly present what the Orthodox Church teaches about baptism and the aspects that cause problems for other denominations. Second, I will comment on the carefully prepared study paper and explain our views of its questions. Third, I will try to point out some suggestions for solutions, knowing very well that while doing so I do not have behind me the authority of any local church, not to mention the authority of the Orthodox world. What I shall present, I do as a scholar oriented to the early history of baptismal ideas and with a standpoint of study that arises inside the Orthodox Church.

1. Aidan Kavanagh has written a very fundamental study: *The Shape of Baptism: The Rite of Christian Initiation,* not found among the texts cited in the study paper. This does not, of course, mean that it is not well known to the writers of the study paper as well as to many others. The author is a member of the Roman Catholic Church, and he presents in his work the basis on which the reforms of baptismal practice were made by the Second Vatican Council. This book, or better, its first part, "The Tradition," is a textbook even in the theological schools of the Orthodox Church. It is noticeable that very many Orthodox theologians can accept what Kavanagh writes concerning the formation of baptism and its first development. The first condition for a common view of baptism is unanimity on the basis of baptism. If some Christian community cannot accept the view the early church had of baptism, it is difficult for it to develop an argument for the suggestion that we should acknowledge the ideas about baptism which have come into being in later times. The problem that we face here is, of course, how the notion of baptism in the early church is to be understood. Kavanagh gives here a detailed and scientifically justified answer of how baptism was based on the Jewish practice of purificatory ablutions.

With the washing of bodies must go the cleansing of hearts, and Saint John the Forerunner practiced this kind of baptism. John's baptism of repentance is preparatory for the messianic work, and it is in water. It will give way to another baptism by One who will baptize with the Holy Spirit. None of the sources reports pneumatic occurrences connected with any baptisms prior to the resurrection.[1] Christian baptism is thus connected with the descent of the Spirit, and the Spirit does things that were not seen earlier.

The early church could have rejected water baptism, saying that it belongs to the Johannine baptism. This could have been done

---

1. Aidan Kavanagh, *The Shape of Baptism: The Rite of Christian Initiation* (New York: Pueblo Publishing Co., 1978), pp. 7, 10, 15.

despite Jesus' baptism in water. The church could have decided that after Pentecost the sufficient rite for receiving the Holy Spirit was the laying on of hands or the anointing derived from the Old Testament. It did not, however, do so, but the water bath was seen as a function of the Spirit. This means that water data concerning Christian baptism are subordinate to pneumatic data: The former are to be understood in terms of the latter. When NT texts refer, especially in passing, to "baptism," they mean something ritually larger and increasingly more sophisticated and complex than the water bath alone.[2]

Heresies plagued the apostolic church from its beginning. In resisting them, the church felt it necessary to specify its understanding of baptism and the benefits the neophytes there received. It was no longer possible to speak in simple terms of a matter which proved to be many-sided and thus open to fatal misunderstanding. The ministers, who performed the rite, had to have the authority of the local church to baptize,[3] in order to make sure that the gifts they transmitted would be those which were intended and thus asked from God. Neophytes were thus also assured that they were being baptized into the *una sancta*, not into one of the many groups outside the church which also practiced baptisms.

Some refer to emergency baptism, noting that it is valid though not performed by an ordained person and arguing that this also justifies baptized laymen transmitting God's gifts. According to early practices, however, such a baptism is not complete but must be completed by anointing by an ordained priest, if the baptized person survives. Emergency baptism was made for death and the anointing is made for life. This demonstrates how baptism consists of two means for one goal: remission of sins as a condition of entry to the kingdom of God, and equipment for Christian living which culminates in deification. By making him "christ" in Christ, by anointing him with the Anointment of the Anointed One, it opens to man the door of *theosis*, of deification.[4]

---

2. Kavanagh, pp. 25-26.

3. "The power to baptize is given only to bishops and presbyters with the assistance of the deacons, not to other clerics as readers, singers and door-keepers." *Apost. Const.* 3.11. Cf. Ignatius of Antioch, *Ep. ad Smyrn.* 8; Tertullian, *de Bapt.* 17.

4. Alexander Schmemann, *Of Water and the Spirit: A Liturgical Study of Baptism* (London: SPCK, 1974), p. 80.

From the earliest times, in receiving baptism the neophytes had to learn and utter one of the creeds;[5] a creed marked the boundaries of the doctrine against those who were seen as heretical. The creeds became longer as more heresies broke out and spread.

The doctrine of salvation appeared in liturgical form before it was verbally determined by the synods. There were no dogmatic declarations except the early creeds. The material the apologies worked with arose from the liturgical life of the church. This means that the Sunday, Pascha, Pentecost, baptismal, and eucharistic celebrations, the evening service and the lectionaries, express the contents of the Christian faith. Salvation was in the early centuries conceived primarily as "rescue," with special consideration given to the factors from which men are rescued: bondage to demons and all that this implies. But one is not only rescued but also cured of the miasma of sin. We are not only redeemed from something, we are also redeemed into something. We are not only "brought from darkness into light" and "from the power of Satan into God," we are also made "partakers of the Divine Nature." This takes place in baptism. If we cannot be saved by ourselves, it is equally clear that we cannot be saved without ourselves.[6]

Two dimensions, or better three, belong to Christian redemption. It is at once an act wrought by God on man's behalf, and an act done by Christ as man before God. The redemption demands the existence of an incarnate Person both human and divine for its accomplishment. But this is in vain if man does not receive it, and the third necessary act is the baptism of the believer.[7]

The words in the baptismal rites, which demonstrate the faith of the church, were important because one had to be sure that the spirit who was going to descend and dwell in the neophyte was the right spirit, who brings salvation. For it was believed that there are many different spirits at work in the world, and not all spirits wished humanity well. In this way there arose in the church an impression that the law of prayer was the law of faith *(lex orandi lex credendi est);* i.e., what we pray in the rite of the church contains also the unanimous faith of

---

5. Trullan Synod, canon 78; Letter to the Laodiceans, 46, 47.

6. Origen, *In Gen. Hom.* 9.3.

7. H. E. W. Turner, *The Patristic Doctrine of Redemption* (London: Mowbray, 1952), pp. 116-21.

the church, and we have the right and also the duty to ask for this, because the Bible teaches: " 'Ask, and it will be given you' "[8] and "You do not have, because you do not ask."[9]

In this way several baptismal rites took shape, which, though being slightly different, strove to express the church's common understanding of the meaning of baptism. The slightly different rites were no problem for the early church. The rite of baptism, which the Orthodox Church even today uses, occurs in its present formula first in the codex Barberini, written circa 790. It is derived from that current in Syria, and in many respects it is similar to that described by Saint John Chrysostom (d. 407).[10] It consists of the following themes: the renunciation of the devil and act of adherence to Christ; exorcisms; anointing with the oil of gladness; baptizing in water in the name of the Holy Trinity; anointing with holy oil, making the sign of the cross on the forehead, eyes, nostrils, mouth, and both ears with the words "The seal of the gift of the Holy Spirit." The divine liturgy follows, including the Eucharist and the first communion of the baptized. This demonstrates his/her full membership in the Christian community, and the Christian way of living: Only with the constant connection to Christ, the life-giver, is one able to fulfill his/her vocation in the world and grow toward the goal — *theosis,* deification.

In the Orthodox Church the anointing, the gift of the Spirit, follows immediately upon baptism, the triple immersion, meaning that the Holy Spirit is operative in both sacraments. He re-creates our nature by purifying it and uniting it to the body of Christ. He also bestows deity — the common energy of the Holy Trinity which is divine grace — upon human persons. It is on account of this intimate connection between the two sacraments of baptism and chrismation that the uncreated and deifying gift, which the descent of the Holy Spirit confers upon the members of the church, is frequently referred to as "baptismal grace."[11]

In the many prayers of the rite we pray, inter alia:

8. Matthew 7:7; cf. 21:22.

9. James 4:2.

10. E. C. Whitaker, *Documents of the Baptismal Liturgy* (London: SPCK, 1970), p. 69.

11. Vladimir Lossky, *The Mystical Theology of the Eastern Church* (New York: St. Vladimir's Seminary Press, 1976), p. 170.

Therefore do thou, our loving king, be present now in the visitation of thy Holy Spirit and sanctify this water. Give it the grace of redemption, the blessing of Jordan. Make it a fount of purity, a gift of sanctification, a way of deliverance from sins, a protection against disease, a destruction to demons. . . . Be present, Lord, in this water and grant that those who are baptized therein may be refashioned, so that they may put off the old man, which is corrupt according to the deceitful lusts (Eph. 4:22) and put on the new man, which is restored after the image of him that created him . . . and guarding the gift of thy Holy Spirit, and increasing the store of grace, they may receive the prize of the high calling (Phil. 3:14) and be numbered among the first-born who are written in heaven (Heb. 12:23).

This is what we pray, this is what we believe too, and we know that we receive what we are praying for.

This baptismal formula contains the Orthodox Church's understanding of baptism. If somebody asks about something that does not occur in our baptismal formula, we cannot answer unambiguously. This is seen in the responses the local Orthodox churches have given to the *BEM* document, since the text of the document does not arise from the liturgical basis. All those churches seem to ask specifications to matters that are pointed to very cursorily. They are asking the same questions the early church asked, before it had the clear baptismal rite, which answered all unclear questions concerning the notion of baptism. It is common to the answers of the Orthodox churches that the *BEM* document does not sufficiently note the aspect of anointing in baptism and does not clarify what is the church to which the neophyte is being joined and what is the faith he/she is to confess. In addition, the Church of Greece, which seems to be most reluctant over against the new ecumenical thinking, does not want to acknowledge the right of the WCC to request reception of the *BEM* document. Those Orthodox churches which for historical reasons are accustomed to cherish the doctrine of the seven sacraments in the same way the Roman Catholics do, emphasize especially the lack of the sacrament of chrismation in the document. The Orthodox Church, however, has never defined the number of its sacraments/mysteries to be precisely seven. Nor is it accustomed to perform confirmation apart from baptism, as the Roman Catholic Church does. Only in cases where a person is baptized in another church, has not received confirmation there, and wishes to join the Orthodox Church is confirmation/chrismation performed separately and is called the supplement to baptism. Thus the mystery of chrismation could be seen, also in theory, as a part of the mystery of baptism, as it mostly has been in practice, when we speak of an unbaptized child or adult. This was the case in the early church, where chrismation could just as well precede the water baptism[12] as follow it, and was clearly a part of the mystery of baptism. Most crucial is the confession that in baptism there is the pouring out of the Holy Spirit and that this is also liturgically demonstrated.

The Orthodox Church has not fully recognized the baptisms of other churches but has decided to follow the principle of economy concerning the baptisms of the Roman Catholic Church and the churches of the Reformation.[13] This demonstrates its belief that these churches strive to teach about baptism in accordance with the teaching of the early church, although it does not yet see that this aim is achieved in the baptismal rites of these churches. The principle of economy can turn into a full recognition only if the Orthodox Church

12. In the Syrian Church before the Council of Chalcedon. See G. Winkler, "The Original Meaning of the Prebaptismal Anointing and Its Implications," *Worship* 52 (1978): 24-45.

13. Economy here means that in theory the Orthodox Church has not fully accepted the baptisms of other churches to be the baptism of the early church, but in practice accepts it so that it does not baptize those who come from these churches into the Orthodox Church.

The commentary of the ninety-fifth canon of Trullo (691-92), made by Bishop Nikodim Milashin in 1910, classifies the nonorthodox groups as those which are (1) to be baptized, (2) to be only anointed, or (3) to have only to declare his/her orthodox faith. The first classification concerns pagans, the second those who have been baptized in the name of the Father and the Son and the Holy Spirit but whose communities do not have legal priesthood and who do not confess the sacrament of anointing. Those are all Protestants. Those Roman Catholics and Armenians, too, who have not received the anointing should be anointed. Totally without baptism and anointing will be received those Roman Catholics and Armenians who are anointed in their own church. They have to reject publicly their former faith and confess the Orthodox faith. In practice this means the sacrament of repentance and communion in the Orthodox Church. See the use of economy today in more detail: John H. Erickson, "The Problem of the Sacramental Economy," in *The Challenge of Our Past* (New York: St. Vladimir's Seminary Press, 1991), pp. 115-32.

can recognize in the baptismal rites of other churches those elements the early church saw as necessary in order to be separated clearly from the groups it held to be heretical. Besides this, I believe that unanimity in the concept of the church and in the ministry of this church is demanded by most Orthodox churches before common baptism can become a true reality. This view is based on the idea that we can baptize into the one church only if we know what this church is and where its boundaries are. In recent times there have been voices that declare that the borders of the church cannot be set by the earlier norms.[14] It is clear, however, that in the *una sancta* which is aspired to, the Orthodox Church has to recognize the features of the earliest Christian church.

2. The study paper separates the question of baptism from its context, the framework where it is exercised, namely, the ecclesiastical communities. From this viewpoint the Orthodox Church constitutes an irritating stone (with other stones) in the shoe, as is implied in II.A.2. We would suggest that in order to come closer to each other, we should look at our practices, because they reveal our true aims. The section "Baptism and Communion as Gift and Call" (I.B.4.) presents the question in a way that arises from Luther's protest and apology, not from the very core of baptism as the church previously had seen and practiced it. It states:

> A personal relation is something that must be *lived* if it is to exist. Thus, precisely as the kind of gift it is, baptism is a call, a call to life in Christ. Most fundamentally, it is a call to receive the gift given, i.e., it is a call to faith. . . . The efficacy of baptism depends on faith in the recipient. We are justified by grace, *through faith.* . . . The gift itself implies a call. . . . We have communion in the Lord who remains the community's true head. . . . Thus, word and sacrament have a theological priority over other forms of communal life. . . .

This view we cannot share, as is well known. For to whom is it given to measure faith, to pass judgment on the degree of "compre-

---

14. J. Karmiris, "Die Universalität des Heils in Christus," *Theologia* 52 (1981): 16-17 (in Greek), ref. D. Papandreou, "Zur Anerkennung der Taufe seitens der orthodoxen Kirche," *Una Sancta* 1 (1993): 48-53.

hension" and "desire" in it? Faith as a word is an attitude: I have faith in this and not in that, but the word in itself does not contain any reality. Faith must be clothed with deeds to be openly seen. We would say that baptism "is a call to faithfulness, and its efficacy depends also on faithfulness" to the voluntarily spoken promise to remain within Christ's troops in the struggle against evil. By this we mean that our faith may fail, but our faithfulness can nevertheless stay. It is hard work, not just feelings. Love is deeds, not words or feelings. We can walk in the dark valley without having any landmark, any faith, any knowledge, even any loving feelings, but still have faithfulness to the promise we once made: to walk within Christ's troops. As the early church put it: "Those who preserved the seal unbroken will inherit the Kingdom." The word was preached and heard in the beginning, before baptism,[15] and it made us to choose faithfulness, but when we are on the way, the word — if this means the word or sentences of the Bible — has no sacramental power in itself to carry us, though it can help us understand the salvation and remind us of it. Only the gift received in baptism or in anointing (whichever expression we are accustomed to use) and renewed in the Eucharist will carry us if we remain faithful to our choice. This is the view of the early church, and it continues in the Orthodox Church, though several times in historical difficulties we have lost the capability to express it clearly.

The important question, whether baptisms can truly occur beyond the church (II.A.2. of the study paper), is easily answered: no! But along with it we must determine the boundaries of the church, and this is more difficult. We can find, however, some guidelines. Patristic thought somehow avoided speaking of the "marks" of the church *in abstracto*. Neither was there among the Fathers a tendency to "hypostasize" and "objectify" the church itself. When they speak of the catholic church, the Fathers say, first of all, that it is the "Body of Christ" and the "Temple of the Spirit." "Where Christ is, there is the catholic Church," says Saint Ignatius of Antioch.[16] Orthodox ecclesiology is based on the idea that a local Christian community, gathered in the name of Christ, presided over by the bishop and celebrating the eucharistic meal, is indeed the catholic church and the body of Christ

15. Trullan Synod, canon 78; Letter to the Laodiceans, 46-47.
16. *Ep. ad Smyrn.* 8.2.

— not a "fragment" of the church, nor only a part of the body. In the ecumenical movement the nature and identity of the church are understood differently by the various Christian groups. The Orthodox Church, however, tries to hold fast to the unity of life and dogma, liturgy and theology, love and truth. Of course, the gap between divine perfection and the deficiencies of sinful men is nothing new in the life of the church.[17]

The doctrine of "catholicity" implies the legitimate possibility of cultural, liturgical, and theological diversity in the church of Christ. This diversity does not mean divergence and contradiction. The unity of the church implies full unity of faith, of vision, of love. The unity of the one body of Christ transcends all legitimate diversity. To quote Saint Gregory of Nyssa: "Truth passes in the mean . . . destroying each heresy, and yet accepting what is useful to it from each."[18]

The new questions about the identity of baptism which are set forth in section II.A.4. of the study paper are from the Orthodox point of view insignificant. New ideas occur all the time in history,[19] but the church cannot chase after them, but must continue preaching the original gospel and holding to the original sacraments and doctrines. Heresies have always tried to confuse the church, as today. Those who seriously suggest new doctrines to the church must first be instructed seriously in the old ones.

The massive nonparticipation referred to in II.B.2. is the result of a lack of faithfulness. It is difficult to be faithful to the baptismal vows if one does not understand what it means to be faithful. Perhaps we need models who demonstrate how this is carried out. The saints of the past time, popular persons of their time, were those models, but they seem to be quite far away from our everyday life. Do we point to them frequently in our instruction? Does the Lutheran church encourage people to look at the models, the saints of the past or present day? Or have we submitted to the reality that the popular persons of

17. John Meyendorff, *Living Tradition: Orthodox Witness in the Contemporary World* (New York: St. Vladimir's Seminary Press, 1978), pp. 81-84.

18. Meyendorff, pp. 89, 91.

19. "If a bishop or presbyter does not baptize according to the commandment of the Lord in the name of the Father and the Son and the Holy Spirit, but in the name of the three without beginning or three sons or three defenders, he shall be discharged." *Const. Apost.* 49.

our time, who are not specially able to stand as our models, have taken this important place? Not just the saints but every member of the church witnesses by his/her life, and indeed we have too few good examples close around us. We have to look at ourselves and nobody else in this question.

A solution to the problem of the participation of the nonbaptized (II.B.3. of the study paper) is to be seen directly in the practice of the early church, where I find no problem. If we consider baptism to be the reception of the Holy Spirit with all its benefits in our life, we simply cannot think that we can be good enough "Christians" even without this grace. There are many stages on the way to perfection. Catechumens had made the decision to strive toward perfection. The way which led to this decision was sometimes long and perhaps took years. Those catechumens whose names were written up in the beginning of the Great Lent sought to be baptized at Easter. They did not even think to stay in the catechumenate longer than was necessary. But if somebody chooses to be a lifelong catechumen, we have to honor his/her decision. We cannot, however, rank him/her among the baptized Christians. By the way, there is in the church a canon ordering that a catechumen had to be baptized immediately if he/she is in danger of death.[20]

The Church of Sweden, which since 1996 no longer counts within its ranks all Swedish people, baptized or not, even atheists and the nonconfessing, is a good example of a church that has noticed on its own that its baptismal theology needs to be rectified.

The communities which do not baptize do not work by the divine power, but by themselves, if their members are not baptized before they enter these communities. The Spirit blows wherever she wants, touching people in different ways, but it is only through baptism that we become partakers of the divine nature and begin to do the deeds of the Spirit. Even unbaptized persons can perform wonderful actions which seem to be truly of divine origin. But if we are faithful to the teaching of the early church, we confess that God does the actions, using baptized persons as mediators of his power. These persons have committed themselves to God, as does the soldier doing his duty at an officer's bidding.

---

20. The fifth canon of Saint Cyril of Alexandria.

To my knowledge, the Methodist church is the original home of the Salvation Army, and the Anglican Church of the Friends. These churches do baptize. In the Nordic countries the Salvation Army is a spiritual organization, not a church as in many other countries, and most of its officers are baptized members of the state church. It seems to me that in the future, the still-growing membership of the Salvation Army will come from various churches and practice their own religious traditions. The idea of the Salvation Army is so good that it is not wise to damage it by holding on to old historical disagreements. The church has always had numerous societies and communities within it, where people who feel close to each other can meet, pray, and work together. This does not influence the structure of the church, nor the local churches where the people are baptized. If a group should arise which does not baptize, totally rejecting the value of water baptism, and which yet insists that its members are Christians and God's children, they are heretics from the point of view of the church, and I do not see any reason why we cannot declare this openly.

3. Finally, I would say some words on a personal level about what I see as solutions to some of our problems.

Is it now time for the so-called old churches — Orthodox, Roman Catholic, Lutheran, Reformed, Anglican — to give up their extreme courtesy and a mutual understanding not based on the facts and start to call heresy heresy? Or would it be better to speak of an error? If we are ready to accept all kinds of new "Christian" ideas and opinions as equal with the old ones, we are causing a difficult confusion which hinders persons from reaching the truth of the catholic church, the *una sancta*, and throws them into the realm of different new and old pagan religions.

The starting point for all considerations must be the life and teaching of the early church, since only there can we find a common basis for the faith to which we wish to commit ourselves. There would be no church today if the early church had not resisted heresy and developed its understanding over against all possible misinterpretations. This does not, however, mean that everybody should return to the realm of the Orthodox Church. The Orthodox Church, such as it exists today, has developed since the early church in its outer manners and symbols. It has never demanded uniformity from the local churches, but is able to comprehend in itself many kinds of national traditions and views, if only we could be reconciled in the main.

# BAPTISMAL RECOGNITION AND THE BAPTIST CHURCHES

## S. Mark Heim

The study paper "Baptism and the Unity of the Church" concisely summarizes the obstacle to mutual recognition of baptism for those in believers' churches: They hold that the baptism of someone incapable of personal confession of faith is simply no baptism, so there is nothing to recognize.[1] The summary is accurate. But it is far from providing a full picture of the situation. This paper will try to outline the problem of mutual recognition from a Baptist perspective. First, I will review the various elements in the Baptist understanding of baptism, attempting to illuminate their interconnections and relative weights. Second, I will offer some reflections on the prospects for mutual recognition of baptism.

Given their polity and principles, Baptists are a notoriously difficult people to represent. I acknowledge that at a few points — specifically in my suggestion of possible future accommodations — my interpretation of Baptist views puts me in a distinct minority within the broader Baptist family, and perhaps within my own communion. However, I believe this approach serves our ecumenical discussion well, since it casts the focus even more strongly on the root problematic, convictions which Baptists maintain on their side with near unanimity and which are unlikely to dissipate.

---

1. "Baptism and the Unity of the Church: A Study Paper," prepared by Michael Root and Risto Saarinen, Institute for Ecumenical Research, Strasbourg, France (1996).

# I

Baptists have long argued their view of baptism on biblical grounds: Believer's baptism by immersion is the only clear New Testament practice. But the issue of baptism clearly turns on three levels, of which the New Testament example is only one. Christians who practice infant baptism argue, rightly, that the New Testament practice cannot be entirely determinative. Two other crucial questions are, What did (and does) baptism *mean?* and What is the nature of the church?

Interestingly, Baptists agree that these two questions are of cardinal importance. Though Baptists often maintain that the New Testament model settles the matter, it would be more accurate to say that Baptists insist on that paradigm because they believe the New Testament practice *exemplifies* the meaning of Christian initiation and the nature of the church. Those who endorse infant baptism believe that for various circumstantial or contextual reasons the acknowledged New Testament practice was only partially illustrative of those underlying truths. The initial converts to Christianity would naturally be those who could make this decision themselves and be initiated accordingly, without precluding the legitimacy of a variant later practice.

I note this in order to stress a point often overlooked: Baptists do not hold that proper performance of the rite of baptism (the right mode, the right subject, the right form) is as such constitutive of the church — so that where the rite is not properly performed the church is not present. It would be more accurate to say that Baptists understand the church to be constituted by God's act in Christ and the free human response to that gracious, initiating act. If it is the nature of the church to be made up of believers, those who experience, acknowledge, and accept God's gracious initiative, then believer's baptism is an instrumental ecclesial imperative, as well as a biblical precedent.

But — and this is the key paradoxical element — for the same reason that Baptists insist on believer's baptism as the only complete or fully valid baptism, they do *not* see it as either necessary for salvation or as a definitive index to the existence of Christ's church. A congregation made up of persons all baptized as infants may also in fact be made up entirely of persons who individually confess their belief in Christ. For Baptists, then, Christian unity, mutual recognition of each other as Christians and as parts of the one church, may exist where "baptismal unity" in the sense of recognition of the full validity of each other's baptismal practice does not.

This is well expressed in a recent document from the Baptist Union of Great Britain:

> [W]e observe that the direction in much ecumenical debate is *from* the act of baptism *to* the nature of the Church and its ministry. The hope is often expressed that once the baptism of *individuals* has been mutually recognized, it might be possible to proceed to what are felt to be the "more difficult" matters of recognition of *ecclesial* realities, such as ministry and sacrament. Bafflement is often expressed as to why Baptists will not apparently take what is widely seen to be the "easiest" step of recognizing a common baptism as the basis for unity.
>
> However, as Baptists our direction of thought is *from* the nature of the church *to* the meaning of baptism: it is because we understand the core of the church community to be committed disciples of Christ . . . that we understand baptism to be the seal of the Spirit for a believing and obedient disciple. At the same time, this means that we can recognize the realities of church and ministry existing among others, regardless of the mode of baptism they exercise. . . .[2]

James Dunn points out in his paper that in the New Testament reception of the Holy Spirit is usually a more important reference point than water baptism. Writers typically argue from the evident work of the Spirit in a person's life *to* baptism. When they argue the other way around (in the sense that we should "live up" to our baptism), they appeal to a sense of incongruity, of departure from the expected sequence in which the manifest action of God's Spirit in an individual's life is already evident in the conversion leading up to the act of baptism, and should hardly be less so afterward. Baptists adopt a similar approach, in essence relating baptism to conversion as an act of obe-

---

2. "Believing and Being Baptized: Baptism, So-Called Re-baptism and Children in the Church," a discussion document by the Doctrine and Worship Committee of the Baptist Union of Great Britain, 1996, pp. 22-23. Published by the Baptist Union of Great Britain, Baptist House, P.O. Box 44, A29 Broadway, Didcot, Oxon, OX11 8RT.

dience and public confession. Baptism is our response, carried out at our initiative, in relation to the historical work of God in Christ and the specific prior work of the Spirit in our lives, both of which took place at God's initiative and without our control.[3]

## II

These general observations can be specified by considering particular aspects that bear on mutual recognition of baptism.

*The mode of baptism.* Baptists universally affirm immersion as the biblical and theologically normative mode of baptism. However, this difference alone is not a powerful obstacle to mutual recognition. Historically Baptists have not insisted on immersion even in their own practice (administering other forms for those who are ill or disabled, for instance) and have very commonly recognized the baptisms of those baptized as believers in other communions, even if they were not immersed.

*The biblical paradigm for baptism.* Baptists have maintained that the New Testament is unequivocal in its explicit examples of baptism, whatever the uncertainty that may attend equivocal texts (regarding "household baptism," for instance). That explicit pattern has the subject of baptism professing belief in Christ and then receiving water baptism in the triune name. The inability to produce a clear biblical mandate for infant baptism is a crucial issue for Baptists.

*The biblical meaning of baptism.* However, Baptists recognize that the simple existence of a predominant practice in the New Testament church does not necessarily constitute a normative command for the church in every age. Though the example given in the New Testament is of great presumptive weight, Baptists in fact put equal or greater emphasis on scriptural accounts of the *nature* of baptism (such as Romans 6;

3. Interestingly, Baptists have had historical disagreements over the laying on of hands for reception of the Spirit as a part of the baptismal rite. These arguments have appeared to depart from a common assumption that an evident, converting work of the Spirit is presumed in baptism, while the varying parties disagree over whether any separate act from immersion is needed to signify this and whether reception of the Spirit should be supposed to come before the act of baptism or to be coincident with it.

Gal. 3:26-27; Col. 2:12).[4] If baptism is participation in Christ's death and resurrection; if the model of baptism is not primarily circumcision, so much as it is Jesus' own baptism by John in the Jordan and his "baptism" in death and resurrection; then the true meaning of baptism is most fully expressed in a practice in which the believer participates through a voluntary personal identification with Christ.

*The sacramentality of baptism.* The whole understanding of "sacrament" has a significant bearing on Baptist perspectives on this issue. One of the rationales for infant baptism which Baptists traditionally rejected was the need for cancellation of original sin. In most cases, this was not because Baptists denied the inheritance of a sinful disposition, but because they denied both that God would attribute guilt for that disposition to those below an age of accountability and that the rite of baptism could itself erase that guilt in any event. Baptism is a sign and seal of cleansing from sin, but this cleansing itself is a distinct reality, inseparable from the response in faith to Christ. In this respect, the difficulty with infant baptism is an instance of a broader difficulty with the ritual application of grace. Baptists affirm the priority of God's grace and initiative, as do those who practice infant baptism, but they resist the notion that its effect can be appropriated or presumed on the basis of the correct performance of a baptismal rite. The idea that baptism as an event apart from the personal confession of the candidate entails some intrinsic ethical effect is problematic for Baptists.

*Ecclesiology.* The keystone Baptist conviction — in common with those in other believers' churches — has to do with the nature of the church. Baptists object more strongly to an ecclesiology based on infant baptism than they do to infant baptism. As Thorwald Lorenzen says, "The name 'Baptist' is unfortunate because it may cover up that for Baptists the decisive issue is not baptism as such but 'the living Church of confessing Christians.' "[5] The Baptist movement began pre-

---

4. A review of these arguments is hardly necessary. Representative sources would be G. R. Beasley-Murray, *Baptism in the New Testament* (Grand Rapids: William B. Eerdmans Publishing Co., 1976) and the chapters on "Baptism in the New Testament," in *Christian Baptism,* ed. A. Gilmore (London: Lutterworth Press, 1959).

5. Thorwald Lorenzen, "Baptists and Ecumenicity with Special Reference to Baptism," *Review and Expositor* 77, no. 1 (winter 1980): 22.

cisely as an alternative ecclesiology, and this is the fundamental issue in questions of baptismal recognition: what are the implications of such recognition for the nature of the church? Baptists generally hold that one is baptized into Christ and into the universal church, not a particular denomination. When the local congregation baptizes, it does so more in its place as an embodiment of the church itself than as part of one communion divided from others. Baptism is in principle distinguishable from membership in a particular church or congregation. The act of baptism does not of itself alone make the recipient a member of the congregation that baptizes: A separate act of reception is required.[6] In this sense, most Baptists affirm a common baptism as a basis for Christian unity. But this unity would be seen as primarily spiritual, since the one church into which we are baptized is itself understood as invisible. As there is no need to identify the church one is baptized into as concretely and visibly the Baptist church, so there is no need to realize a single institutionally unified church to which baptism would correspond.

*Baptism and communion.* Baptists do not agree with each other on the relation between baptism and communion. Many hold to closed communion: Only those baptized as believers by immersion — sometimes only those so baptized in the individual congregation — partake in the Lord's Supper. Others hold to open communion, inviting to the Lord's Table all fellow Christians or all those who are committed to follow Christ (not even specifying that one must be baptized in any form to come). Thus it is quite possible in many Baptist congregations to receive communion without being a member of that congregation, without meeting the criteria for membership, without being a member of any other church, or without being baptized at all.

6. This is commonly designated the "right hand of fellowship" and precedes participation in communion. Many Baptist baptismal services may include all three — baptism, reception, participation in communion — in one worship event. But in many other churches the second two would follow later over days or weeks. Some representative body of the congregation (usually the diaconate) normally votes to approve candidates for baptism and for membership. It is usual for the entire congregation or the congregation's governing body to have the opportunity to vote to accept the baptized as new members. Though baptism and membership may often be conflated in this process, they remain discernibly distinct.

*The subjects of baptism.* It is the combination of all the elements noted above — most notably biblical precedent, biblical meaning, and ecclesiology — that leads Baptists to restrict baptism to those who are able to make a personal profession of faith. This of course is the point at which mutual recognition becomes difficult. It is important to note that the baptism of believers is not a single, detachable belief in a list of several, but represents the intersection of several different convictions, each of which leads toward it.

The two key issues regarding the subject of baptism are the baptism of infants and so-called rebaptism. Baptists question whether infants are proper subjects for baptism, while paedo-baptists question whether adults who were baptized as infants are proper subjects for baptism in believers' churches.

## III

For Baptists the fundamental issue of recognition turns on baptism's relation to the nature of the church. The question of whether Baptists may recognize infant baptism as a valid (if less than ideal) baptism is difficult but not intractable. A minority would already be willing to do this in at least some cases. The much harder issue turns on *what* one expects to be entailed in the recognition of baptism. If recognition of other churches' baptisms requires Baptists to relinquish the capacity to regulate their own membership so as to constitute their congregations as communities of professed believers, then this recognition will not be forthcoming.

The issue is framed well, I believe, in the *Baptism, Eucharist and Ministry* section on baptism when it states (in para. 15): "Churches are increasingly recognizing one another's baptism as the one baptism into Christ when Jesus Christ has been confessed as Lord by the candidate or, in the case of infant baptism, when confession has been made by the church (parents, guardians, godparents and congregation) and affirmed later by personal faith and commitment."[7] Inter-

---

7. *Baptism, Eucharist and Ministry,* Faith and Order Paper 111 (Geneva: World Council of Churches, 1982).

pretations of this paragraph vary, but it suggests an approach which Baptists can seriously entertain.

Clearly most who practice infant baptism regard it as complete and valid, a sufficient condition of initiation into the church. Baptists do not agree. But the sentence I quoted says churches are increasingly *recognizing* each other's baptism as the one baptism when it is believer's baptism or infant baptism accompanied by confirmation (or some equivalent). What is suggested here is a distinction between what may be the internal conviction of a church in which baptized infants are fully initiated and what will be claimed ecumenically in terms of recognition from other churches. This ecumenical recognition is not to be expected until personal confession has been associated with one's baptism. Such an approach would require Baptists to accept the administration of infant baptism in other Christian churches as valid in providing all the appropriate outward elements of baptism and thus, when conjoined with the personal confession of the person baptized, making unnecessary any repetition of the rite.

Those baptized in other churches would then routinely be accepted by Baptist churches on the basis either of their baptism and confirmation in those churches or of their baptism and a current personal confession of faith. This approach would allow paedo-baptist churches to continue to function in their internal life according to their present convictions — that infant baptism represents full Christian initiation — but it would require them to agree that they would not insist that believers' churches' standards for membership be bound by this assumption. Among paedo-baptist churches, some draw a sharper line than others between "confirmed baptized members" and the baptized who have taken no individual step to carry their baptism into active life in the church. The perspective in the paragraph quoted from *BEM* suggests the possibility of moving the issue of baptism to a point where the difference between Baptists and others could become analogous to this tension *within* churches that practice infant baptism, a tension over full Christian initiation. Indeed, the ecumenical interest today in an "integrated" or "unified" rite of initiation points to an awareness that whatever our various traditions might emphasize as the key moment of initiation, each of those traditions presumes a more expansive set of elements for full membership or participation.[8] A "folk church" like that in Sweden recognizes a need both for evangelization of the baptized and a more purposeful catechumenate for those who are registered within the church and yet remain unbaptized.[9] Neither a baptism unfulfilled by participation in the Eucharist and the broader life of the church nor an active association with the church's activities which is as yet unspecified through baptism or personal confession can be the fullness of entry into the body of Christ.

However, the difficult question of "rebaptism" remains. If Baptists were willing to accept baptized believers from other traditions, they would still face the cases of those baptized as infants who, confirmed or not, wish now to be baptized as believers by immersion. Even ecumenical Baptists are very reluctant to endorse a blanket denial of such requests.[10] The only way forward I can see in this area relates to the fact I noted earlier — that Baptists do not really focus supremely on the rite itself. Therefore the believer's participation in the rite of immersion does not itself constitute an absolute condition for entry into the church. This being so, Baptists might eventually be willing to retain the freedom to carry out in some cases the immersion of those baptized as infants, while marking this as an event of affirmation, an appropriation of an *act* of baptism that has taken place earlier.

Paedo-baptists bristle generally at the notion of a "completion" of infant baptism — suggesting as it does that the baptism was not full or effective as it stood. But on the other side it is important to grasp that Baptists believe that baptism is "completed" by the personal act of faith . . . not by the "correct" performance of the rite which happens

---

8. See the discussion on a unified rite of initiation, with particular emphasis on the relation between baptism and the Eucharist, in Susan Wood's paper "Baptism and the Foundations of Communion."

9. See the paper by Ragnar Persenius, "Baptism and Membership in the Church of Sweden."

10. See, e.g., the response of American Baptists to *BEM* on this point: ". . . American Baptists have been — and largely still are — unwilling to commit themselves to deny the ordinance of baptism to those who may in all sincerity seek it in accordance with the biblical practice of combining personal confession of faith with the experience of baptism." Max Thurian, ed., *Churches Respond to BEM*, vol. 3, Faith and Order Paper 135 (Geneva: World Council of Churches, 1987), p. 259.

to include individual confession. In believer's baptism this crucial element of completion *precedes* the act of baptism and is reflected and embodied in that act.[11] It is the physical act of baptism itself which "completes" — in the sense of making public and visible — the acceptance in faith of God's grace.

## IV

The ecumenical difficulties and possibilities can be illustrated by considering the differences among Baptists themselves in this area. Baptists draw different conclusions about the relation of baptism and membership: closed membership, open membership, and modified open membership.[12] Most Baptist churches practice closed membership: Baptism as a believer by immersion is a necessary prerequisite for church membership. (Most of these churches practice open communion, where baptism is *not* a prerequisite for communion, though some practice closed communion.) A small proportion of Baptists practice open membership: Membership is open to all who will profess their faith in Jesus Christ and commit to the church's life. The only form of baptism administered is believer's baptism by immersion, and anyone who enters the congregation by baptism enters in this way. But those baptized as believers in other churches, those baptized

11. The term J. D. G. Dunn coined to express the New Testament characterization of the total event of becoming a Christian, "conversion-initiation," nicely expresses the Baptist perspective here, with emphasis on the personal conversion that precedes or coincides with baptism. See J. D. G. Dunn, *Baptism in the Holy Spirit* (London: SCM, 1970), p. 5.

12. Baptist manuals of polity and practice generally note three means by which persons may be received into membership: baptism (meaning believer's baptism), experience, and letter. "Experience" refers to a direct personal confession of faith in Christ, a testimony to one's saving experience of relationship with Christ. "Letter" refers to documentation from another Christian communion that one is a baptized and confirmed member in good standing (which communions' letters will be accepted varies among Baptists). Closed membership Baptist churches would limit themselves essentially to entrance through believer's baptism, open membership Baptist churches would limit themselves essentially to entrance through baptism or experience, and modified open membership congregations would utilize any of the three means.

as infants, and even those never baptized at all may all be received into membership on the basis of confession of faith in Christ. Baptism itself, let alone a particular form of baptism, is regarded as a desirable but not essential mark of the church.[13] An intermediate number of Baptists practice a modified open membership policy: accepting into membership those baptized as infants in other churches if they testify that they have appropriated that act by faith or if they present evidence of having already done so in another church by confirmation or testimony (though these Baptist churches would generally freely grant believer's baptism to any in the situations described who would request it). Some would restrict recognition of other baptisms more severely — accepting only some form of believer's baptism administered in another tradition.

In those cases where Baptists have entered into united churches or seriously pursued ecumenical unions, they have generally done so through some arrangement that protects the ecclesiological principle of the believers' church. In the Church of North India (CNI), for example, two elements are crucial. Congregations of a Baptist tradition (as well as those from Disciples and Brethren background) are entitled to continue to practice only believer's baptism by immersion, though they are likewise committed to provide baptism for infants if it is requested (turning to a CNI pastor from another congregation if they wish). And the full communicant membership of the entire Church of North India is limited to those who are baptized and "give evidence of repentance, faith and love toward Jesus Christ. . . ."[14]

Variations on this approach can be found on a smaller scale. My own denomination counts some individual congregations which are "federated" or "united" with another, paedo-baptist denomination (most often United Church of Christ or Methodist). Within these congregations both believer's baptism and infant baptism are administered and recognized, but full membership rests upon baptism and

13. This is an ironic *internal* issue among Baptists that bears on ecumenical relations. Some Baptists have objected to this (rare) practice in which a small number of congregations may admit persons who have never undergone Christian baptism, and called upon Baptists themselves to insist on a common baptism in this respect. See, e.g., "Believing and Being Baptized," p. 29.

14. *Forward to Union: The Church of North India: A Handbook* (Delhi: ISPECK and LPH, 1968), p. 19.

personal confession.[15] Thus, although infant baptism is unequivocally "recognized" in these contexts — in the sense that no other rite of baptism need be substituted for it — it is not recognized as entailing membership. Personal confession of faith is still requisite for full Christian initiation. The crux of the ecumenical question here seems to be whether such a situation must be interpreted as implying that infant baptism is defective or whether it can be understood from the perspective of a fullness of Christian initiation which goes beyond baptism itself — whether infant or believer's.

*What* are Baptists to recognize in the baptism of infants? A witness to the prevenient and objective grace of God toward us? An expression of the faith of the church? An obedient performance of the biblical command to baptize in water and the triune name, a performance that *need not* be repeated ever again? It is possible Baptists could recognize all of these.[16] What Baptists cannot recognize in infant baptism is full initiation into the church of Jesus Christ, in both the spiritual and the structural sense. Those churches which put emphasis upon confirmation express in essence a similar view.

"Common baptism" is a confusing phrase, since it can be taken in a restricted and in a maximal way. In the restricted sense it can refer to the barest mechanical features of the rite, and in this sense Baptists can recognize a common baptism. In the most maximal sense baptism can mean a whole integral complex of Christian initiation encompassing not only the fundamental rite but also rejection of evil, reception of the Holy Spirit, confession of faith, and participation in the Eucharist. Interestingly, if taken in this maximal sense, Baptists can also recognize a common baptism with other confessing Christians — meaning that in those other believers Baptists recognize all of these features to be present. The problem of recognition arises in the "in between" area, where Baptists believe a claim for recognition of something like the latter reality is being made on the basis of the former alone. To put the matter differently, for believing individuals who present themselves seeking a

15. In some cases membership may be recorded on two different rosters and may be marked at different points, so that the congregation itself does not have a single membership standard.

16. Here is one of those points, indicated in my opening paragraphs, where I go beyond what the vast majority of Baptists today would accept. However, I believe the inner logic of Baptist convictions allows a development in this direction.

recognition for their Christian baptism in infancy, a baptism which they themselves now claim as their own, Baptists have only a limited problem. The very request itself has gone much of the way to meet the primary objection Baptists might raise. This problem is real, but I believe it can eventually be resolved. But if the ecumenical claim is for an omnibus recognition of baptisms whose subjects themselves make no such claim, then the gap remains immense.

Frequently in ecumenical discussions of baptism there has been suggestion that a revived catechumenate might be helpful. I believe this is true. From a Baptist perspective the existence of a catechumenate — which in paedo-baptist churches must normally be a post-baptism catechumenate — is itself an acknowledgment of a major portion of the Baptist conviction. Though the task of the catechumenate may be posed — and in part rightly — in terms of "becoming what you already are," still it recognizes that one must progress to a further point to enter actually into the confessing community. Such a process, which culminates in a confirmation of one's baptism, would in principle meet Baptists' ecclesiological concerns.[17]

When I speak of common baptism in a minimal sense, I reflect the common ecumenical notion that what we have in common by subtraction is where we might start: In baptism this means the fact that we all baptize, with water, in the triune name, in obedience to biblical mandate and example, as a means of initiation. This is what is "common" about our baptism in the sense that it is what is left when

---

17. There are two areas here where Baptists themselves are in need of reform if their own witness is to be credited. The first is in their preparation of candidates for baptism (an area in which attention to the character of the catechumenate in the early church would be merited). The second is in their articulation of the place of children within the body of the church. The practice of infant dedication is widespread among Baptists, but it is often insufficiently developed or interpreted so as to encompass those dimensions of infant baptism which Baptists can accept as legitimate. The most notable aspect, in my view, is recognition that the child now has a real place within the life and community of the church (similar, one might say, to the place of a catechumen). The development of a child's life in the church is not simply a matter of waiting to confess and be baptized. Appreciation of a unified rite of initiation means, for most churches, attention to the elements that follow on baptism and fill out entry into the church. For Baptists, it must mean primarily a "working back" from baptism to affirm the initiatory character of various elements within congregational life leading up to it.

you subtract the aspects of our various baptisms which are not in common: that the subjects here are infants, there adolescents or adults; that some involve chrismation and some do not; that some are by immersion, some by pouring or sprinkling; that some admit the subject to the Eucharist and some do not; and so on. I suspect that all we can truly "recognize" in common baptism so defined is an intention to incorporate persons into the one body which is Christ's church. This is no small matter, but its ecumenical value is limited.

I believe that a more fruitful approach would be to view mutual recognition from the perspective of full Christian initiation. There seems to be agreement among most Christian traditions that the fuller model of Christian initiation involves at least baptism, personal confession, and participation in the Eucharist. Could we agree to recognize Christians from each of our traditions as *ecumenically* part of the one church when these three are present? This would mean that if all three have taken place within another tradition, we would be challenged to recognize that other church's baptism, mode of personal confession, and celebration of Eucharist as valid *at least for the purpose of Christian initiation.* And it could mean that if one or more of the three were lacking, the lack could be supplied in the church in which recognition is sought, according to its traditions, as a prerequisite to membership. In some ways, this is a maximal approach to Christian initiation, while at the same time a minimalist approach to ecumenical unity. That is, it does not entail affirmation of the full ecclesial validity of other communions but does recognize their legitimacy as avenues by which we become members of one body.

I am well aware of the difficulties my proposal raises for many churches, and the disappointment it casts on hopes to progress by emphasis on "simple" baptism. However, at the very least it provides a picture of the way this question looks when reflected in the mirror of a Baptist perspective. At most, it may be a contribution to the process by which the members of still-divided churches claim their unity as beginners on the Christian path, even if we cannot yet claim to live out that journey as one church.

# BAPTISMAL RECOGNITION AND AFRICAN INSTITUTED CHURCHES

## John Pobee

This paper is given as part of a process of study probing further the learnings of the ecumenical process of study which becomes crystallized in the document *Baptism, Eucharist and Ministry*. This paper attempts to address the question of baptism as perceived by African Instituted Churches (AICs) and to see how it relates to the finding of the ecumenical process. The specific focus is how through beliefs and affirmations regarding baptism there can be *koinonia*, fellowship, and communion between the historic churches and the African initiatives in Christian mission.

## Multivocal and Polysemous World Christianity

Scholars have for some time come to acknowledge the phenomenal, geometric growth of Christianity on the continent of Africa.[1] It is not just a matter of numerical growth but also of vibrancy. Whatever else we may wish to say of so-called mother churches, there is also need to say that Christianity that matters is one which is alive, vibrant. So African Christianity represents something more significant than the language of mother-daughter churches and the history of power a parent would suggest. Of course, we need to be more guarded in conclusions we may draw from such assembly, for the reasons are diverse, some on grounds of rational, calculated utility, pleasure, and practical needs.

---

1. E.g., Andrew F. Walls, "Africa's Place in Christian History," in *Religion in a Pluralistic Society*, ed. John S. Pobee (Leiden: E. J. Brill, 1976), p. 180.

The indisputable shift of the center of gravity of Christianity from the North and West to the Third World reminds us of the multivocal and polysemous nature of world Christianity today. Christianity today is found in many languages, with each people hearing God's speech to them in their own language. God speaks to peoples of every race and tongue and tribe. But it is equally important to remember that the peoples too are putting their questions to God and the gospel. And in our dialogues, let us hear these questionings too.

Inside this general picture of African Christianity is the growth at varying rates and in varying degrees of a particular group variously called separatist churches, spiritual/Pentecostal churches, the Ethiopianist movement/church, Zionist churches, messianic churches, the prophetic movement, the syncretist movement, the witchcraft eradication movement, nativist churches, etc.[2] The number of this group of self-styled Christians in sub-Saharan Africa is put at 39 million, 26 million of whom are Pentecostal "charismatics."[3] Already in 1968 David Barrett painted the following picture of these independent churches: in western Africa they had 938,000 members; in northern Africa, 12,000 members; in southern Africa, 3,179,000; in central Africa, 1,212,600, and in eastern Africa, 980,000 — a total membership of 6,662,200.[4] Today they are far more, even if facts and figures are difficult to attain.

## A Plea for an Emic Approach

The language scholars use of the aforementioned names reveals part of the problem in dealing with these churches. For not infrequently *etic* interpretation is applied to describing them; i.e., scholars impose interpretations on the phenomena they observe, reading meanings into them which often reflect their own biases. For example, in the

2. John S. Pobee, "African Instituted Churches," in *Dictionary of the Ecumenical Movement,* ed. J. N. Lossky et al. (Geneva: WCC, 1991), p. 81; D. B. Barrett, *Schism and Renewal* (London and Nairobi: OUP, 1968).

3. Patrick Johnstone, *Operation World* (Carlisle, UK: OM Publishing, 1993).

4. Barrett, p. 98, table II: "Statistics of Independency Adherents in Thirty Four African Nations," 1967.

1948 publication *Bantu Prophets in South Africa,* Bengt Sundkler spoke of them as a return to heathenism. G. C. Oosthuizen, and to some extent Marie Louise Martin, followed him in so categorizing them. Happily, in a later revision of his work, Sundkler retracted that judgment.[5] With such etic interpretations, "the historic churches, at best, have been suspicious of AICs, regarding them as a heathenization of Christianity. Not surprisingly the AICs have rarely found a place in the ecumenical movement."[6] However, for the health of the discussion it is better and more important to employ an *emic* approach, i.e., to interpret them through the eyes of the actors/participants, because etic approaches mislead the discussion.

However, there is a deeper issue, namely, the understanding of being church and ecclesiology. Their presence, especially as they are so vibrant and on the increase, raises the question of the tests of being church. Scholars from the Reformed tradition, e.g., all too quickly invoke the *notae ecclesiae* to assess these African initiatives in mission. In other words, they consciously or unconsciously apply to them the three tests: (a) "incorruptible proclamation of the Word"; (b) use of the sacraments, especially baptism and Eucharist; (c) the exercise of discipline.[7] On the other hand, a Roman Catholic or Anglican scholar, with determined commitment to the ecumenical councils of the first five centuries, is tempted to apply the criteria of unity, holiness, catholicity, and apostolicity. Thus, even in so-called mainline Christianity there are varying, if not different, criteria for evaluating church. In other words, our respective theological evaluations of the other (church) tradition are often, if not always, subject to and dependent on our own theology regarding the teaching of Christ, of the Holy Spirit, of the church. In that, we often use *etic* categories for judging the other. Indeed, frequency of celebration of the Eucharist in one's own church is often used to determine that another tradition and practice is deficient in ecclesiology.

5. B. E. H. Sundkler, *Bantu Prophets in South Africa,* rev. ed. (London: International Africa Institute, 1961; originally published 1948); Sundkler, *Zulu Zion and Swazi Zionists* (London: OUP, 1976); G. C. Oosthuizen, *Post-Christianity in Africa* (Stellenbosch: Werer, 1968).

6. Pobee, "African Instituted Churches," p. 11.

7. M. L. Daneel, *Quest for Belonging* (Gweru: Mambo, 1987), pp. 22, 25; Oosthuizen, *Post-Christianity in Africa.*

Thus the task in hand invites us to seek clarity with regard to the theological criteria we use for evaluating the life and mission of African Instituted Churches, indeed, of the other church. In this regard we must be on our guard against the consequences of long years of division. Permit me also to draw attention to a truism which is often forgotten by scholars: Only believers and participants can understand their religions. This is a reminder that there are epistemological problems entailed in any attempt to make abstractions regarding the meaning of a belief system, especially when one does not subscribe to it.[8]

## Celebrated Theology Rather Than Cerebrated Christianity

This meeting is an assembly of ecumenists and professional theologians, or, at least, persons who dabble in theology. In the face of AIC, there is limited value in the theological approach we dabble in. The constituency of AIC is largely simple people, poor, theologically nonliterate. It is expecting too much to call for neatly defined and articulated theological positions. They represent enacted theology done in other than Hellenistic philosophical categories. So we may have to glean their positions from their practices. Permit me to recall the incisive identification of belief, religious experience, and ritual as the three cornerstones of religion.[9] Their theology may have to be gleaned from their practices, their beliefs, ritual and religious experience rather than from any clearly articulated or defined statements of belief or creeds. Ipso facto silence on any particular thing may not necessarily be equated with denial. Harold Turner, whose monumental study of the Church of the Lord, Aladura, is classic, affirms the Aladura church as African yet universal, possessing the notes of the true church "similar to the historic creeds and formulations." But he also admits that that church is "devoid of theological or historical understanding."[10]

8. J. M. Fernandez, "Rededication and Prophetism in Ghana," *Cahiers d'Etudes Africains* 10, no. 2 (1970): 228-305; R. A. Hahn, "Understanding Belief," *Current Anthropology* 14, no. 3 (1973): 207-29.

9. I. M. Lewis, *Ecstatic Religion* (Harmondsworth: Penguin, 1971).

10. Harold W. Turner, *African Independent Church*, 2 vols. (Oxford: OUP, 1962), 2:326. See also W. F. Shenk, "The Contribution of the Study of New Religious

## AICs, a Variety in a Genre

They are deemed to be protest movements, analyzed in connection with acculturation, cultural revival, proto-political action. Some represent prophetic and charismatic phenomena of a protest type or proto-political cultism. These descriptions mentioned earlier essentially see them as a challenge to "true" principles of Christianity, and more so, in an age of ecumenism. We also need to remember that there is often a gap between the ideal and reality in people's conception of religions and proper social order, often calling for purification. Whatever else we may wish to say of them, they represent vibrant African initiatives in mission, which we shall ignore to our own impoverishment.

The brief listing of designations suggests that they represent a variety of initiatives in a genre. For that reason they do not constitute a single entity and may not be lumped together. They do, however, represent dissatisfaction with and protest against the expressions of Christianity which have been minted through the traditions of the West (Latin) and North and, to some extent, the East (Greek). We also recall the study done by sociologists suggesting that people are born into a denomination but sects like the AICs and cults are joined voluntarily. There is thus an issue of who joins what cult and for what reasons. This is an issue theologians and ecumenists must bear in mind before they dare to pass judgment on AICs.[11] This issue must be borne in mind when addressing issues of ownership and accountability.

In the context of AICs the religion, indeed their theology, is less cerebral; it is more celebrated. The AICs continue the situation in the preindustrial African societies where religions did not have formally formulated and written theologies and, therefore, no corresponding dogmas and rigid interpretations of myths surrounding such tenets, and wherein most rites may be seen basically as solidarist mechanisms.

---

Movements to Missiology," in *Exploring New Religious Movements,* ed. A. F. Walls and W. F. Schenk (Indiana: Mission Focus, 1990), p. 194.

11. Richard H. Niebuhr, *The Social Sources of Denominationalism* (Connecticut: Shoe String Press, 1954); Joiachim Wach, *The Comparative Study of Religion* (New York: Columbia Press, 1963).

## Call to Be Mindful of Interpenetration of Various Phases of the Ecumenical Movement

This study is undertaken at a particular stage of the ecumenical pilgrimage. John Hotchkin has divided the ecumenical movement into three stages. The first stage is "the pioneering and organizational stage." At that stage, I would add, AICs were not in sight. In any case, churches in Africa were present largely, if not only, through the so-called mother churches. The D. T. Nileses, the C. G. Baetas, etc., were there through churches initiated from the North and West. The second stage, according to Hotchkin, is "the stage of dialogue." At this stage there was a move from a predominantly Protestant story to engage the Orthodox and Roman Catholic traditions. At this stage the AICs are not players in the ecumenical debate. But when they were acknowledged, the language of heresy, syncretism, etc., often appeared. The third stage is "phased reconciliation." Hotchkin writes,

> [T]he "stages" of ecumenism are not discrete segments; rather they interpenetrate and overlap. . . . Dialogue among churches must be a permanent feature of our life together, one not less necessary because we are becoming more united than in the past. . . . [In ecumenism's third stage] churches have coming before them proposals to redefine their relationships by decisive mutual action leading in the end to increased direct participation in one another's ecclesial lives, though without corporately merging. It is these proposals which characterize the ecumenical movement today and indicate its overall direction.[12]

It is the mood and orientation of this third stage of ecumenism that compels me to plead for emic approaches to facilitate "decisive mutual action leading . . . to increased direct participation in one another's ecclesial lives, though without corporately merging." I submit that a sensitive and sympathetic focus on baptism can facilitate that goal. To what extent do the respective teachings with regard to baptism — both in agreements and disagreements — indicate the areas of pro-

12. Fr. John Hotchkin, "The Ecumenical Movement's Third Stage," *Origins* 25, no. 21 (9 November 1995).

found agreement and accords between the churches of the West and North, as well as the traditions of the East, on the one hand, and the African Christian initiatives on the other hand?

## Sociological Significance and Implications of Religion and Culture

Calling this genre a "protest movement" and AICs "African initiatives" reminds us that the study of AICs is more complex than if we were treating them as just a religion or even a church. This is not new insight but is true of all religions and traditions. Calling a particular tradition "Anglican" is an admission that it is a particular cultural expression, in this case English, of the one holy catholic and apostolic church. AICs have distinctive African characteristics in terms of form, rhythm, emotion, structures, and symbolism, while at the same time exhibiting intra-African differences in respect of language and other cultural patterns not unrelated to political organization, kinship system, and religion. As a late Ghanaian sociologist put it of African cultures as a whole, "obvious differences of language, dress, customs, exist alongside obvious similarities, common interests, and experiences, shared aspects of culture."[13] These churches have come into being as responses, in varying degrees, to the challenge of culture, colonial experience, technology, morality, and common humanity.

For this last reason and several others I propose not to make general statements regarding AICs but to take particular churches. One has to take seriously not only the fact of religious and denominational pluralism but also the pluralism within the one genre of African initiatives in mission. Belonging to the one genre "does not mean that all the members of such groups share exactly the same beliefs or engage in exactly the same practices; it means that such differences as exist are regarded as complementary in nature, not contradictory."[14] We may dare to make our ecumenical judgments not so

13. K. A. Busia, *The Challenge of African Culture* (New York: Praeger, 1962), p. 42.

14. Gerald Laski, "Religious Pluralism in Theoretical Perspective," in *International Jahrbuch für Religionssoziologie*, I.1 (1965), p. 29.

much in terms of polarities, truth and falsehood, truth and heresy, but in terms of complementarities of expression.

The convergence document *Baptism, Eucharist and Ministry* was produced when AICs were not there; they were not part of the discussion. In a sense it is a misnomer to use the language of convergence *post facto* of what could be the relationship, accord, compatibility, and consensus. So part of the exercise here is attempting to seek language that will make it possible to hold dialogue and also engage the globalization of the church in which the growing unity of Christians goes with a greater sense of cultural diversity of the churches and more contact with other faith traditions which are there not only to be combated and converted but also to be dialogued with in the one household of the one Creator God.

## Snapshot 1: The African Church (AFC), Lagos, Nigeria

AFC, founded by Jacob Kehunde Coker (in the nineteenth century) and others, was a breakaway church from the Church Missionary Society (CMS), now the Anglican Church of Nigeria. The actual break occurred on 13 October 1890 when some six hundred worshipers at Saint Paul's Breadfruit Church, Lagos, walked out partly because of the arrogance of Bishop Herbert Tugwell and the incipient racism that characterized CMS missionaries, as well as the treatment of Rev. (later Bishop) James Johnson, one of the founding fathers of the Ethiopianist movement. Coker declared that the founders of AFC "decided to establish the African Church, in which Africans would worship God as Africans, independently, both in spirit and in truth, applying Christianity to African customs, not repugnant to Christ's teaching."[15] In view of what was said earlier about Anglicanism, this rationale for the schism is unexceptional. But it also means that some aspects of Anglicanism remained in that AFC. Thus, for example, no unbaptized person was regarded as a member — baptism was the rite by which a candidate became a member of the Christian community.

However, three issues came up for debate in that context. The first was whether to baptize with or without the sign of the cross. The

15. Coker Papers. File 4/1/28, p. 112.

second issue was whether baptism was by ceremonial washing or by dipping into water. A third issue was whether polygamists could be admitted to baptism. As the debate progressed, it was clarified that baptism was a dipping into the Holy Spirit and fire and in the name of the Father, the Son, and Holy Spirit. In other words, baptism was an outward sign with an inner grace and there was some emphasis on Spirit. Certainly, without saying so in so many words, baptism was for *koinonia* and thus an entry rite into the fellowship of believers. Further, the Spirit is what effected the fellowship and communion. This is to be expected of Africans who have a religious and spiritual epistemology and ontology. Baptism was a rite which initiates into the one communion, and the effectiveness of the rite is achieved by the Holy Spirit.

## Snapshot 2: *Musama Disco Christo Church (MDCC), Ghana*

Founded by Joseph William Egyankaba Appiah (1893-1948), a Methodist teacher and catechist, this church understandably has some of its roots in Methodism. The self-description of the church is that it is a "spiritual church" — indeed, it is one of the large spiritual churches in Ghana committed to experience the Holy Spirit and God as the early church did and in consonance with African culture, which has spiritual and religious epistemology and ontology. Thus the church put a high premium on dreams, visions, and trances, and some of its activities read very much like those of the Montanists of Asia Minor. But Appiah was forced out of the Methodist church for "occult practices," i.e., for engaging in alleged curious magical practices and customs as well as medicine and special drugs from India and America. He believed in, and practiced by prayers, what may be called divine healing.

With regard to baptism, there are two rites that need to be considered together. The first is the naming ceremony. In African tradition there is on the eighth day after birth a rite called the Outdooring Ceremony. On that day the child, who until then had been indoors with the mother, is brought out ceremonially into the open to officially join the rest of the family (extended) to which it belongs by definition and which is an essential part of its identity and identification. It is on this occasion that the child is named, and the name is always after a relative. MDCC has Christianized this traditional rite of initiation into the family. Though traditionally the naming was done by the family head who is the paterfamilias, in this new form it is a priest of the MDCC who is the celebrant of the ceremony. Here we see the coming together of aspects of African culture; we see, first, the working out of the African epistemology and ontology expressed as *cognatus sum, ergo sum*, i.e., I am because I am related to others by blood, thus stressing the sense of belonging and community. From that starting point the priest becomes "not just an officiant or mediator, but a kind of lineage head, to whom both spiritual and secular problems are brought for advice and resolution. He is a type of community head, a general factotum. . . ."[16] Needless to recall that here the (extended) family is the paradigm for understanding the church.

The rite is itself interesting. The priest begins the ritual while the mother holds the baby by saying: "O holy King Jesus, we thank Thee this day also that Thou protected Thine handmaid and her baby, and that Thou hast delivered them from the evil snares of the devil and hast saved them from falling into danger or mishaps. We beseech Thee to guide them and grant them love and unity; that by the tender care of Thy Holy Spirit they may live in Thy Peace, for Thy Holy Name's sake. Amen." Grace is said then and the father takes the baby from the mother to give to the priest, who then names the child. As in the African naming rite, the priest for the first time calls the child's name three times and says, ". . . this day I name you in the Name of our Lord, Jesus Christ" and that "henceforth, when thou sayest it is water, it must be water." Amen. This last reference to water is the traditional language for calling to truthfulness. The concern for the good and upright life, then, is a theme intoned by the ritual of baptism.

There is a very interesting and striking rubric: To the rubric referring to the priest calling the name of the child is added the phrase "and baptize it." Thus it is reasonable to interpret the whole naming rite as the African version of infant baptism in the name of the Trinity and as initiation into the family or the community. But that family is more than the biological, blood relation; it is the family

16. John S. Pobee, "African Spirituality," in *Dictionary of Spirituality*, ed. Gordon S. Wakefield (London: SCM, 1983), p. 6.

of God the Creator through Christ and the experience of the Holy Spirit.

There is another rite which takes place for adults, or when these children "named" in infancy become adults. That second rite is baptism by immersion. For that rite the biblical readings are Matthew 3:1-17 (the proclamation of John the Baptist and the baptism of Jesus), John 3:1-8 (the visit of Nicodemus to Jesus), and Acts 8:22-39 (the encounter between Peter and John and Simon in Samaria, and the encounter between Philip and the Ethiopian eunuch that led to the latter's baptism). The readings, like the rite, attest to adult baptism by immersion and a commitment to the demands of the kingdom of God. The accompanying rite of the immersion gives further confirmation of our interpretation: "Brother/sister. As our Lord Jesus Christ commandeth us to do to them that believe in the Gospel, this day, I baptize you in the name of Jesus who is also the Father: the Son: and the Holy Spirit. Amen." The ritual is a symbol of accepting the gospel of Christ as the basis for belonging in the community of faith.

The rite is accompanied by joyful singing, which is, of course, a mark of African spirituality that, I dare say, itself is biblical. After the joyful singing, the newly baptized pray seven times with one accord, asking for purity. The prayers for purity attest to a commitment to the ethical imperative of the gospel.

Let us attempt to sum up the story of the MDCC as it relates to the subject in hand. First, MDCC practices two baptisms, infant and adult. Second, the rites on these two occasions have been accommodated to the African culture, the former to the traditional naming ceremony which introduces the recipient into the community of the family, and the latter to African spirituality. Third, the rites stress the ethical demands of baptism. Hence, the biblical readings, especially Matthew 3 and the prayers for purity. Fourth, baptism is into the Trinity, though the language can be problematic, talking as it does of "Jesus who is also the Father: the Son: and the Holy Spirit."

There are two more things to lay out. First, there are some questions to the postulant at adult baptism, at the end of which he/she is told, "you have accepted to become as the Soldier of Christ." This language underscores the obligation to discipline and to raise up the ethical demands of the gospel. But it also underscores baptism as a rite which initiates into a community, for there is a play on the expression "soldiers of Christ." MDCC means the Army of the Cross of Christ Church. But that name also highlights the commitment to a vigorous missionary policy and program.

The second is a creed that is said. The creed said on the occasion is the Apostles' Creed with a curious addition. After the affirmation of Christ coming again to judge the quick and the dead, there is the following insertion: "I believe in the Holy Musama Disco Christo Church, and all the True Christian Churches of the world." There is an affirmation of the MDCC as well as of all true Christian churches. Presumably that church complements other churches. But for now, let me flag this variation of the Apostles' Creed to return to it in a little while. But the issue is whether that insertion is comparable to the insertion of the *filioque* clause into the Nicene Creed, which became the last straw causing the East and West to go their several ways. But before we turn to another church, let MDCC speak for itself.

The summary of what that church believes and teaches includes three particular statements. Article 2 states, "We believe in the Holy Trinity as God the Father, the Son and the Holy Spirit." With that clear statement, the earlier, seemingly problematic trinitarian statement need not be a problem. Article 8 states, "We believe in all other Christian Churches." This verges on an inbuilt ecumenical spirit. Finally, article 11 states: "we believe in the Holy Baptism in any form — Mt. 3:16, Mt. 28:19; Acts 2:36-38; Acts 10:47; Col. 2:12."

In all that we have laid out above, there is nothing in particular that goes against *BEM*. Indeed, MDCC in its own way and style intones the key elements of *BEM* regarding baptism. But it calls us to seek ecumenical convergence not so much by signing on the dotted line but by complementing others, which allows for different styles of language and ritual.

### Snapshot 3: *Apostolowo Fe Dede fia Hiabobo Nuntimya (Apostolic Revelation Society Todzevu, near Keta, Volta Region, Ghana)*[17]

This church came out of the Evangelical Presbyterian Church, formerly Ewe Presbyterian Church, which grew out of the missionary activities of the North German Evangelical Missionary Society, commonly known as Bremen Mission, begun in 1847 in the east of Ghana, in the then German colony of Togoland. As the church states it: There is "no difference between our doctrine and that of the Ewe (now Evangelical) Presbyterian church." This church states that "members of other Christian denominations may join our Society and retain their membership in their own church. But we do not accept pagans, Muslims and other non-Christians." There is a further expatiation of this in its catechism, questions 23 and 24.

Catechism question 23: "Which church is the divine one of Christ and the church abiding in its fellowship?" The response is: "The Christian Church which is divine and pleasing to God is every Church in which God alone is worshiped and His laws are strictly adhered to. For Christ said, 'Not everyone that saith unto me Lord, Lord, shall enter into the Kingdom of heaven, but he that doeth the will of my Father...' Mt. 7.21. For this cause, the apostles with one accord in the confession of the Faith of the Creed declared to their Lord and God that it is only in the Holy Church they believed."[18] The marks of the church are, first, the worship of the one God who in question 18 is referred to as "the living God . . . the Father, the Son and the Holy Spirit" and, second, faithful living of the tenets of Christianity. The reference to the creed is not necessarily to the Apostles' Creed but to the earliest kerygma.

For our purpose catechism question 24 is also instructive. The question put there is: "Is the holy Church established at any one particular place?" The response is: "Never; This Holy Church is everywhere or it is every assembly of people who adhere to the laws and precepts of the one God and denounce Satan and his wicked ways."[19] Exclusivism is not part of its self-understanding. The church is any community of people who obey God's commandments and make war on Satan and his wiles. The heavy, convoluted theology of the church is not here. The Apostles' Creed is taken for granted as a heritage from the Evangelical Presbyterian Church.

With regard to baptism, the answer to catechism question 17 is on baptism of repentance. It states:

17. "Apostolowo Fe Dede fia Hiabobo Nuntimya 1939-1954" (Cape Coast: Mfantisiman Press); Fernandez, "Rededication and Prophetism in Ghana."
18. C. G. Baeta, *Prophetism in Ghana* (London: SCM, 1963), pp. 164ff.

[B]aptism is a mark of redemption, administered by means of water to those who have been Christians. There are two forms of baptism. The first form is the one in which water is sprinkled on the person as a sign or mark of his redemption in the name of the Holy Trinity. This form is best suitable for babies, children and those who are wearied through ill health. The second form is that in which the person is immersed in water as an ablution mark of redemption. It is suitable for grown-ups. These two forms are good as they are outward and visible signs administered on the redeemed to cleanse them and make them worthy followers of God and Christ so that they escape the anger of God as is accorded the disobedient and wicked children of God. For, the Lord Jahweh is merciful towards those who love him and keep his commandments. Ex. 20. 6.[20]

What comes out of these statements and their practices is the concept of the church functioning as a community holding allegiance to the living God, Father and Son and Holy Spirit. At the headquarters in Tadzewu are a shrine, a school, a postal facility, and an infirmary, all of which are cared for by village development groups. They may not say the creed or articulate the sense of *koinonia*, but they live communal solidarities.

## General Conclusions

Permit me now to draw some threads together. First, the AICs represent a different style from historical churches in the respect of being church and reflecting on the faith. Being largely but not exclusively nonliterate, and largely the "poor" of society, they are not so beholden to the methods of the North and West, especially to the Enlightenment style of reflecting on faith. We, therefore, should not impose our styles on them, especially in the light of the learnings from sociology (cf. Fernandez, Wach, Niebuhr).

Second, these churches are many and varied. It is dangerous to extrapolate from one church to a general statement. Third, those we

19. Baeta, p. 164.
20. Baeta, p. 163.

examined have baptism as a rite of entry into the community. But not infrequently they have more than one baptismal rite — infant and adult, sprinkling and immersion. The water symbolism is important for them to focus on the need for purity and cleanliness as a crucial element of relationship and communication with the Supreme Being. The second baptism may be like confirmation in some traditions, at which adults renew their baptismal vows.

Fourth, the idea of community, or solidarity, is often not articulated in particularly Christian language. It owes a lot to traditional African epistemology and ontology that *cognatus sum, ergo sum.* And many adherents of new religions like AICs appear to opt for a religious system which takes account of traditional and/or perennial fears and aspirations. The search for wholeness and identity includes the examination of viable aspects of the traditional past, and that kind of rediscovery is a kind of baptism of items from the past.

*Koinonia* may not be talked about articulately, but it is lived: They live together in one compound as village, as at Tadzewu in the case of the Apostolic Revelation Society or Mozano of MDCC. But there is also a general feeling of communal cohesion coming from attendance at services which are able to bring together the entire community to assist each other at funerals, weddings, and other activities. The bonds of solidarity also include sharing symbols and secrets among members, such as the peculiar language of the MDCC.

Two comments by scholars articulate what this sense of community is about. Galloway,[21] an expatriate who worked in Nigeria, asserts that in Africa "there is an understanding of man's unity with the whole Natural order of God's creation which is not just a thing of the intellect, but also of the heart." May our discussions on *koinonia* be more than intellectual matter; *koinonia* is perhaps, more importantly, a thing of the heart. The theology of communion was articulated in the historic churches in a manner which did not satisfy the Africans. So they moved out. Maybe we in the historic churches can learn from their living of communion, even if they do not talk so much about it. After all, experience is one of the cornerstones of religion.

African scholar Bolaji Idowu, a Nigerian, also has written that in

---

21. A. D. Galloway, "The Universality of Christ," *Orita* (Ibadan Journal of Religious Studies) 1, no. 1 (June 1967): 25.

African religions "man's problems — personal, domestic, social, politi-cal, relational, national and international — will never be solved until he has learnt to think of one God and one universe, and of his fellow-men as persons with identical basic values and spiritual urges like himself."[22] What other intimation of the ecumenical vision do we need to convince us that those AICs are ecumenical, starting from the tradi-tional ideas and aspirations and rebaptizing them into Christ?

The religious movements I have dealt with here represent African versions of the one holy catholic and apostolic church. Several of them are African initiatives which, though with some background from some historic churches, express not only dissatisfaction with the European captivity of these churches, but also are a search "for a place to feel at home."[23] This does not mean a total break with or rejection of all the things of their background. Second, because the constituency of AICs is largely nonliterate, symbolism is an important way of com-munication. Baptism is such an important symbol. It is a rite which symbolizes the believer's identification with Jesus Christ in his death and resurrection. Third, water baptism is a rite of entry into the church, a family, a community. The rite is not only symbolism; in the African holistic understanding of reality, the rite represents the inte-gration of the symbol and reality of the baptism. In the same spirit, baptism is a symbol of renewed life and the means of effecting the renewal.

## A Dialogue with Alan Falconer

I shared this draft with my colleague, Alan Falconer, of Faith and Order, WCC. While welcoming my insights and especially the effort to listen to the experience and practice of AICs, he also put some questions to me: "How far is baptism seen as incorporating into Christ? (ii) How far is it seen as a sign of life which relates to the Kingdom and thus

---

22. E. Bolaji Idowu, "The Study of Religion — with Special Reference to Afri-can Traditional Religions," *Orita* (Ibadan Journal of Religious Studies) 1, no. 1 (June 1967): 12.

23. R. B. Welbourn and B. A. Ogot, *A Place to Feel at Home* (London: OUP, 1968).

challenges the particularity of all cultures and their modes of life? (iii) What are the processes of nurture? — Is baptism seen as a once-for-all event or as initiation into a process of growth — perhaps marked by another rite of commitment? (iv) How far is mutual recognition of baptism practised? (I noticed in one case you speak of members of other churches being able to join the particular AIC; but is there a sense of mutuality and common accountability with those of other churches? (not simply the immediate extended family of the clan?)" He adds: "forgive me, if these seem particular Northern questions."

I cite these *in intenso,* because I believe they are valid questions in the ecumenical dialogue, which all across the cultural and ecclesial lines must hear and engage. First, these questions touch the issue of the difficulty of speaking for the AICs as a mass and category. On a specific issue we may make a case for an affirmative answer with regard to a particular question, while one may not have the courage to give the same answer in respect of another tradition. Second, because the case studies in this paper come from breakaways from the Anglican, Methodist, and Presbyterian traditions, I dare to say they imply the received tradition of incorporation into Christ. My reason for giving them the benefit of the doubt is the oft-repeated reference to baptism in the *name* of Christ. In African societies, a name is more than a label of identification; it is about incorporation. The collapse of the Outdooring and infant baptism in the case of MDCC attests to baptism being seen as incorporation into the natural family, the extended family — the church — and with Christ.

With regard to the second question, baptism as a sign of life relating to the kingdom and, therefore, challenging cultural particularities, the answer is more implicit than explicit. An axiom of African life is that one may not dare to approach Divinity in sin, whether moral or ritual. For that reason the rite of water baptism is a drama of a washing away of sins that obstruct nearness to God. The terms of that are the values of the kingdom, which are not particularly articulated, though the churches' catechisms have catalogues of evils/sins to be avoided. Two particular issues concern me in this regard. African churches are very much beholden to the Old Testament, precisely because Semitic cultures and African cultures are not dissimilar. So the values of the kingdom tend to be in very much Old Testament terms. Second, and for the same reason, they tend to be rather legalistic. We need them in dialogue to attempt to deepen the language of values of the kingdom.

As to the challenge to cultural particularities, I would draw attention to the AFC and indeed the MDCC, which raise the question of polygamy. Their struggle is to come to some coherent understanding of how far the gospel affirms and challenges the culture and vice versa. Here, too, there is quite a spectrum of responses. Whether there is sufficient grounds to unchurch them, I am not sure.

AICs have strict processes of nurture. The two baptisms, infant and adult, are, in a way, their attempt to get people to take ownership of their faith. Here we must recall the distinction between church and sect in terms of being born into one and choosing to belong to the other. The second baptism represents a rite of commitment after a period of nurture. Further, those who fall short of the norms of the church are publicly rebuked and subjected to disciplinary action, including exclusion, until they show signs of penitence.

With regard to mutual recognition of baptism, the three case studies seem to affirm it, as long as it is in the threefold name. However, I have a little concern. In African societies it is often said that "we, i.e., all humans, worship the same God." This is a crude way of stating their belief in the one Creator God, though in practice they do not seem to live the implied vision in respect to Muslims and adherents of African traditional religions. But between Christians, they for their part have a culture of hospitality. The difficulty is that in their historic circumstances the historic churches have discriminated against them. So they start from embattled positions. Furthermore, often being simple people, they tend to have a complex before the doctors of the historic churches. This being the case, we need in ecumenical debates to be attentive to the psychological aspects of dialogue, in any event to avoid talking down at them and browbeating them.

Finally, having taken AICs seriously, we are challenged as to how we theologize. The long-cherished propositional style which dominates ecumenical dialogues today cannot be the only ecumenical methodology. The AICs have a Pentecost paradigm for doing theology. In this paradigm knowledge is a relationship relating the intertextuality of our world and the Word of God. The Pentecost paradigm offers a radical epistemological reordering, inverting the fund of knowledge as well as of subject-object dichotomy. It may be that their style of stating their beliefs and living them has a word or two for us, and that if we learn from them our ecumenical dialogue may be more viable, vital, and vibrant.

# Baptism and the Complexities of Church Life

## BAPTISM AND MEMBERSHIP IN THE CHURCH OF SWEDEN

*Ragnar Persenius*

### Historical Background

In the tradition and history of the Church of Sweden there has always been a close link between baptism and church membership. In the Church Code of 1686 this connection was expressed by the rule that the parents were obliged to baptize their child within eight days after birth. In 1864 the time limit was extended to six weeks. Nevertheless, there never was a complete identity between citizenship and church membership.

This obligation to be baptized was expressed within a society where it was the duty of all citizens to belong to the Church of Sweden — in principle no Swedish citizen should remain outside the church. Since then society gradually has changed. The legal development in

Sweden has led to a situation where there are a certain number of unbaptized members formally belonging to the church. The number has been estimated at 500,000 out of 7.6 million members, but nobody knows for sure. A comparison with the closely connected Lutheran sister church in Finland illustrates the importance of a continual reform of church law in order to safeguard the identity of the church in a rapidly changing society.

As the unity between church and society now is broken, the position of the Church of Sweden within society also is different. In the year 2000 it will be an independent, completely self-governing folk church with a new role in relation to the state.

Due to immigration the religious map of Sweden has changed rather dramatically, particularly during the last decade. Until 1970 Sweden was very much a monoreligious society where the religious scene was shared by the one great majority church and the old Free Churches with their origin in the nineteenth-century revival movements. The first major change came in the late 1960s when the Roman Catholic Church began to grow, mainly due to immigration from southern Europe and Latin America. This church now has 150,000 members and is the largest of the minority churches. Although it is multiethnic in character, it has gradually become more of an integrated Swedish church.

During the 1980s Sweden developed into a multicultural and multireligious society. The main reason for this was immigration from countries such as Iran and the former Yugoslavia, from the Middle East, and from a number of African countries. There are now in Sweden several small Orthodox churches of different nationalities. The most profound social change is the living presence of the Muslim community of about two hundred thousand, with about one hundred thousand active believers. It is a sign of a new religious era in Sweden that a mosque recently has been built in Uppsala, the capital of the Church of Sweden. And not only that — it was inaugurated in the presence of representatives of the church.

About 88 percent of the population of Sweden still belongs to the established Lutheran Church. The bonds between people and church are strong. They are most evidently displayed in the many rites and traditions which are closely connected to particular milestones in life. The statistical figures of baptisms, confirmations, weddings, and funerals in the church are still very high, even though regular attendance at Sunday services is comparatively low from an international viewpoint.

Due to the social and legal development the church no longer can demand anything of the parents on the basis of an authority given by the state. The only reasons for bringing the children to baptism are of a spiritual and social nature.

## Initiatives for a Reform, 1929-51

The full recognition of the individual's right to religious freedom came rather late in Sweden. In 1929 a united Bishops' Conference made a proposal to the General Synod in which they expressed a wish to give the individual citizen the choice of leaving the Church of Sweden. Such a proposal was not adopted, however, until 1951. The bishops wanted the religious identity of the Church of Sweden to be more consciously manifested. The bishops stated in their proposal that the Church of Sweden is bearer and instrument of "the unmerited, universal and prevenient grace of God." The grace of God is the foundation and primary principle of the folk church, the bishops wrote.

The proposal rejected the idea that the personal faith of individuals could be a normative principle for the organization of the Church of Sweden. It was important, however, that they should be free to leave the church. Thereby the identity of the folk church as a communion of grace would be more evident. This perspective has been important also in the work leading up to the recent reform.

The 1929 proposal from the bishops is of particular interest in relation to the reception of adults into the Church of Sweden. The bishops accepted the proposal by a governmental commission of 1925 that baptized adults could be members of the church without any further requirement. But they insisted that an unbaptized adult could be accepted as a member only on the basis of a serious decision to enter into a sacramental communion with the Church of Sweden.

## The 1951 Law on Religious Freedom

In this respect the government's action two decades later did not follow the proposal made by the bishops. It was said that unbaptized
adults, after having received Christian education, only had to make
assurance that their entrance into the church was "based upon serious
religious reasons." On the basis of such an assurance, the adult had
to be given church membership.

The baptized could enter without any action by the Church of
Sweden. A person coming from an Evangelical Lutheran Church was
automatically incorporated as a member of the church when Swedish
citizenship was granted. Only when an explicit wish not to enter the
church was stated did this not occur. Clearly the law sought to express
the view that normally a Swedish citizen is a member of the Church
of Sweden.

The focus at that time was on the freedom of individuals to resign
their membership in the Church of Sweden, not on the conditions for
those becoming members. Especially after the Parliament adopted a
new Constitutional Act in the early 1970s, the state often expressed
the intention to change the membership regulations so that nobody
would be a member of the church without expressing some personal
intent or wish. The main argument remained the religious freedom of
the individual for and from religion.

The regulation of church membership as specified in the Law on
Religious Freedom stated that if parents were themselves members of
the Church of Sweden, their children became members of the church
automatically at birth. In the years just before the recent reform, about
90 percent of such children were baptized.

When church leaders and others in the Church of Sweden since
the 1950s have argued for a reform, they have emphasized the theological interconnection between baptism and church membership.
The legal separation of the two was regarded as unacceptable, especially in the modern Swedish society. But most responsible people in
the church, both those in favor of and those against reform, also
stressed the fundamental connection between a child and its parents
within the framework of the folk church.

The different opinions within the Church of Sweden and its de-
cades-long difficulty in finding a solution were to a significant degree

a function of the debate over the future relation between church and state. Those in favor of a new membership regulation tended to be in favor of a new relation, and there was a corresponding tendency in the opposite direction among those against new membership rules.

## The Crucial Question: The Church of Christ and the Church of Sweden

Both the Church of Sweden as a whole and individual theologians and ministers have always taught that it is through baptism that a person is incorporated into Christ, the kingdom of God, and becomes a member of the church of Christ — a part of the body of Christ. In the baptismal certificate given at the service of baptism, it has been clearly stated that holy baptism means an incorporation into the church of Christ. It has also been taught that baptism is a necessary requirement for admittance to the Eucharist. No theological decision in any other direction has ever been taken. But as time went by without any change in formal membership rules, individual theologians began to defend the absence of a formal requirement of baptism. Different arguments were put forward.

One set of arguments was related to ecclesiology. If the church is to remain an open, inclusive folk church, the way into the church must not be blocked by spiritual demands on the individual. The identity of the church is not dependent on the beliefs or religious status of individuals but on the fact that the gospel is proclaimed and the sacraments are administered in the Church of Sweden. These arguments were of an extremely functional nature, often seeking support in article 7 of the Augsburg Confession. That this article deals with the assembly of all believers (communion of saints) was regarded as a description of an invisible entity. The visible church is then only an instrument. This theological argumentation was often combined with an extreme stress on the folk church as a witness to and a reflection of the grace of God. The individual receives the grace of God without merit and without encountering demands. In the same way he or she must be received as a member of the church. The form of incorporation that most avoided merit was that of the Church of Sweden — to become a member at birth.

Needless to say, the arguments were not wholly consistent theologically. It was difficult to explain how grace per se can be separated from the means of grace, how this argumentation is compatible with the statement of article 7 of the Augsburg Confession that the preaching and administering of sacraments take place within the communion of saints, and how grace can be dependent on having a parent who belongs to the Church of Sweden.

Another set of arguments outlined an almost symbolic understanding of baptism. The prevenient grace of God meets the human being before he or she knows or realizes it. The unconditional membership rules manifest this. When a person is baptized, this is a sign of grace already having met the person. Baptism is not primarily seen as renewal and incorporation, but as an outer sign of the will of God. The inner status of a person — baptized or not — is solely a question for God. On the basis of these arguments, the objective saving act of God in baptism was almost denied. In order to avoid making baptism the acquisition of a quality, baptism was theologically spiritualized, as if its content, like a person's faith, were evident only to God. No judgment whatsoever may be made about the religious status of anyone.

Although this theological argumentation may seem odd if related to the confessional documents of the Lutheran Church and to the faith of the church catholic, its purpose was well intended, namely, to safeguard the universal, open character of the folk church. Nevertheless, the membership regulation was questioned within the church itself, as well as by sister churches and the ecumenical movement.

The main question for the Church of Sweden to consider was: What is the relation between the church of Christ and the Church of Sweden? Is the church of Christ a visible communion? Is it necessary for a specific church to manifest the constitutive factors of the church of Christ?

## The 1992 Meeting of the General Synod: Membership Is Always Related to Baptism

At the 1992 General Synod the initial principal decisions were taken concerning reform. A commission on baptism and membership was to be appointed with the task of proposing a new set of membership regulations to the General Synod. The final decision, however, had to be taken by Parliament.

The Doctrinal Commission of the General Synod had already declared that membership always must be related to baptism, so that either the individual through baptism has become a member of the church or the membership is intended to be fulfilled in a forthcoming baptism. In the specific social and legal situation of the Church of Sweden, the commission sought a way of solving the situation by, on the one hand, reestablishing the theologically motivated connection between baptism and membership and, on the other, avoiding doing something which could be regarded as closing the door to the church.

Principally the Doctrinal Commission and later the General Synod itself made a clear statement answering the question about the relation between the church of Christ and the Church of Sweden. Since the latter is and must be a manifestation of the former, membership in both is founded in baptism. Baptism and the open character of the church belong together, because baptism is a means of grace.

The General Synod declared that the following principles must direct the work for reform:

1. There is a fundamental connection between baptism and membership. Either the individual is incorporated through baptism or the membership is intended to be completed with baptism.

2. The Church of Sweden is a community of grace and stands in a folk church tradition. Therefore the church may not be legally regulated as depending on the beliefs of individuals or as a community of like-minded individuals. On the other hand, the regulation must safeguard the church as a community of grace and, therefore, any regulation which can give the impression that the individual is compulsorily enrolled must be avoided.

3. The Church of Sweden sprang from a particular history and situation. For pastoral reasons, the question must be explored as to how it can be possible to belong to the church while still on the way to baptism.

4. The family is of great religious significance. The relation between children and parents is important in questions of church membership and spiritual nurture.

## The Church of Sweden Commission
## on Baptism and Membership

During the course of one year, a commission of bishops, priests, and laypeople completed its work. After discussions and study in every parish, diocese, and national organization, a final proposal was laid before the General Synod of 1994.

The commission on baptism and membership emphasized that the identity of the Church of Sweden as a folk church must be made clearer. Therefore the role of baptism as a constitutive factor of the church has to be expressed in regulating membership. This is a consequence of the fact that the Church of Sweden as a community of grace is founded by Word and sacraments, not by the beliefs or union of individuals, the commission declared.

The commission suggested baptism as the regular way to membership. The regulation sought to express baptism as an adoption into the church by an act of God, not by an act determined by the personal confession of faith of the individual. The baptismal candidate can confess the saving act of God but can add nothing extra to it.

The task of proposing a regulation defining a type of membership "on the way to baptism" did, of course, create difficulties. Previous commissions had proposed an eighteen-year limit for the preparatory membership of unbaptized children, a solution similar to the possibility for children to be "within the bounds" of the Church of Norway. But the Norwegian church has no unbaptized members.

The commission found it pastorally difficult to suggest anything that could question the right of already unbaptized members to remain as members. The main intention was to suggest a catechumenate within the membership regulation without giving up the theologically motivated principle of the close connection between baptism and membership.

The commission did not accept an eighteen-year limit for the catechumenate. The important thing according to them was that the individual was on the way to baptism, not that this process must be limited to a specific age or time period. There certainly was a pastoral dilemma. For those acting on behalf of the church or taking part in parish, diocesan, or national councils of the church, baptism must be a requirement. The in-principle openness of the church had to be combined with clear rules about participation in the church's sacramental life for those being ordained deacons, priests, and bishops as well as for elected laypersons. There must be an interrelation between duties and demands in this respect.

## Baptism as Gift, Incorporation into the Church, and Basis for the Life of the Church

The commission and the 1992 and 1994 General Synods emphasized the sacramental character of baptism. Baptism is a divine gift, an offer and mediation of grace. It is the act of God in order to incorporate people into his communion, and therefore it is the foundation for the sacramental life in the church.

The following motives were stressed:

- Baptism is a sacrament. By the word of God the baptismal act in water becomes a divine saving act. Earthly means are used in the act of God. The divine is hidden in the visible baptismal act but is realized by faith.
- Baptism is an incorporation into Christ. To belong to Christ in baptism also means to belong to the communion of the church of Christ (Rom. 12:5).
- Baptism gives the forgiveness of sins and means the reception of the gift of the Spirit (Acts 2:38).
- Baptism means participation in the death and resurrection of Christ and anticipation of the death and resurrection of the individual. It gives participation in the divine context of resurrection and life (I Pet. 1:3).
- Baptism gives the model for the Christian life, i.e., to die and rise with Christ daily through repentance and renewal (Rom. 6:4). It gives interpretation to life: through death to life. To live in faith is equivalent to living in personal baptism.
- Baptism has the same content and grants the same gifts to a child or to an adult being baptized. The practice of baptizing children expresses in a radical way the prevenient grace of God and the value of the human being irrespective of personal merits or deeds. Baptism gives the blessing of God to the child for life in a

dangerous world and gives evidence of the will of God to guide the child along God's paths.

# The 1994 General Synod Decisions on Baptism and Membership

The decision of the General Synod contains three main parts: baptism as the regular way into the church, the catechumenate on the way to baptism, and a compulsory pastoral program for work on the parochial level.

All decisions were made by the 1994 General Synod, but the final decisions on the membership regulation, which was to be included in the Church Code as a new chapter, were made by the Parliament in 1995.

## *Baptism as the Regular Way to Membership in the Church of Sweden*

Beginning 1 January 1996 baptism became the regular requirement for children and adults to become members in the Church of Sweden. The main regulation says:

> A person being baptized in the order of the Church of Sweden is thereby adopted as member in the Church of Sweden.

No certificate is required. The membership need only be noted.

Children also may be admitted on their way to baptism if their parents express such a wish. Even adults have the same opportunity if they ask for teaching on the faith, confession, and doctrine of the Church of Sweden in preparation for baptism. But normally they are adopted when baptized.

## *The Catechumenate — On the Way to Baptism*

The openness of the church is marked by the possibility for children to belong to the church on their way to baptism — a form of regulated catechumenate. For the General Synod it was important to safeguard that baptism is conceived as inclusive, not exclusive. The solution for a catechumenate within the membership regulation was pastorally motivated.

The regulation expresses the church as a communion of faith. Therefore, the responsibility to safeguard the bond between baptism and membership lies mainly on the church and the parish and not so much on the individual. This responsibility cannot be regulated in detail by law. The church found it decisive that there be a strategy for evangelization among nonbaptized members. The new regulation of membership thus has as a precondition an active pastoral program.

The catechumenate in the early church was usually, though not always, time limited. A period of preparation of varying lengths was concluded by confession of faith, which was followed by baptism as the full incorporation into the church. In the particular situation within the Church of Sweden, with a great number of unbaptized members, it is important that the principle of the catechumenate influences how the church approaches these members. Since most of the catechumens already belong to the church, and are not only on their way into the church, as in the early church, the commission and the Synod found it pastorally difficult to introduce a time limit.

## The Pastoral Program

An important sign of renewal of the identity and outlook of the church is the pastoral program of evangelization which the church has laid down in connection with membership reform. According to the program, every parent belonging to the church is to be contacted by the local parish with information about membership rules and teachings and is to be given an invitation to baptize the newborn child.

"God wants us to live in communion with Him." These words from the 1986 Service Book express what the church does and is. God calls and invites people to his church, a communion that transcends all human limitations. This must characterize the attitude of the church and its representatives in the encounter with people of our time.

Sweden is a secularized society. Many people are quite far away from active participation in church life, although most Swedish citizens belong to the Church of Sweden. Many of those encountering the church in relation to some of the sacramental acts are not familiar with regular worship, and their knowledge of the faith and life of the church is often fragmentary and dated. Some are seekers, some are doubtful about the work of the church, and some pursue a wait-and-see policy. Others have a secret longing for a deeper communion with the life of faith.

The church has to meet people precisely where they are. Those who doubt must also have the opportunity to express their hesitation; those who long, their yearning; the unaware, their ignorance. The church must always proclaim the will of God on such occasions so that people feel invited to live in communion with him.

The new membership regulation has as a precondition the stipulation that the church and the parishes have a strategy of invitation to baptism and membership and of education for those on the way to baptism.

When parents belonging to the Church of Sweden receive a child, they will be invited to baptize their child, who is thereby incorporated into the church. The local vicar is obliged to contact the parents before the child is six months old. He or she has to inform the parents about the membership regulation.

When an unbaptized child belonging to the Church of Sweden becomes eighteen years old, the parish also has an obligation to invite him or her to Christian education and baptism.

## Concluding Remarks

Attention should be drawn to the view of the church behind the new membership regulation. The Church of Sweden wants to remain an open and inviting folk church, offering membership in the church to persons at different stages of belief and phases in life. The focus is not on the borders of the church but on the way into the church. If the Church of Sweden is to fulfill its mission as a folk church in a multicultural and multireligious society, the openness cannot be played off against the distinctiveness of the church. Thus it is not possible to have the same regulation for those representing the church as for those on their way into the church. The commission to serve as a representative of the church must be founded in baptism, if more than just ministers are to be allowed to speak on behalf of the church. Such a regulation also points to baptism as the foundation for church membership and the sacramental life of the church.

The Church of Sweden has become more theologically unified, not least due to this process of rediscovering and redefining the basics of church membership and developing the compulsory pastoral program. This seems to imply that the Church of Sweden will be able to meet the future within the modern pluralistic Swedish society. In this society the relation between the church and her members must be strengthened. This is possible if the church is an evangelizing church with sincere interest in the individual.

The regulation of baptism and membership in the Church of Sweden from 1 January 1996 has resulted in a quite new situation for the church. Baptism is the regular way into the church. But the possibility of a membership on the way to baptism — a catechumenate — has given the church an important pastoral task of evangelization. It seems to me that the reform has been successful. The figures of baptism are increasing. But most important of all, the attitude and teaching of the church have changed. Both baptism and membership have become more important than ever.

# BAPTISM AND THE UNITY OF THE CHURCH IN INDIA TODAY

## J. Jayakiran Sebastian

In the introduction to "Baptism and the Unity of the Church: A Study Paper," the writers lament the fact that "Baptism as a bond of unity is mentioned and then left to the side." This reality of being left aside has practical and theological implications for the life and witness of the church in India. This paper[1] makes an attempt to spell out the repercussions of such a situation within the Indian context and to raise questions, not with the intention of getting "answers," but rather in an attempt to seek a better understanding and appreciation of the particular situation in India within a wider ecumenical framework.

\*     \*     \*

The issues and themes that challenge and confront the churches in India today are captured by the words of M. M. Thomas:

> [T]he Church's future lies in evolving new non-communal forms of fellowship in Christ which can spiritually penetrate the life of India at all levels. Here we need to clarify what are the essentials and what are less-essential and non-essential to Christian faith and Church life. Above all the mission to witness to the truth and meaning of the Cross for the life of the world must be the criterion for evaluating forms of the Church of the future. Today we are burdened with too

1. The essence of this article is extracted from my doctoral dissertation entitled "'. . . Baptisma Unum in Sancta Ecclesia . . .': A Theological Appraisal of the Baptismal Controversy in the Work and Writings of Cyprian of Carthage" (submitted to the University of Hamburg, Germany).

much Christian communal luggage which hinders our witness to the Crucified Christ in terms of the Christ-centred fellowship in the Church, and the Church's identification with victims or the Church's search for secular forms of community in the religious and ideological pluralism of our nation.[2]

In the Indian context the word "communalism" has come to acquire ugly overtones, since this word and all that it entails has been linked to the expression of exclusive group identity, leading to hostility and intolerance over against those perceived to be outside the boundaries of this group. This has led to a deepening of prejudice which has manifested itself in social conflicts, colored with religious overtones, including riots; has fermented discrimination and quick stereotyping of those not seen as "belonging"; and has also resulted in an attitude of triumphal exclusivism on the part of those considered to be the "insiders." Given this background, when the observations of Thomas are applied to the meaning, relevance, and importance of baptism, several issues can be raised:

- whether baptism belongs to the essential, the less-essential, or the nonessential element of Christian faith and church life;
- whether baptism plays any role in the evolution of new, noncommunal forms of fellowship in Christ;
- whether baptism has contributed to the communal baggage which burdens the witness of the churches today;
- whether baptism has any relevance in the search for secular forms of community; and
- whether baptism is a stumbling block in the religious and ideological pluralism of the Indian nation.

This theme of "Baptism" has been discussed not only by individual theologians, but also at a national level. In November 1971,

2. M. M. Thomas, "The Church in India — Witness to the Meaning of the Cross Today," in *The Future of the Church in India,* ed. Aruna Gnanadason (Nagpur: National Council of Churches in India, 1990), p. 11. This book contains the major papers and presentations given at a National Consultation on the theme "The Future of the Church in India," organized on the occasion of the platinum jubilee (1914-89) of the National Council of Churches in India, in December 1989.

the Christian Institute for the Study of Religion and Society organized a consultation on the theme "Meaning of Conversion and Baptism in the Cultural Context of India." The papers and findings coming from this consultation, along with correspondence that it generated, were published in the bulletin of the Christian Institute for the Study of Religion and Society.[3] The writer of the editorial commented:

> If Baptism is to be retained in Indian Christianity, the churches that retain it should be constrained to find in it (or for it) a meaning that is strongly supportive of Christian life and faith. Otherwise its liability to the Gospel in India can hardly justify its continued practice.[4]

These are indeed strong words and have to be listened to, and responded to, seriously. The questions that can be raised from these comments are:

- whether baptism, as practiced in the Indian churches today, has become a liability because of its social function and understanding, and if so, whether its relevance and meaning, if any, could be recaptured and reinterpreted;
- whether baptism has been understood as a ritual or ceremony (e.g., a name-giving ceremony); and
- whether baptism in its relationship to the gospel has indeed become a liability.

In November 1982 an ecumenical conference on the theme "Baptism and Conversion in the Context of Mission in India" was organized by the National Council of Churches in India.[5] This conference followed a major study project initiated by the National Council of Churches in India to stimulate reflection on this theme in the current Indian context. In the introduction, Godwin R. Singh writes:

> One of the major questions that loomed large in the discussions and deliberations of the Conference was that the Christian baptism has

3. *Religion and Society* 19, no. 1 (March 1972).
4. *Religion and Society* 19, no. 1 (March 1972): 4.
5. Godwin R. Singh, ed., *A Call to Discipleship: Baptism and Conversion* (Delhi: ISPCK, 1985).

often been presented as a total repudiation of one's socio-cultural heritage and accepting a name, a style of life alien to one's own. This sort of idea and practice of baptism has kept many from accepting baptism. For many, baptism, particularly as presented in our churches, does not seem to be essential for the faith, response and commitment to Christ. In the light of the cultural and social demands that baptism has wrongly demanded from many, it may be important to ask the question whether the rite of baptism could be the necessary condition for the entry into the fellowship of the Church.[6]

This situation raises the following questions:

- whether baptism has functioned, or continues to function, as an initiation ceremony or rite of passage into the church;
- whether faith and commitment to Christ can be de-linked from baptism; and
- whether baptism, which in this quotation has been called a "rite," has anything to offer when understood as a sacrament.

At this point, rather than analyzing each of the questions that I have raised, I would like to highlight some of the responses to the issues raised by baptism in the Indian context.

1. It is clear from the themes of both the consultations mentioned above that the issue of *conversion* plays a significant role in any discussion about baptism in India. This takes on added significance because of the understanding that after baptism the "converted" person has not only changed his or her religion but also social milieu, habits, customs, and manners, in addition to forfeiting several legal rights, especially with regard to the inheritance of property.[7] This led to the formation of "mission compounds" and social ghettos where Christians could take their place as one more subcaste or subsect among the thousands of such subcastes and subsects in India. J. R. Chandran writes:

---

6. Singh, p. 2.

7. See Gauri Viswanathan, "Coping with (Civil) Death: The Christian Convert's Right of Passage in Colonial India," in *After Colonialism: Imperial Histories and Postcolonial Displacements,* ed. Gyan Prakash (Princeton: Princeton University Press, 1995), pp. 183-210.

The traditional image of separation which has created the impression of the "baptised" being a loss to his original Hindu or Muslim family or community needs radical re-thinking. Separation can only be from sin and not necessarily from one's community. Baptism seeks to bring unity and not disunity.[8]

That is why, as D. A. Thangasamy writes:

[T]he pioneers in indigenous Christian thinking have exercised their mind over what conversion should mean in terms of retaining or giving up social and cultural practices of the past and of maintaining or repudiating the religious ideas and spiritual experiences the "convert" had before he became a Christian.[9]

We have to recognize that the caste system in India not only functioned to legitimize divisions and hierarchy under the idea that it was intended to organize and orient society, but also that it perpetuated a religiously sanctioned system of economic degradation linked with social exploitation, and thrived by keeping the oppressed separated and divided.[10] The emergence of Dalit theology[11] and the quest

8. In *Religion and Society* 19, no. 1 (March 1972): 58.

9. *Religion and Society* 19, no. 1 (March 1972): 37. See also the article by Christopher Duraisingh, "Some Dominant Motifs in the New Testament Doctrine of Baptism" (pp. 5-17). In the course of this article he quotes from an unpublished article by Samuel Amirtham, whose title captures the issue aptly: "Baptism: Solidarity or Separation?" (p. 15). Duraisingh himself writes that when baptism "works against the formation of a 'united, loving, peaceful life together' of all men, breaking the barriers of organised natural structures secular or ecclesiastical, it ceases to be *baptisma* in the New Testament sense of the term and remains only a baptismos — a ritual" (pp. 15-16).

10. For detailed analysis see John C. B. Webster, *The Dalit Christians: A History*, 2nd ed. (Delhi: ISPCK, 1994), pp. 1-32, and James Massey, *Dalits in India: Religion as a Source of Bondage or Liberation with Special Reference to Christians* (Delhi: ISPCK, 1995), pp. 21-80.

11. There is a fast-growing amount of literature on the emergence of the Dalit identity and Dalit theology in India. The fundamental article remains that by Arvind P. Nirmal, "Towards a Christian Dalit Theology," reprinted in the collection of his essays, *Heuristic Explorations* (Madras: Christian Literature Society, 1990), pp. 138-56. I have reviewed the two volumes edited by Arvind P. Nirmal, *A Reader in Dalit Theology* and *Towards a Common Dalit Identity*, both published by the

Gurukul Lutheran Theological College and Research Institute, Madras, in 1991, in the *National Council of Churches Review* 111 (1991): 1453-56. A recent, important book on the theme is the *Habilitationsschrift* of James Massey, *Dalits in India.* In my article "Die indische Kirche vor der Kastenfrage heute: Die neue Zuspitzung aus protestantischer Sicht," Theologische Stimmen, in *Zeitschrift für Mission* 20, no. 1 (1994): 47-50, I have attempted to spell out what the implications of Dalit theology are for the churches and the ecumenical movement.

For the history of Dalit Christians in India, Webster, *The Dalit Christians,* is not only methodologically sound but also indispensable, not least for its extensive bibliography. To get a feeling for the "raw" reality of Dalit existence, the booklets of D. Manohar Chandra Prasad are important: *Dalit Christian Consciousness* (Bangalore: Rachana Publications, 1994) and *Broken God, Broken People: The Plight of Dalit Christians* (Bangalore: Rachana Publications, 1996).

Important collections of essays on various aspects of Dalit theology and identity include the two volumes edited by Arvind P. Nirmal mentioned above. An earlier volume, which is programmatic in nature, is that edited by M. E. Prabhakar, *Towards a Dalit Theology* (Delhi: ISPCK, 1988). The journals *Religion and Society* 34, no. 3 (1987) and *Journal for Dharma* 16, no. 1 (1991) have devoted an entire issue to various aspects of *Dalitsein.* Theme-oriented collections of essays are found in V. Devasahayam, ed., *Dalits and Women: Quest for Humanity* (Madras: Gurukul, 1992); James Massey, ed., *Indigenous People — Dalits: Dalit Issues in Today's Theological Debate* (Delhi: ISPCK, 1994); and Bhagwan Das and James Massey, eds., *Dalit Solidarity* (Delhi: ISPCK, 1995).

For studies of the Dalit movement in a particular context, in this case in the state of Kerala, see the pioneering work of J. W. Gladstone, "Protestant Church and Peoples Movement in Kerala: A Study of Christian Mass Movements in Relation to Neo-Hindu Socio-Religious Movements in Kerala (1850-1936)" (Diss., Hamburg Ev.-Theol. Fakultät, 1983). Another notable contribution is that by George Oommen, "Communist Influences on Dalit Christians — the Kerala Experience," *Bangalore Theological Forum* 26, nos. 3-4 (September-December 1994): 43-62.

On the importance of Dr. B. R. Ambedkar (1891-1956) and his movement for Dalit consciousness, the collection of essays edited by Arvind P. Nirmal and V. Devasahayam, *Dr. B. R. Ambedkar: A Centenary Tribute* (Madras: Gurukul, 1991), is significant.

A recent publication contains excellent articles on "practical" theologizing with the traditions of the tribal and Dalit people: Joseph Patmury, ed., *Doing Theology with the Poetic Traditions of India: Focus on Dalit and Tribal Poems* (Bangalore: PTCA/SATHRI, 1996).

In concluding this brief bibliographical survey, I would like to quote from the collection of Kannada poems, *Hole Madigara Haadu,* of the Dalit poet-politician, Siddalingiah:

> This bone that I am,
> I will not remain like this for ever,
> I will howl, explode, and become a human being.

for Dalit identity[12] are the most significant manifestations of the desire for liberation, which includes challenging and questioning various forms of theologizing in the Indian context. John C. B. Webster, in his fine survey of the history of the Dalit Christians, points out that "Between ten and fifteen percent of all Dalits in India are Christians. Between two-thirds and three-quarters of all Christians in India are Dalits."[13] In this context, where those who have often been provided answers to questions that they neither asked nor were permitted to ask, and who now question the very basis on which theologizing has been done in the Indian context, would it be too presumptuous to claim that the quest for community takes a different form among those for whom baptism, on the one hand, did mean being added to the community, but on the other hand meant realizing only too quickly the bitter reality that this new community mirrored and reflected the deep divisions that existed in the Indian society?[14] It is in this context that we must seek to understand the desire of Samuel Rayan to rediscover the deeper meaning of conversion as "conversion from individualism in religion and society to corporate existence; from spiritual and economic selfishness to the truth of the community and of the world which God loves. . . ."[15]

2. Another major issue to be addressed is that of the so-called *unbaptized believers in Christ.* This issue was highlighted by research carried out in Madras in 1976, which showed that 10 percent of Hindus in Madras believed that the only true God was Jesus. The survey pointed out that if this were true, then there were more nonbaptized believers in Christ in the city than there were baptized Christians.[16] The reasons given for refusing baptism included caste customs like marriage alliances, funeral customs, loss of status; financial concerns

---

12. A helpful article which clarifies much of the terminology is that by Simon Charsley, " 'Untouchable': What Is in a Name?" *Journal of the Royal Anthropological Institute* 2, no. 1 (March 1996): 1-23.

13. Webster, back cover.

14. On the persistence of caste divisions in the church, see Massey, *Dalits in India,* pp. 81-84 and passim, as well as Webster, pp. 179-87.

15. In *A Call to Discipleship,* pp. 176-77.

16. This was published in *Gurukul Perspective,* March 1981, and reprinted in *A Call to Discipleship* as Appendix 2, "Research among Non-baptized Believers in Christ," pp. 206-11.

like loss of privileges from the government or jobs; and problems with the organized church like the persistence of caste feelings within the church.[17]

While this raises major issues regarding the pastoral ministry of the church in such a context, and issues relating to faith and order,[18] we must note another phenomenon: the phenomenon of movements growing around charismatic preachers or healers who, while proclaiming or claiming the good news offered through Jesus, vehemently deny the efficacy or the necessity of baptism. The most famous of such movements is probably that around K. Subba Rao (1912-81) in Andhra Pradesh. Subba Rao sought to proclaim a Christ disentangled from controversy, doctrines, rituals, and denominational rivalries, and said that the only qualification a person needed to become the pupil of Jesus was renunciation. Regarding the "madness of baptism," he said baptism does not qualify anyone for admission into the school of Christ; rather, it is the conversion of the heart which is the true baptism.[19] The attraction that this and other movements have for many people is not only a matter of sociological interest, but also a matter of theological interest, since the detachment of baptism from the message being proclaimed leads to the question as to how baptism has been perceived by the so-called nonbaptized believers in Christ. In one of his books, *Retreat Padre*, Subba Rao questions the cheapening of the gospel by padres to a show, a religion, a jugglery, a business, and a baptism.[20] That is to say, he sees baptism as a ritual that has been used to legitimize unjust and unnecessary structures within the church and wants to have nothing to do with it.[21] In this context it is

17. *A Call to Discipleship*, p. 210.

18. See the comments and analysis of other writings on this theme by Christine Lienemann-Perrin in her article "Zwischen verfaßter Kirche und Hinduismus: Anmerkungen zu einer indischen Ekklesiologie im Anschluß an eine Studienreise," *Theologische Zeitschrift* 52, no. 2 (1996): 100-107 and passim.

19. Cf. K. P. Aleaz, "The Theology of K. Subba Rao," *Bangalore Theological Forum* 23, no. 4 (December 1991): 41-63. This article not only includes an analysis of Subba Rao's theology, a bibliography of his writings, and articles and books on him, but it also assesses his writings from an Advaita Vedantic standpoint.

20. Quoted and analyzed in Aleaz, pp. 48-49.

21. In his article "The Church — the Fellowship of the Baptised and the Unbaptised?" in *Literating Witness: Dr. K. Rajaratnam's Platinum Birthday Anniversary Commemoration, Vol. 1*, ed. Prasanna Kumari (Madras: Gurukul, 1995), pp.

necessary to raise the question as to what the word "church" itself means and to explore the relationship between the organized churches and movements like those around Subba Rao. Stanley Samartha, in an article entitled "The Church of the Future," writes:

> When we speak of the future of the Church in India, which Church do we have in mind? This tension between the Church as it is in the mystery of God and the Church as a sociological reality cannot be resolved in history. Perhaps it should not be resolved because to be aware of this tension is to accept that we are constantly under the mercy and judgement of God.[22]

3. The cluster of themes, *secularism, communalism, and fundamentalism,* which are interrelated to each other,[23] constitutes another area which has implications for a study of baptism in India today. It must be made clear that in considering these concepts, baptism as such cannot be taken as an isolated phenomenon without taking into consideration the whole gamut of Christian life, practice, worship, and witness in India. Nevertheless, it must be recognized that the understanding and perception of baptismal practices within the Indian churches is an important indicator in constituting the image of Christianity in the following areas:

- within the officially secular democratic republic that is India;[24]

---

8-15, which surveys this and similar issues, analyzes certain case studies, and comments on various consultations that have been held, M. M. Thomas pointedly remarks that "the question of giving to the unbaptised Christ-bhakts in other religious communities a sense of full belonging to the spiritual fellowship of the church, including participation in the sacrament of the Lord's Supper, needs exploration" (p. 13).

22. In *The Future of the Church in India,* p. 13.

23. See the analysis of Sandeep Shastri, "Secularism, Fundamentalism and Communalism: An Attempt at Understanding the Indian Experience," in *Fundamentalism and Secularism: The Indian Predicament,* ed. Andreas Nehring, Gurukul Summer Institute 1994 (Madras: Gurukul, 1994), pp. 99-117.

24. See, e.g., the section on "Religious Identities in a Secular State," in S. J. Samartha, *One Christ — Many Religions: Toward a Revised Christology* (Maryknoll, N.Y.: Orbis, 1991), pp. 45-57. Samartha asks, "What role do religious communities have in a secular democratic state? Has the secular state provided opportunities

- with reference to fermenting and fostering communal riots and disturbances, and aiding and abetting communal feelings and attitudes within the churches;[25] and
- in fostering and nurturing fundamentalistic tendencies coupled with a closed mind and fixed attitudes toward people of other faiths or of no faith at all.[26]

4. A final point to be made is that of the relationship between baptism and *salvation*. If, as R. Panikkar writes, "the Church is by definition the locus of salvation, so that wherever salvation takes place

---

for different religions to make their contributions to undergird the value bases of a nation in the making?" (p. 46).

25. See, e.g., the comments of Gnana Robinson: "The churches in India, through their internal life and through their relation to others have not proved to the outside world that the Church of Christ is 'a Church for others.' For the non-Christians in India, Christianity is a communal group, just like other caste-groups in India, which care for its own members." In "The Church and People's Development: A Critical Look into the Life and Witness of the Church in India," in *Adventurous Faith and Transforming Vision: Essays in Honour of Kunchala Rajaratnam*, ed. Arvind P. Nirmal (Madras: Gurukul, 1989), p. 91. The distinguished diplomat-administrator P. C. Alexander writes, "We thought that with partition and independence, religious differences would cease to divide people, but we find the emergence of communalism in a much more dangerous form today." In "Promoting Communal Harmony — a Mission of the Church," in *Towards a New Humanity: Essays in Honour of Dr. Paulos Mar Gregorios*, ed. K. M. George and K. J. Gabriel (Delhi: ISPCK, 1992), p. 23.

26. See the articles in John S. Augustine, ed., *Religious Fundamentalism: An Asian Perspective* (Bangalore: South Asia Theological Research Institute, 1993), especially those by Ashis Nandy, "Fundamentalism" (pp. 1-10); George Mathew, "Fundamentalism in India: A Sociological Perspective" (pp. 20-24); John S. Augustine, "Dimensions of Fundamentalism: Sociological Soundings Emerging from an Empirical Probe into the Evangelical Upsurge in Madras" (pp. 109-80).

The Sri Lankan theologian R. S. Sugirtharajah, in an article entitled "Reconceiving Jesus: Some Continuing Concerns," writes about the Christian response to the revival of religious fundamentalism in Asia and asks, "In this increasingly tension filled situation what sort of Jesus should the Christian church project? Should one respond to one fundamentalism with another and create even greater tension and disharmony? Or should one look for alternative images of human solidarity that would mediate hope in the midst of communal tensions, religious bigotry and social disruption?" In R. S. Sugirtharajah, ed., *Asian Faces of Jesus* (London: SCM Press, 1993), p. 261.

there is the Church,"[27] then in the pluralistic context of India this raises questions not only regarding the meaning of the sacrament of baptism but also regarding the self-understanding, witness, and on-going life of the church within the context of Indian suffering and hope, especially regarding its claim to be the mediator of the salvation offered in and through Jesus the Christ.

Concluding on a personal note: My research on the baptismal controversy in the work and writings of Cyprian of Carthage has con-vinced me both of the importance of *situating* the issue of baptism in the early church within its historical parameters and, at the same time, of the necessity of keeping in mind the *specific* ecumenical movement, so that such studies do not have only an "antiquarian" value but rather *illuminate* our attempts to comprehend the ongoing flow of tradition and interpretation within the faith and order of the contemporary life of the church. The point made by Robert M. Grant regarding the writ-ers of the second century cannot be overlooked:

> They reached no solutions with direct "relevance" for twentieth- or twenty-first-century theology, but they stated perennial problems in fresh ways that only later became classical and offered possible moves toward dealing with them. Later Christians need to review their exegetical search in order to continue it.[28]

Reviewing the exegetical search of the early writers involves, then, for those of us who have come into the inheritance of these traditions, the *responsibility* not only to interact with these inherited

27. In an article entitled "The Dream of an Indian Ecclesiology," in *Searching for an Indian Ecclesiology*, ed. G. van Leeuwen (Bangalore: Asian Trading Corpora-tion, 1984), p. 33.

For a clear and systematic presentation of the thinking of R. Panikkar, see Origen Vasantha Jathanna, "Das Verhältnis von Christentum und Hinduismus im heutigen indisch-christlichen theologischen Denken. Ein Beispiel: Raimundo Panikkar," *Theologische Zeitschrift* 52, no. 2 (1996): 129-49. O. V. Jathanna also raises several pertinent questions regarding the question of baptism in an article entitled "Ecclesiology in Context: Reflections from an Indian Perspective in the Light of Current Ecumenical Deliberations," *Bangalore Theological Forum* 28, nos. 3 and 4 (September-December 1996), especially pp. 10-11.

28. In the "Preface" to his *Jesus after the Gospels: The Christ of the Second Century* (London: SCM Press, 1990), p. 14.

traditions, but also to interpret them in the context of the "extratextual hermeneutics that is slowly emerging as a distinctive Asian contribution to theological methodology [which] seeks to transcend the textual, historical, and religious boundaries of Christian tradition and cultivate a deeper contact with the mysterious ways in which people of all religious persuasions have defined and appropriated humanity and divinity."[29]

29. R. S. Sugirtharajah, "Introduction," in R. S. Sugirtharajah, ed., *Frontiers in Asian Christian Theology: Emerging Trends* (Maryknoll, N.Y.: Orbis Books, 1994), p. 3.

# Contributors

ANDRÉ BIRMELÉ is Professor of Systematic Theology, University of Strasbourg, France.

EUGENE L. BRAND is Distinguished International Professor in Residence at Trinity Lutheran Seminary, Columbus, Ohio, and formerly Assistant General Secretary for Ecumenical Affairs, Lutheran World Federation, Geneva, Switzerland.

JAMES D. G. DUNN is Lightfoot Professor of Divinity, University of Durham, England.

S. MARK HEIM is Professor of Christian Theology, Andover Newton Theological School, Newton Centre, Massachusetts, USA.

PEDER NØRGAARD-HØJEN is Professor of Systematic Theology, University of Copenhagen, Denmark.

RAGNAR PERSENIUS is Director for Theology and Ecumenical Affairs, Central Board of the Church of Sweden, Uppsala, Sweden.

JOHN POBEE is Programme Coordinator for Ecumenical Theological Education, World Council of Churches, Geneva, Switzerland.

MERJA MERRAS is Lecturer in the Orthodox Theological Faculty, University of Joensuu, Finland.

MICHAEL ROOT is Research Professor, Institute for Ecumenical Research, Strasbourg, France.

RISTO SAARINEN is Research Professor, Institute for Ecumenical Research, Strasbourg, France.

J. JAYAKIRAN SEBASTIAN is Lecturer in the Department of Theology and Ethics, United Theological College, Bangalore, India.

SUSAN K. WOOD, SCL, is Associate Professor of Theology, St. John's University, Collegeville, Minnesota, USA.